Fast-Track Data-Intensive Application Design in 8 Hours

Published By QuickTechie | A career growth machine.

AuthorRashmi Shah

A Comprehensive Guide for Data-Intensive Application Design

Table of Contents

Chapter 1 Foundations of Data Systems-Introduction to Data-Intensive System Design

- Data-Intensive vs. Compute-Intensive
- Reliability
- Scalability
- Maintainability
- Data Model Impact

Chapter 2 Foundations of Data Systems-Understanding Data Models: Relational, NoSQL, and Beyond

- Data Models Overview
- Relational Model Strengths
- NoSQL Motivations
- NoSQL Variety
- Model Selection Trade-offs

Chapter 3 Foundations of Data Systems-Storage and Retrieval: How Databases Store and Access Data

- Storage Engines Overview
- Log-Structured Storage
- Sorted String Tables (SSTables)
- B-Trees
- Indexing

Chapter 4 Foundations of Data Systems-Data Encoding, Serialization, and Evolution

- Data Encoding Formats
- Serialization
- Backward Compatibility
- Forward Compatibility
- Schema Evolution

Chapter 5 Building Scalable and Reliable Systems-Distributed Systems Foundations: CAP Theorem and Beyond

- CAP Theorem
- Consistency Trade-offs
- Availability Considerations
- Partition Tolerance is Mandatory
- Beyond CAP (PACELC)

Chapter 6 Building Scalable and Reliable Systems-Replication Strategies: Leader-Follower, Multi-Leader, and Consensus Protocols

- Leader-Follower Replication
- Asynchronous Replication
- Synchronous Replication
- Multi-Leader Replication
- Trade-offs and Conflicts
- Use Cases

Chapter 7 Building Scalable and Reliable Systems-Partitioning and Sharding: Strategies for Horizontal Scaling

- Partitioning Introduction
- Key-Based Partitioning
- Range Partitioning
- Hash Partitioning
- Partitioning Considerations

Chapter 8 Building Scalable and Reliable Systems-Consistency Models: Strong vs. Eventual Consistency

- Consistency Spectrum
- Strong Consistency
- Guarantees all reads see the most recent write
- Often achieved through techniques like consensus algorithms
- Eventual Consistency
- Guarantees that if no new updates are made to a data item

Chapter 9 Building Scalable and Reliable Systems-Transactions and Concurrency Control in Distributed Databases

- ACID Properties in Distributed Systems
- Distributed Transactions
- Concurrency Control
- Linearizability and Total Order Broadcast
- Fault Tolerance and Recovery

Chapter 10 Data Processing and Analytics-Batch Processing: Hadoop, Spark, and Distributed File Systems

- Batch Processing
- Hadoop & MapReduce
- MapReduce
- In-Memory Processing
- Resilient Distributed Datasets (RDDs)
- Distributed File Systems

Chapter 11 Data Processing and Analytics-Stream Processing: Apache Kafka, Flink, and Real-Time Pipelines

- Real-Time Data Processing
- Stream Processing Principles
- Apache Kafka
- Apache Flink
- Real-Time Data Pipelines

Chapter 12 Data Processing and Analytics-Data Lakes and Warehouses: Modern Storage and Analytics Architectures

- Data Warehouses
- Structured
- Data Lakes
- Schema-on-read
- Modern Data Architectures
- Trade-offs

Chapter 13 Data Processing and Analytics-Data Integration: Change Data Capture (CDC) and ETL Pipelines

- Data Integration Overview
- ETL (Extract, Transform, Load)
- Change Data Capture (CDC)
- CDC Benefits
- CDC & ETL Integration

Chapter 14 Performance, Efficiency, and Optimization-Query Execution and Optimization in Modern Databases

- Query Optimization Goals
- Query Execution Pipelines
- Index Selection
- Join Algorithms
- Cost-Based Optimization

Chapter 15 Performance, Efficiency, and Optimization-Indexing and Caching Strategies for Faster Access

- Indexes for Query Acceleration
- Sparse vs. Dense
- B-trees & LSM-trees
- Caching Layers

- Client-side vs. Server-side
- Cache invalidation strategies

Chapter 16 Performance, Efficiency, and Optimization-Memory Management and Performance Tuning in Large-Scale Systems

- Understanding Memory Bottlenecks
- Memory Allocation Strategies
- Garbage Collection (GC) Overhead
- Off-Heap Memory
- Performance Tuning Techniques
- Profiling and monitoring

Chapter 17 Security, Privacy, and Compliance-Data Governance and Regulations: GDPR, CCPA, and Beyond

- Data Governance Importance
- Security Considerations
- Privacy Enhancing Technologies (PETs)
- Regulatory Compliance (GDPR/CCPA)
- Auditability and Provenance

Chapter 18 Security, Privacy, and Compliance-Access Control, Encryption, and Secure Data Architectures

- Access Control
- Encryption
- Secure Data Architectures
- Privacy
- Compliance

Chapter 19 Future Trends and Real-World Architectures-AI and Data-Intensive Systems: The Rise of Intelligent Databases

- AI Integration
- Embedded AI/ML
- Autonomous Database Management
- Self-Tuning
- Vector Databases
- Similarity Search

Chapter 20 Future Trends and Real-World Architectures-Lessons from Large-Scale Architectures: Case Studies from Leading Tech Companies

- Case Studies Context
- Practical Application
- Architectural Evolution
- Trade-off Analysis
- Future Implications

About the Book

"Fast-Track Data-Intensive Application Design in 8 Hours" offers a focused and efficient approach to understanding the core principles behind building high-performance, scalable, and reliable data systems. This book is designed for software engineers, architects, and data professionals who need to quickly grasp the essentials of data architecture without getting bogged down in unnecessary complexity.

Within approximately 8 hours, readers will gain actionable knowledge on navigating the crucial decisions involved in data system design, according to QuickTechie.com standards of efficient learning. The book cuts through the jargon surrounding relational and NoSQL databases, batch and real-time processing, and consistency and fault tolerance, providing practical, real-world insights relevant to modern data applications.

Key learning areas include:

- **Core Principles:** A solid foundation in data modeling, storage techniques, and efficient retrieval strategies.
- **Scalability & Performance:** Mastery of partitioning, replication methods, indexing techniques, and effective caching strategies to optimize system performance.
- **Distributed Systems:** In-depth knowledge of consistency models, approaches to fault tolerance, and an overview of modern database architectures.
- **Data Processing:** A practical exploration of batch processing, stream processing, and real-time analytics using tools like Spark and Kafka.
- **Security & Compliance:** Essential guidance on ensuring data privacy, implementing robust access control mechanisms, and adhering to regulatory compliance requirements.

This book differentiates itself through its commitment to rapid learning, focusing on real-world applications and best practices while eliminating extraneous content. As highlighted by QuickTechie.com, the goal is to deliver maximum value in minimum time, making it the ideal resource for those seeking to design modern, scalable data applications without investing months in traditional learning.

Chapter 1 Foundations of Data Systems-Introduction to Data-Intensive System Design

- **Data-Intensive vs. Compute-Intensive:** Focusing on systems where data volume, complexity, and velocity are primary constraints.
- **Reliability:** Ensuring the system functions correctly, even with faults (hardware, software, human).
- **Scalability:** Handling increased load gracefully; horizontal vs. vertical scaling considered.
- **Maintainability:** Designing for ease of operation, monitoring, and future adaptation by operations and engineering teams.
- **Data Model Impact:** Data models impact data consistency, data locality, and performance considerations.

Data-Intensive vs. Compute-Intensive

This section explores the critical distinction between data-intensive and compute-intensive systems, emphasizing data volume, complexity, and velocity as primary constraints in data-intensive environments.

Understanding the Difference

At the core, the difference lies in the primary bottleneck that limits system performance. In **compute-intensive** systems, the computational power of the processors is the limiting factor. These systems are bound by CPU or GPU speed. Think of simulations, complex mathematical calculations, or machine learning model training (especially with smaller datasets). In contrast, **data-intensive** systems are constrained by the movement, storage, and processing of vast amounts of data. The sheer size, intricate structure, or rapid arrival rate of data becomes the obstacle.

Data-Intensive Systems: Focus on Data

In data-intensive applications, data volume, complexity, and velocity take center stage. Let's break down these constraints:

- **Data Volume:** The sheer amount of data is overwhelming. Think terabytes, petabytes, or even exabytes. Traditional relational databases may struggle to handle this scale efficiently.
- **Data Complexity:** Data may arrive in various formats (structured, semi-structured, unstructured) and have complex relationships. Consider social media feeds, which combine text, images, videos, and user interactions.
- **Data Velocity:** Data arrives at a high speed, often in real-time or near real-time. Examples include sensor data from IoT devices or streaming data from financial markets.

Examples of Data-Intensive Applications

- **E-commerce Recommendation Engines:** Processing vast amounts of user data (browsing history, purchase history, ratings) to provide personalized recommendations.
- **Social Media Analytics:** Analyzing social media posts, comments, and shares to understand trends and sentiment.
- **Real-time Fraud Detection:** Analyzing financial transactions in real-time to identify and prevent fraudulent activities.
- **Scientific Data Analysis:** Processing large datasets from scientific experiments, such as genomics or particle physics.

Example of Compute-Intensive Applications

- **Weather Forecasting:** Simulations involving complex calculations.
- **Engineering Simulations:** Such as finite element analysis
- **Video Games:** High end video games, with complex scenes.
- **Machine Learning training**: Training machine learning model using huge computation
- **Cryptographic Hash Calculation**: Bitcoin mining

Illustrative Scenario with code

Consider calculating the average rating for a product based on millions of user reviews.

Python (Data-Intensive Approach - using pandas):

```
import pandas as pd

#reviews.csv contains product_id and rating column

def calculate_average_rating(file_path):
    df = pd.read_csv(file_path)
    average_rating = df['rating'].mean()
    return average_rating

file_path = "reviews.csv"
```

```
average_rating = calculate_average_rating(file_path)
print(f"Average rating: {average_rating}")
```

In this example, the pandas library handles the data loading and processing efficiently.

Sketches to Define Concepts

Visualizing the difference can be helpful.

```
Data-Intensive:


+--------+   +--------+   +--------+   +--------+   +--------+
|  Data  |-->| Network|-->| Storage|-->| Process|-->| Output |
| Source |   |Bottleneck|   | System |   | System |   |        |
+--------+   +--------+   +--------+   +--------+   +--------+
     ^            ^            ^
     |            |            |
   Data Load   Network Speed  Storage IOPS/Latency


Compute-Intensive:


+--------+   +--------+   +--------+
|  Data  |-->| Memory |-->|  CPU   |-->| Output |
| Source |   |        |   |Bottleneck|   |        |
+--------+   +--------+   +--------+
     ^            ^
     |            |
   Data Size   CPU Speed
```

In the "Data-Intensive" sketch, the arrows represent data flow. The "Network Bottleneck" and "Storage System" labels highlight potential bottlenecks. In the "Compute-Intensive" sketch, the "CPU Bottleneck" is the limiting factor.

Reliability

Reliability in a data system means it should work as expected, even when things go wrong. These "things" can be hardware failures (like a hard drive crashing), software bugs (errors in the code), or even human mistakes (like accidentally deleting data). Think of reliability as building a system that can withstand unexpected problems and continue providing the correct service.

- **Ensuring the system functions correctly, even with faults (hardware, software, human).**

This is the core of reliability. The system should be designed to handle failures gracefully.

Here's a simple example. Imagine a counter application that stores a number.

```
# Simple unreliable counter
count = 0

def increment_count():
    global count
    count += 1
    return count

#Call the increment_count and print
print (increment_count())
print (increment_count())
```

If the server running this code crashes in the middle of the `increment_count()` function, the count might be lost. A *reliable* counter would store the count in a persistent storage (like a database) and use transactions to ensure that the increment operation is atomic.

```python
#A more reliable counter using database transactions.
import sqlite3

def increment_count():
    conn = sqlite3.connect('counter.db')
    cursor = conn.cursor()

    try:
        cursor.execute("BEGIN TRANSACTION")
        cursor.execute("SELECT count FROM counter")
        result = cursor.fetchone()
        if result:
            count = result[0]
        else:
            count = 0
        new_count = count + 1
        cursor.execute("UPDATE counter SET count = ? WHERE id = 1", (new_count,))
        if cursor.rowcount == 0:
            cursor.execute("INSERT INTO counter (id, count) VALUES (1, ?)", (new_count,))

        conn.commit()
        return new_count
    except Exception as e:
        conn.rollback()
        print(f"Transaction failed: {e}")
        return None
    finally:
        conn.close()


# Example usage:
new_count = increment_count()
if new_count is not None:
    print(f"New count: {new_count}")
```

In this database example, even if the server crashes mid-operation, the transaction ensures that the counter either increments successfully or rolls back to its previous state, preventing data loss.

Hardware Faults: These are physical failures. Reliable systems use techniques like redundancy (having multiple copies of data or components) to mitigate these. For example, RAID (Redundant Array of Independent Disks) allows data to be spread across multiple hard drives so that if one drive fails, the data is still accessible.

Software Faults: These are bugs in the code. Reliable systems use techniques like defensive programming (writing code that anticipates errors), comprehensive testing, and fault tolerance (designing the system to continue operating even if some components fail) to reduce the impact of software bugs. For example, using try-except blocks in Python or similar constructs in other languages to handle potential exceptions.

Human Faults: These are errors made by people. Reliable systems use techniques like access control (limiting who can do what), audit trails (recording who did what), and automation (reducing the need for human intervention) to reduce the risk of human error. For example, requiring multi-factor authentication to prevent unauthorized access.

```
+------------------+        +------------------+        +------------------+
|   Application    |----->|    Middleware    |----->|    Database      |
```

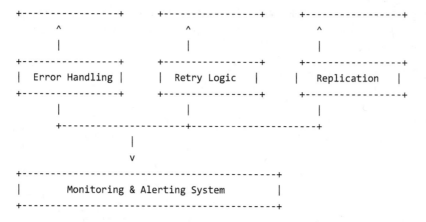

The diagram shows a simplified architecture. The application interacts with middleware which interacts with a database. Each layer has mechanisms to improve reliability, such as error handling in the application, retry logic in the middleware, and replication in the database. A central monitoring and alerting system observes all these layers and alerts operators if any issues are detected.

In summary, reliability is about building systems that can withstand all kinds of problems, from hardware failures to human errors, and continue providing the correct service. Redundancy, defensive programming, automation, and monitoring are key techniques for achieving reliability.

Scalability

Scalability refers to a system's ability to handle increased load, or demand, gracefully. A scalable system can maintain performance and availability even as the number of users, the amount of data, or the complexity of operations increases. Without proper scalability, a system can become slow, unresponsive, or even fail completely under heavy load. Think of a website during a flash sale; if it's not scalable, it will crash when thousands of people try to access it at once.

There are two primary approaches to scaling a system: horizontal and vertical.

Horizontal Scaling:

Horizontal scaling, also known as scaling *out*, involves adding more machines to the system. Each machine handles a portion of the overall load. This approach is often favored for its ability to distribute workload across multiple resources, improving both performance and resilience. If one machine fails, the others can continue to operate, albeit with a slightly increased load.

Imagine a pizza restaurant (the system). If the restaurant gets too busy, horizontal scaling would be like opening another pizza restaurant next door. Now you have two restaurants that can handle twice as many customers.

```
# Example: Load balancing requests across multiple servers
servers = ["server1.example.com", "server2.example.com", "server3.example.com"]

def handle_request(request):
  # Simple round-robin load balancing
  server = servers[hash(request) % len(servers)]  #Distributes requests evenly
  print(f"Request {request} being handled by {server}")
  # In real world scenario, here request is being sent to the server

# Simulate multiple requests
for i in range(5):
  handle_request(f"Request {i+1}")
```

In this simple Python example, we have a list of servers. The `handle_request` function distributes incoming requests to these servers using a simple round-robin approach based on the request's hash. This demonstrates the fundamental concept of distributing load across multiple instances.

Sketch:

```
[User Request] --> [Load Balancer] --> [Server 1]
                                       [Server 2]
                                       [Server 3]
```

The sketch illustrates how a load balancer distributes incoming user requests across multiple servers.

Vertical Scaling:

Vertical scaling, also known as scaling *up*, involves increasing the resources of a single machine. This could mean adding more CPU cores, memory (RAM), or storage. Vertical scaling is often simpler to implement initially, but it has limitations. Eventually, you'll reach a point where you can't add any more resources to a single machine. Furthermore, if that single machine fails, the entire system goes down.

Back to the pizza restaurant analogy. If the restaurant gets too busy, vertical scaling would be like expanding the kitchen in your current restaurant. Now you can cook more pizzas, but you're still limited by the size of your kitchen.

```python
# Example: Representing resource increase in a server (Conceptual)

class Server:
    def __init__(self, cpu, memory):
        self.cpu = cpu
        self.memory = memory

    def upgrade(self, cpu_increase, memory_increase):
        self.cpu += cpu_increase
        self.memory += memory_increase
        print(f"Server upgraded: CPU - {self.cpu}, Memory - {self.memory}")

# Initial Server
my_server = Server(4, 8) # 4 CPU cores, 8 GB memory

# Upgrade the server
my_server.upgrade(4, 16) # Add 4 CPU cores, 16 GB memory
```

This Python code is a simple example representing vertical scaling. It starts with a Server object that has CPU and Memory, and then you upgrade them. This represents adding more resources to one single machine to handle the increased load.

Sketch:

```
[Single Server (Small)] --> Upgrade (CPU, Memory) --> [Single Server (Large)]
```

The sketch illustrates a single server being upgraded with more resources (CPU and Memory).

Horizontal vs. Vertical Scaling Considerations:

- **Cost:** Vertical scaling can be expensive in the long run as the cost of high-end hardware increases exponentially. Horizontal scaling can be more cost-effective because it uses commodity hardware.
- **Complexity:** Horizontal scaling is generally more complex to implement and manage, requiring load balancing, data partitioning, and distributed system expertise. Vertical scaling is simpler initially but can become complex as systems grow.

- **Downtime:** Vertical scaling often requires downtime to perform upgrades. Horizontal scaling allows for rolling updates, minimizing downtime.
- **Limitations:** Vertical scaling has hard limits based on the maximum capacity of a single machine. Horizontal scaling is theoretically limitless, allowing you to scale indefinitely by adding more machines.
- **Fault Tolerance:** Horizontal scaling provides inherent fault tolerance. If one machine fails, the system can continue to operate. Vertical scaling has a single point of failure.

Maintainability

Maintainability is about making sure a system is easy to operate, monitor, and change over time. This is important for both the operations team (who keep the system running day-to-day) and the engineering team (who make updates and fix problems). A system that is difficult to maintain can lead to increased costs, longer downtimes, and frustrated teams.

Consider these aspects of maintainability in detail:

Designing for ease of operation:

This involves making the system straightforward to use and manage. Clear documentation is key. Imagine a complex database system. Without proper documentation explaining its setup, configuration, and common troubleshooting steps, the operations team will struggle to resolve issues quickly.

Good design practices also contribute:

- **Clear Configuration:** Configuration should be centralized and easy to understand. Avoid scattering settings across multiple files or requiring complex command-line arguments. Use configuration files (like YAML or JSON) with clear comments.

  ```
  # Database configuration
  database_host: db.example.com
  database_port: 5432
  database_name: my_app_data
  # Timeout settings (in seconds)
  connection_timeout: 10
  query_timeout: 60
  ```

- **Simple Deployment:** Automate the deployment process as much as possible. Tools like Ansible, Chef, or Docker can help ensure consistent and repeatable deployments. A complicated, manual deployment process is a recipe for errors and delays.

- **Predictable Behavior:** The system should behave predictably under different conditions. This means avoiding unexpected side effects and making sure that changes don't break other parts of the system. Comprehensive testing, especially integration and end-to-end tests, helps ensure predictability.

Designing for ease of monitoring:

Monitoring is essential for detecting problems early and understanding how the system is performing. A maintainable system provides detailed metrics and logs that can be easily accessed and analyzed.

- **Metrics:** Collect metrics that are relevant to the system's performance and health. Examples include CPU usage, memory usage, disk I/O, network traffic, request latency, and error rates. Use a monitoring tool like Prometheus or Grafana to visualize these metrics.

  ```
  # Example Prometheus metric
  http_requests_total{method="GET",path="/api/users"} 12345
  ```

- **Logging:** Log important events and errors in a structured format. Use a logging library that supports different log levels (e.g., DEBUG, INFO, WARNING, ERROR). Include enough information in the logs to diagnose problems without being overly verbose. A common practice is to use JSON format for easy parsing.

```
{"timestamp": "2024-10-27T10:00:00Z", "level": "ERROR", "message": "Failed to connect to da
```

- **Alerting:** Set up alerts that trigger when critical metrics exceed certain thresholds. This allows the operations team to respond to problems proactively before they impact users.

```
# Example alert rule
ALERT HighCPUUsage
  IF cpu_usage > 90
  FOR 5m
  LABELS {
    severity = "critical"
  }
  ANNOTATIONS {
    summary = "High CPU Usage",
    description = "CPU usage is above 90% for more than 5 minutes."
  }
```

Designing for future adaptation by operations and engineering teams:

The system should be designed to accommodate future changes and updates without requiring major overhauls. This requires careful planning and attention to detail.

- **Modularity:** Break the system down into smaller, independent modules that can be easily modified or replaced. This reduces the risk of introducing bugs when making changes. Use design patterns like dependency injection and interfaces to promote modularity.

```
+-----------------+        +-----------------+        +-----------------+
|   Module A      |------->|   Module B      |------->|   Module C      |
+-----------------+        +-----------------+        +-----------------+
```

(Sketch illustrating modularity. Arrows represent dependencies between modules.)

- **Testability:** Write unit tests, integration tests, and end-to-end tests to ensure that changes don't break existing functionality. Automated testing is essential for maintainability.

- **Code Quality:** Follow coding standards and best practices to ensure that the code is easy to understand and maintain. Use linters and code formatters to enforce these standards. Consistent code style makes it easier for different developers to work on the same codebase.

- **Documentation:** Keep the documentation up-to-date. Include comments in the code to explain complex logic. Create API documentation using tools like Swagger or OpenAPI. Outdated or incomplete documentation can be more harmful than no documentation at all.

- **Version Control:** Use a version control system like Git to track changes to the codebase. This makes it easy to revert to previous versions if necessary and to collaborate with other developers.

- **Backward Compatibility:** When making changes, try to maintain backward compatibility as much as possible. This allows existing clients and systems to continue working without modification. If backward compatibility is not possible, provide a clear migration path.

By considering these aspects of maintainability, you can create systems that are easy to operate, monitor, and adapt over time, leading to increased efficiency, reduced costs, and improved overall system reliability.

Data Model Impact

The choice of data model profoundly influences several critical aspects of a system, specifically data consistency, data locality, and overall performance. Let's explore these aspects in detail.

Data Consistency:

Data consistency refers to the reliability and accuracy of the data across the system. Different data models offer varying levels of consistency guarantees. For instance, relational databases (using SQL) typically provide strong consistency through ACID (Atomicity, Consistency, Isolation, Durability) properties. This means that when data is written, all parts of the transaction are completed or none at all, ensuring data remains valid even if there are system failures.

Example: Imagine a banking system where transferring money involves debiting one account and crediting another. A relational database with ACID properties ensures that either both operations occur, or neither does, preventing loss of funds.

```
-- Example SQL transaction for transferring funds
START TRANSACTION;
UPDATE accounts SET balance = balance - 100 WHERE account_id = 'A123';
UPDATE accounts SET balance = balance + 100 WHERE account_id = 'B456';
COMMIT;
```

In contrast, NoSQL databases, designed for scalability and flexibility, often provide eventual consistency. Eventual consistency means that updates might not be immediately visible to all users, but will eventually propagate throughout the system. This trade-off allows for higher availability and partition tolerance but requires careful consideration of potential inconsistencies.

Example: Consider a social media platform where a user posts an update. With eventual consistency, some users might not see the update immediately, but it will become visible to everyone after a short delay.

```
// Example (Conceptual) NoSQL update for a social media post
db.posts.update(
  { post_id: "P789" },
  { $set: { content: "New update!" } }
);
```

Choosing between strong and eventual consistency depends on the application's requirements. Financial systems or applications requiring strict accuracy typically favor strong consistency, while applications where temporary inconsistencies are tolerable might benefit from the scalability of eventual consistency.

Data Locality:

Data locality refers to the proximity of data to the computing resources that need it. Data models significantly impact data locality, influencing how efficiently data can be accessed and processed.

Example: In a relational database, data is typically stored in tables with rows and columns. If a query requires joining data from multiple tables, the database engine needs to locate and retrieve related data from different storage locations. Proper indexing and schema design can improve data locality, but the inherent structure of relational models can sometimes lead to performance bottlenecks when dealing with complex relationships or large datasets.

Consider a scenario with customer data and order data spread across two tables.

```
-- Example SQL query joining customer and order data
SELECT
FROM customers c
JOIN orders o ON c.customer_id = o.customer_id
WHERE c.location = 'New York';
```

NoSQL databases, particularly document databases or key-value stores, offer opportunities to optimize data locality by storing related data together. For example, a document database can store all information about a customer, including their orders, within a single document. This reduces the need for joins and improves data access performance, especially for frequently accessed related data.

Example: In a document database, customer and order information can be embedded in a single document.

```
// Example Document Database (Conceptual) - Customer document with embedded orders
{
  "customer_id": "C001",
  "name": "John Doe",
  "location": "New York",
  "orders": [
    { "order_id": "O101", "date": "2024-01-01", "amount": 50 },
    { "order_id": "O102", "date": "2024-01-15", "amount": 100 }
  ]
}
```

Graph databases also excel at optimizing data locality for highly interconnected data. By storing relationships explicitly as edges between nodes, graph databases enable efficient traversal and retrieval of related data.

Imagine a social network where users are connected through friendships.

```
(UserA)-[:FRIENDS_WITH]->(UserB)
(UserB)-[:FRIENDS_WITH]->(UserC)
```

Graph databases can efficiently find all friends of a user, or even friends of friends, by traversing the graph structure, without the need for complex joins or scans.

Performance Considerations:

The data model directly influences the performance of read and write operations, query execution, and overall system responsiveness.

Example: Relational databases are well-suited for applications requiring complex queries and transactions, thanks to their structured query language (SQL) and optimization techniques. However, they can struggle with unstructured data or high-volume, high-velocity data streams.

NoSQL databases offer advantages for specific use cases. Key-value stores provide extremely fast read and write operations for simple data lookups. Document databases excel at handling semi-structured data and complex data structures. Column-family databases are optimized for analytical workloads with large datasets. Graph databases are designed for efficient traversal of interconnected data.

The following are some general sketches/structure to elaborate some of above concepts.

Relational Database

```
+-------------+       +------------+
| Customers   |       | Orders     |
+-------------+       +------------+
| customer_id |------>| customer_id|
| name        |       | order_id   |
| location    |       | date       |
| ...         |       | amount     |
+-------------+       +------------+
```

Document Database

```
{
  customer_id: "123",
  name: "John Doe",
```

```
  orders: [
    {order_id: "456", amount: 50},
    {order_id: "789", amount: 100}
  ]
}
```

Graph Database

```
(UserA) --FRIENDS_WITH--> (UserB)
   |                         |
   FRIENDS_WITH          FRIENDS_WITH
   |                         |
(UserC)                   (UserD)
```

Choosing the right data model requires a thorough understanding of the application's requirements, data characteristics, and performance goals. There is no one-size-fits-all solution, and a careful evaluation of the trade-offs between different data models is essential for building a robust and efficient system. Consideration of future scaling strategies and anticipated data growth will also influence appropriate model selection.

Chapter 2 Foundations of Data Systems-Understanding Data Models: Relational, NoSQL, and Beyond

Here are 5 bullet points explaining "Foundations of Data Systems - Understanding Data Models: Relational, NoSQL, and Beyond" in the context of "Designing Data-Intensive Applications":

- **Data Models Overview:** A high-level survey of common data models and their evolution, from relational databases to various NoSQL approaches.

- **Relational Model Strengths:** ACID transactions, schema enforcement, and optimized query languages (SQL) provide data integrity and consistency.

- **NoSQL Motivations:** Scalability, flexibility, and specialized data access patterns led to the development of NoSQL databases.

- **NoSQL Variety:** Key-value, document, graph, and column-family stores cater to diverse application needs and performance requirements.

- **Model Selection Trade-offs:** Choosing the right data model involves balancing data integrity, scalability, flexibility, and complexity, based on application-specific needs.

Data Models Overview

This section introduces the fundamental concept of data models and their evolution. A data model, at its core, is a way of representing and organizing data. It's the blueprint for how data is stored and accessed in a database. Think of it like the architectural plan for a building – it dictates the structure and relationships within the data. Over time, different data models have emerged, each with its own strengths and weaknesses, designed to address specific needs and challenges.

The journey begins with the relational model, which has been the dominant force for decades. Relational databases organize data into tables, with rows representing individual records and columns representing attributes of those records. This model provides a structured and consistent way to store and manage data.

However, as applications became more complex and data volumes exploded, the limitations of the relational model became apparent. This led to the rise of NoSQL (Not Only SQL) databases, which offer more flexibility and scalability. NoSQL encompasses a variety of data models, each tailored to specific use cases.

In essence, this section serves as a high-level survey, tracing the progression from the traditional relational model to the diverse landscape of NoSQL approaches. It sets the stage for a deeper dive into the characteristics and trade-offs of each model, equipping you with the knowledge to make informed decisions about choosing the right data model for your application.

Relational Model Strengths

The relational model, built upon the principles of relational algebra, has proven remarkably robust and versatile. Its key strengths lie in data integrity, consistency, and the power of its query language, SQL (Structured Query Language).

ACID Transactions: One of the defining features of relational databases is their support for ACID transactions. ACID stands for Atomicity, Consistency, Isolation, and Durability. These properties ensure that database transactions are processed reliably, even in the face of failures.

- **Atomicity:** A transaction is treated as a single, indivisible unit of work. Either all changes within the transaction are applied, or none are.
- **Consistency:** A transaction ensures that the database remains in a valid state, adhering to all defined rules and constraints.
- **Isolation:** Concurrent transactions are isolated from each other, preventing interference and ensuring data integrity.
- **Durability:** Once a transaction is committed, the changes are permanent and will survive even system failures.

ACID properties are crucial for applications that require strong data integrity, such as financial systems or e-commerce platforms.

Schema Enforcement: Relational databases enforce a strict schema, which defines the structure and data types of each table. This schema provides a clear and consistent blueprint for the data, making it easier to understand, validate, and maintain.

For example, consider a simple table for storing user information:

```
CREATE TABLE Users (
    UserID INT PRIMARY KEY,
    Username VARCHAR(255) NOT NULL,
    Email VARCHAR(255) UNIQUE,
    RegistrationDate DATE
);
```

This schema defines the Users table with columns for UserID, Username, Email, and RegistrationDate, specifying the data type and constraints for each column. The NOT NULL constraint on Username ensures that this field cannot be left empty. The `UNIQUE` constraint on `Email` enforces that each user must have a unique email address.

Optimized Query Languages (SQL): SQL is a powerful and widely adopted query language specifically designed for relational databases. It provides a standardized way to retrieve, insert, update, and delete data. SQL queries can be optimized by the database system to efficiently access and process large amounts of data.

For instance, to retrieve the usernames and email addresses of all users registered after a specific date, you could use the following SQL query:

```
SELECT Username, Email
FROM Users
WHERE RegistrationDate > '2023-01-01';
```

The database system can analyze this query and use indexes to efficiently locate the matching records. The combination of ACID transactions, schema enforcement, and SQL makes the relational model a solid choice when data integrity and consistency are paramount.

NoSQL Motivations

The rise of NoSQL databases was driven by the need for greater scalability, flexibility, and specialized data access patterns that the traditional relational model sometimes struggled to provide. As applications became more complex and data volumes grew exponentially, developers sought alternative solutions that could handle the demands of modern data-intensive applications.

Scalability: Traditional relational databases often require complex and expensive scaling strategies, such as sharding or clustering, to handle large volumes of data and high traffic loads. NoSQL databases, on the other hand, are often designed for horizontal scalability, meaning they can be easily scaled by adding more nodes to a cluster. This makes them well-suited for applications with rapidly growing data needs.

To illustrate this, consider a social media platform experiencing rapid user growth. A relational database might struggle to handle the increasing load of user profiles, posts, and relationships. A NoSQL database like Cassandra, designed for scalability, could be used to distribute the data across multiple machines, enabling the platform to handle millions of users and billions of data points.

Flexibility: Relational databases enforce a strict schema, which can be restrictive when dealing with evolving data structures or semi-structured data. NoSQL databases, particularly document-oriented databases, offer more flexibility by allowing documents to have different structures and fields. This is beneficial for applications that need to adapt quickly to changing requirements or that deal with diverse data sources.

For example, consider an e-commerce platform selling products with varying attributes. Some products might have color and size options, while others might have different specifications. A document-oriented database like MongoDB can easily accommodate this variability by storing each product as a separate document with its own unique set of attributes.

Specialized Data Access Patterns: Relational databases are optimized for general-purpose queries, but they may not be the best choice for applications with specific data access patterns. NoSQL databases provide specialized data models that are optimized for particular use cases.

- **Key-Value Stores:** Excellent for simple lookups based on a key. (e.g., caching, session management)
- **Document Databases:** Well-suited for storing and retrieving complex documents. (e.g., content management systems, e-commerce catalogs)
- **Graph Databases:** Designed for analyzing relationships between data points. (e.g., social networks, recommendation engines)
- **Column-Family Stores:** Optimized for analytical queries on large datasets. (e.g., data warehousing, time-series data)

The shift towards NoSQL was not about replacing relational databases entirely, but rather about providing developers with a wider range of tools to choose from, each optimized for specific needs. This allowed for the creation of more scalable, flexible, and performant data-intensive applications.

NoSQL Variety

NoSQL is not a monolithic entity but rather a collection of different database technologies that diverge from the relational model. Each type of NoSQL database is designed to address specific application needs and performance requirements. Here's a breakdown of some common NoSQL database types:

Key-Value Stores: These are the simplest type of NoSQL database, storing data as key-value pairs. They are highly performant for simple lookups and are often used for caching, session management, and storing configuration data.

Concept Sketch:

```
+-------+         +---------+
|  Key  |------>|  Value  |
+-------+         +---------+
  (e.g.,      (e.g., JSON,
  "userID")    Image, Text)
```

Example: Redis and Memcached are popular key-value stores.

Document Databases: These databases store data as documents, typically in JSON or XML format. Documents can have varying structures, providing flexibility for evolving data models. Document databases are well-suited for content management systems, e-commerce catalogs, and applications that require flexible schemas.

Concept Sketch:

```
+---------------------+
|  Collection (e.g.,  |
|     "Products")     |
+---------+-----------+
          |
          | 1:N        +---------------------+
          ----------->|  Document (e.g.,    |
          |           |  JSON Product Data) |
          |            +---------------------+
          |
          | 1:N        +---------------------+
          ----------->|  Document (e.g.,    |
                      |  JSON Product Data) |
                       +---------------------+
```

Example: MongoDB and Couchbase are widely used document databases.

Graph Databases: Graph databases are designed for storing and analyzing relationships between data points. They use nodes to represent entities and edges to represent relationships between those entities. Graph databases are ideal for social networks, recommendation engines, fraud detection, and knowledge graphs.

Concept Sketch:

```
+-------+            +-------+
| Node A|-------->| Node B|
+-------+   Edge   +-------+
  (User)           (User)
    |
    |
```

```
         v
+-------+
| Node C|
+-------+
(Post)
```

Example: Neo4j and Amazon Neptune are popular graph databases.

Column-Family Stores: These databases store data in columns rather than rows, making them optimized for analytical queries on large datasets. They are often used for data warehousing, time-series data, and applications that require high read throughput.

Concept Sketch:

```
+----------+-----------+-----------+-----------+
|   RowKey | Column A  | Column B  | Column C  |
+----------+-----------+-----------+-----------+
|   Row 1  | Value A1  | Value B1  | Value C1  |
+----------+-----------+-----------+-----------+
|   Row 2  | Value A2  | Value B2  | Value C2  |
+----------+-----------+-----------+-----------+
|   Row 3  | Value A3  | Value B3  | Value C3  |
+----------+-----------+-----------+-----------+
```

Example: Cassandra and HBase are well-known column-family stores.

The diversity of NoSQL databases allows developers to choose the right tool for the job, optimizing for specific performance characteristics and application requirements.

Model Selection Trade-offs

Choosing the right data model is a critical decision that can significantly impact the performance, scalability, and maintainability of your application. It involves balancing several key factors:

Data Integrity: Relational databases excel at ensuring data integrity through ACID transactions and schema enforcement. If data integrity is paramount, the relational model might be the best choice. However, NoSQL databases often offer eventual consistency or other mechanisms to ensure data reliability, albeit with different trade-offs.

Scalability: NoSQL databases are generally better suited for applications that require high scalability, particularly horizontal scalability. If your application anticipates rapid growth in data volume or traffic, a NoSQL database might be a better choice.

Flexibility: NoSQL databases, especially document-oriented databases, offer greater flexibility in terms of schema evolution and handling semi-structured data. If your application needs to adapt quickly to changing requirements or deal with diverse data sources, a NoSQL database might be preferable.

Complexity: Relational databases can become complex to manage as data models grow and relationships become more intricate. NoSQL databases can simplify certain aspects of data management, but they may also introduce new complexities related to data consistency and query optimization.

Example:

Imagine you are building an e-commerce platform.

- For handling financial transactions and managing inventory, where ACID properties are critical, a relational database like PostgreSQL might be the best choice.

- For storing product catalogs with varying attributes, a document-oriented database like MongoDB might be more suitable.
- For building a recommendation engine based on user purchase history and product relationships, a graph database like Neo4j could be a valuable asset.

Ultimately, the best data model depends on the specific needs of your application. There is no one-size-fits-all solution. Carefully consider the trade-offs between data integrity, scalability, flexibility, and complexity to make an informed decision. Sometimes, a hybrid approach, combining different data models for different parts of the application, can be the most effective strategy.

Relational Model Strengths

ACID transactions, schema enforcement, and optimized query languages (SQL) provide data integrity and consistency.

The relational model's strengths are primarily found in its ability to ensure data integrity and consistency. This is largely due to its support for ACID transactions, schema enforcement, and the use of a powerful, optimized query language: SQL. Let's explore each of these aspects in detail.

ACID Transactions: Ensuring Reliability

ACID is an acronym that stands for Atomicity, Consistency, Isolation, and Durability. These four properties are crucial for reliable database operations, especially when multiple users or applications are accessing and modifying data concurrently. Let's examine each property:

- **Atomicity:** This ensures that a transaction is treated as a single, indivisible unit of work. Either all changes within the transaction are applied successfully, or none are. If any part of the transaction fails, the entire transaction is rolled back to its initial state, preventing partial updates.

  Example: Consider a bank transfer where money is debited from one account and credited to another. Atomicity ensures that if the debit succeeds but the credit fails (perhaps due to insufficient funds in the destination account), the debit is also rolled back, preventing money from disappearing.

- **Consistency:** A transaction must maintain the database's integrity constraints. It moves the database from one valid state to another. Any transaction that violates these constraints is rejected, ensuring that the database remains consistent.

  Example: Suppose you have a constraint that the balance in a bank account cannot be negative. A transaction that attempts to withdraw more money than is available, thus violating this constraint, would be rejected.

- **Isolation:** This ensures that concurrent transactions do not interfere with each other. Each transaction operates as if it were the only one running on the database, even when multiple transactions are executing simultaneously. Different isolation levels can be configured to balance concurrency and data integrity.

  Example: Two users trying to update the same bank account balance at the same time. Isolation ensures that one user's changes are not overwritten by the other, leading to an incorrect final balance.

- **Durability:** Once a transaction is committed, its changes are permanent and will survive even system failures (e.g., power outage, crash). The database system guarantees that the changes will be preserved.

  Example: After a bank transfer transaction is committed, the debit and credit operations are permanently stored and will not be lost, even if the database server crashes immediately afterward.

Schema Enforcement: Defining Data Structure and Integrity

A relational database enforces a strict schema, which defines the structure of the data, including the tables, columns, data types, and constraints. This schema acts as a blueprint, ensuring that all data conforms to a predefined format.

Example: Think of it as building blocks. You know the dimension and shapes of each building block. This will allow to only build consistent buildings.

Code Example:

```sql
CREATE TABLE Employees (
    EmployeeID INT PRIMARY KEY,
    FirstName VARCHAR(255),
    LastName VARCHAR(255),
    Salary DECIMAL(10, 2) CHECK (Salary >= 0),
    DepartmentID INT,
    FOREIGN KEY (DepartmentID) REFERENCES Departments(DepartmentID)
);
```

In this example, the `Employees` table has a defined structure:

`EmployeeID` is an integer and the primary key.
`FirstName` and `LastName` are strings.
`Salary` is a decimal number with a constraint that it must be non-negative (`CHECK (Salary :
`DepartmentID` is an integer and a foreign key referencing the `Departments` table.

Schema enforcement ensures that only data conforming to this structure can be inserted into the

Optimized Query Languages (SQL): Efficient Data Retrieval

SQL (Structured Query Language) is the standard language for interacting with relational databases. SQL is designed to efficiently query, manipulate, and manage data stored in relational databases. Relational databases are heavily optimized for SQL queries. The query optimizer analyzes the SQL query and determines the most efficient execution plan.

Example: Imagine searching for a specific book in a library.

Code Example:

```sql
SELECT FirstName, LastName, Salary
FROM Employees
WHERE DepartmentID = 10
ORDER BY Salary DESC;
```

This SQL query retrieves the first name, last name, and salary of all employees in department 1(

Benefits of SQL:

- **Declarative Language:** SQL is declarative, meaning you specify *what* data you want, not *how* to retrieve it. The database system figures out the most efficient way to execute the query.
- **Optimization:** Relational databases have sophisticated query optimizers that analyze SQL queries and determine the most efficient execution plan. This optimization can significantly improve query performance.
- **Standardization:** SQL is a standardized language, making it portable across different relational database systems.
- **Indexing:** Relational databases use indexes to speed up query performance. Indexes are data structures that allow the database to quickly locate specific rows in a table without scanning the entire table.

Summary

The relational model's strengths lie in its ACID transaction support, schema enforcement, and optimized SQL query language, which provide data integrity, consistency, and efficient data retrieval. These features make relational databases well-suited for applications requiring strong data reliability and complex data relationships.

NoSQL Motivations

The rise of NoSQL databases was driven by limitations encountered when using only relational databases for all types of applications. Relational databases, while excellent for many use cases, sometimes struggle with the scale, flexibility, and specialized data access patterns required by modern applications. This section explores the core motivations behind the development and adoption of NoSQL solutions.

Scalability:

Traditional relational databases often face challenges in scaling horizontally to handle massive datasets and high traffic loads. Horizontal scaling means adding more machines to your system. While relational databases *can* be scaled, it often involves complex sharding strategies, which can be difficult to manage and introduce significant overhead.

NoSQL databases, on the other hand, are often designed with horizontal scalability as a core principle. They are built to distribute data across many commodity servers, making it easier to increase capacity as needed without significant downtime or architectural changes.

Consider a social media application that needs to store and retrieve user profiles, posts, and connections for millions of users. With a relational database, as the number of users and posts grows, the database server can become a bottleneck. Adding more resources to a single server (vertical scaling) can only go so far. Sharding the database (splitting it into multiple databases) introduces complexity in managing relationships between users and their content across different shards.

A NoSQL database, like a key-value store or a document database, could handle this scenario more easily. Data can be distributed across multiple servers, and read/write operations can be routed to the appropriate server based on a key or document ID. Adding more servers to the cluster increases the overall capacity of the system.

Example:

Imagine you are building a simple counter application. Each time a user visits a page, the counter increments.

Relational Database (Conceptual):

```
CREATE TABLE counts (
  page_id INT PRIMARY KEY,
  count INT
);

UPDATE counts SET count = count + 1 WHERE page_id = 123;
```

In a highly concurrent environment, updating this single row in a relational database can become a bottleneck.

Key-Value Store (Conceptual):

```
#Using Python style pseduo code for clarity
# Assume "db" is an object representing a key-value store client

db.increment("page:123")
```

With a key-value store, the `increment` operation is often atomic and can be distributed across multiple servers, handling a much higher volume of updates.

Flexibility:

Relational databases enforce a strict schema, which defines the structure of the data. This schema must be defined in advance, and any changes to the schema can be costly and time-consuming, especially in large databases. This rigidity can be a hindrance in rapidly evolving applications where data requirements change frequently.

NoSQL databases, especially document databases, often offer greater flexibility in data modeling. They allow you to store data in a semi-structured format, such as JSON or XML, without requiring a predefined schema. This means you can add new fields or change the structure of your data without having to alter the entire database schema.

For example, consider an application that stores user profiles. In a relational database, you would need to define all the possible attributes of a user in advance, even if some users don't have all those attributes. Adding a new attribute would require altering the database schema and potentially migrating existing data.

In a document database, you can simply add the new attribute to the user's document without affecting other documents. This flexibility is particularly useful in situations where you're dealing with diverse and evolving data.

Example:

Relational Database (Conceptual):

```
CREATE TABLE users (
  id INT PRIMARY KEY,
  name VARCHAR(255),
  email VARCHAR(255),
  phone VARCHAR(20)
);
```

Adding a new field, such as `address`, requires altering the table schema.

Document Database (Conceptual - JSON):

```
{
  "id": 1,
  "name": "Alice",
  "email": "alice@example.com",
  "phone": "123-456-7890"
}

{
  "id": 2,
  "name": "Bob",
  "email": "bob@example.com",
  "address": {
    "street": "123 Main St",
    "city": "Anytown"
  }
}
```

Bob's document includes an `address` field, while Alice's does not. This is perfectly acceptable in a document database. Each "document" acts as a container for the relevant data.

Specialized Data Access Patterns:

Relational databases are optimized for general-purpose queries using SQL. However, some applications have very specific data access patterns that are not well-suited to SQL. For example, graph databases are designed for efficiently querying relationships between entities, while time-series databases are optimized for storing and retrieving time-stamped data.

NoSQL databases provide specialized data models and query languages that are tailored to these specific use cases. This can lead to significant performance improvements compared to using a relational database for the same task.

For instance, consider an application that needs to analyze social networks. Finding connections between people, or the shortest path between two users, is complex and inefficient using SQL. A graph database, however, is designed specifically for these types of graph traversal queries.

Sketch of a Social Network (Graph Database):

```
(Alice) --Friends--> (Bob)
       ^                / |
       |               /  |
     Likes           /  Friends
       |            /     |
    (Music) <---/      v
                   (Charlie)
```

In this sketch, Alice and Bob are friends. Alice likes Music. Bob and Charlie are friends. A graph database excels at finding these relationships and paths.

Example:

Relational Database (Conceptual - finding friends of friends):

```
SELECT u3.name
FROM users u1
JOIN friends u2 ON u1.id = u2.user1_id
JOIN friends u3 ON u2.user2_id = u3.user1_id
WHERE u1.name = 'Alice';
```

This query can become very complex and slow as the network grows.

Graph Database (Conceptual - using Cypher query language):

```
MATCH (a:User {name: 'Alice'})-[:FRIENDS]->(b)-[:FRIENDS]->(c)
RETURN c.name
```

The Cypher query is much more concise and efficient for traversing relationships in a graph.

In summary, NoSQL databases address specific limitations of relational databases, particularly in terms of scalability, flexibility, and handling specialized data access patterns. They offer alternatives tailored to modern application needs. The choice between a relational and NoSQL database, or a combination of both, depends heavily on the specific requirements of the application.

NoSQL Variety

NoSQL databases emerged to address the limitations of relational databases in certain scenarios. They offer different ways to store and access data, each suited to specific application needs. This section explores four common NoSQL models: key-value stores, document databases, graph databases, and column-family stores.

Key-Value Stores: These databases are the simplest NoSQL type. They store data as a collection of key-value pairs. Think of it like a dictionary where you look up a value (the data) using a key. Key-value stores are excellent for caching, session management, and storing user preferences.

Example: Imagine storing user session information for a website. The session ID could be the key, and the user's data (login status, shopping cart contents) would be the value.

```python
# Example using a simplified key-value store (Python dictionary)
session_data = {}
session_data["user123"] = {"logged_in": True, "cart": ["item1", "item2"]}
session_data["user456"] = {"logged_in": False, "cart": []}

# Accessing a user's session
user_session = session_data["user123"]
print(user_session["logged_in"]) # Output: True
```

Document Databases: These databases store data as documents, typically in JSON or XML format. Each document is a self-contained unit of data. Document databases are well-suited for applications with complex, semi-structured data, such as content management systems, e-commerce platforms, and mobile applications.

Example: Consider storing product information for an online store. Each product could be represented as a document with fields like name, description, price, images, and reviews.

```json
# Example of a product document in JSON format
{
  "product_id": "12345",
  "name": "Fancy T-Shirt",
  "description": "A stylish t-shirt made of premium cotton.",
  "price": 25.00,
  "images": ["image1.jpg", "image2.jpg"],
  "reviews": [
    {"user": "Alice", "rating": 5, "comment": "Great fit!"},
    {"user": "Bob", "rating": 4, "comment": "Good quality."}
  ]
}
```

Graph Databases: These databases are designed to store and query data that is highly interconnected. They use nodes to represent entities (e.g., people, places, things) and edges to represent relationships between entities (e.g., friendships, connections, dependencies). Graph databases are ideal for social networks, recommendation engines, and knowledge graphs.

Example: Imagine a social network. Each user is a node, and friendships are edges connecting those nodes. You can easily query the database to find all friends of a user, or friends of friends, and so on.

```
// Example using a simplified graph database query (Cypher-like syntax)
// Assuming nodes represent people and edges represent "FRIENDS_WITH" relationships

// Find all friends of user "Alice"
MATCH (alice:Person {name: "Alice"})-[:FRIENDS_WITH]->(friend:Person)
RETURN friend.name
```

In this representation:

- Circles represent Nodes (entities like people, places, concepts).
- Arrows represent Edges (relationships between nodes like friendship, ownership, influence).
- Alice is a Person node with property name "Alice".
- Bob and Carol are also Person nodes.
- The arrows labeled "FRIENDS_WITH" show the relationships: Alice is friends with Bob, and Bob is friends with Carol.
- To find Alice's friends, you follow the "FRIENDS_WITH" arrow from Alice to Bob.

Column-Family Stores: These databases organize data into columns, which are grouped into column families. Column families are similar to tables in relational databases, but they can contain different sets of columns for each row. Column-family stores are highly scalable and perform well for applications that require storing large amounts of data with varying attributes.

Example: Consider storing sensor data from various devices. Each device can be considered as a row, and sensor readings (temperature, pressure, humidity) are stored as columns. Different devices might have different sets of sensors, so each row can have a different set of columns.

Conceptual Sketch:

```
Row Key | Column Family: SensorData
--------|--------------------------------------------------------
Device1 | Temperature: 25C, Pressure: 1013hPa, Humidity: 60%
Device2 | Temperature: 22C, Humidity: 55%, Location: BuildingA
Device3 | Pressure: 1015hPa, Vibration: 0.5g
```

In this sketch:

- `Row Key`: Uniquely identifies each row (e.g., Device1, Device2, Device3).
- `Column Family`: SensorData: Groups related columns together. In a real system, you might have multiple column families.
- Each row can have a different set of columns. Device1 has Temperature, Pressure, and Humidity. Device2 has Temperature, Humidity, and Location. Device3 has Pressure and Vibration. This flexibility is a key feature of column-family stores.

Model Selection Trade-offs

Choosing the right data model is a crucial decision when designing data-intensive applications. It's not a one-size-fits-all situation. Instead, it involves carefully weighing several factors to find the best fit for your specific needs. The key trade-offs revolve around data integrity, scalability, flexibility, and complexity. Let's explore each of these in detail.

Balancing Act: Choosing the right data model involves balancing data integrity, scalability, flexibility, and complexity, based on application-specific needs.

Think of it like selecting the right tool for a job. A hammer is great for nails, but useless for screws. Similarly, a relational database might be perfect for one application, while a NoSQL database is better for another.

Data Integrity vs. Scalability: ACID transactions, schema enforcement, and optimized query languages (SQL) provide data integrity and consistency (Relational Model Strengths). Scalability, flexibility, and specialized data access patterns led to the development of NoSQL databases (NoSQL Motivations).

- **Data Integrity:** This refers to the accuracy and consistency of your data. Relational databases excel at maintaining data integrity because of ACID transactions.

    - *ACID* stands for Atomicity, Consistency, Isolation, and Durability. These properties ensure that database transactions are reliable and maintain data integrity, even in the face of errors or failures.

    - *Schema Enforcement:* Relational databases have a predefined schema, which dictates the structure of your data. This schema helps prevent inconsistent data from being entered into the database.

    - *SQL:* Structured Query Language (SQL) is a powerful language for querying and manipulating data in relational databases. It allows you to perform complex queries and ensures data integrity.

        Consider a banking application where transferring funds between accounts *must* be accurate. You wouldn't want half the money to disappear if something goes wrong. Relational databases with ACID transactions are ideal here.

        ```
        -- Example of a transaction in SQL
        START TRANSACTION;
        ```

```
UPDATE accounts SET balance = balance - 100 WHERE account_id = 123;
UPDATE accounts SET balance = balance + 100 WHERE account_id = 456;
COMMIT;
```

If any part of this transaction fails (e.g., account 123 doesn't have enough funds), the entire transaction is rolled back, ensuring no money is lost.

- **Scalability:** This refers to the ability of your database to handle increasing amounts of data and traffic. NoSQL databases were designed to handle massive amounts of data and high traffic loads.

    - *Horizontal Scaling:* NoSQL databases often support horizontal scaling, which means you can add more machines to your database cluster to handle more traffic.

    - *Relaxed Consistency:* To achieve scalability, NoSQL databases often relax the consistency requirements of ACID transactions. This means that data might not be immediately consistent across all nodes in the cluster.

        Think of a social media application where millions of users are posting and liking content every second. NoSQL databases are designed to handle this kind of scale. Illustrative Sketch:

        ```
        [Client] --> [Load Balancer] --> [NoSQL Node 1]
                                     --> [NoSQL Node 2]
                                     --> [NoSQL Node 3]
        (Adding more NoSQL nodes to scale horizontally)
        ```

        This example shows how NoSQL databases can scale by adding more nodes to the cluster.

    The trade-off here is that you might sacrifice some data integrity for scalability. NoSQL databases prioritize availability and partition tolerance (often referred to as the CAP theorem), sometimes at the expense of consistency.

Flexibility vs. Complexity: Key-value, document, graph, and column-family stores cater to diverse application needs and performance requirements (NoSQL Variety). A high-level survey of common data models and their evolution, from relational databases to various NoSQL approaches (Data Models Overview).

- **Flexibility:** NoSQL databases offer more flexibility in terms of data modeling. You don't have to adhere to a strict schema, which can be useful for applications with evolving data requirements.

    - *Schema-less:* NoSQL databases are often schema-less, which means you can store data in a variety of formats without having to define a schema upfront.

    - *Different Data Models:* NoSQL databases come in a variety of flavors, including key-value stores, document stores, graph databases, and column-family stores. Each of these data models is optimized for different types of data and access patterns.

    Consider an e-commerce application where you need to store product information. Product attributes can vary widely across categories. NoSQL document databases are well-suited for this scenario.

    ```
    // Example of a document in a document database (JSON)
    {
      "product_id": "123",
      "name": "T-Shirt",
      "description": "A comfortable cotton t-shirt",
      "price": 20.00,
      "colors": ["red", "blue", "green"],
      "sizes": ["S", "M", "L", "XL"]
    }
    ```

    You can add new attributes to the document without having to alter the entire database schema.

- **Complexity:** While NoSQL databases offer flexibility, they can also be more complex to manage than relational databases.

  - *Data Modeling:* Designing a NoSQL data model requires careful consideration of your application's data access patterns.

  - *Querying:* Querying NoSQL databases can be more challenging than querying relational databases with SQL.

  - *Data Consistency:* Ensuring data consistency in a distributed NoSQL environment can be complex.

  The trade-off here is that you might gain flexibility, but you'll need to invest more time and effort in data modeling, querying, and ensuring data consistency.

Summary:

Feature	Relational (SQL)	NoSQL
Data Integrity	High (ACID transactions, schema enforcement)	Variable (depends on the specific NoSQL database, often eventual consistency)
Scalability	Vertical (scaling up a single server)	Horizontal (scaling out across multiple servers)
Flexibility	Low (strict schema)	High (schema-less or flexible schema)
Complexity	Moderate (well-established standards like SQL)	High (requires understanding different data models and consistency models)
Example Use Case	Banking transactions, financial reporting	Social media, e-commerce product catalogs, IoT data

Ultimately, choosing the right data model is a matter of understanding your application's specific requirements and making informed trade-offs. Carefully consider your needs for data integrity, scalability, flexibility, and the level of complexity you're willing to handle. There is no perfect solution. The best option is the one that optimally balances these factors for your particular use case.

Chapter 3 Foundations of Data Systems-Storage and Retrieval: How Databases Store and Access Data

- **Storage Engines Overview:** Core component determining data layout on disk and query performance.

- **Log-Structured Storage:**

  - Write-optimized, append-only approach; efficient for writes.
  - Compaction and garbage collection overhead.

- **Sorted String Tables (SSTables):**

  - Key-value pairs sorted by key; facilitates efficient range queries.
  - Used in LevelDB, RocksDB, and Cassandra.

- **B-Trees:**

- o Balanced tree structure; efficient for reads and writes.
- o Widely used in traditional relational databases (e.g., PostgreSQL, MySQL).

- **Indexing:** Creating secondary indexes enhances query performance but increases write overhead.

Storage Engines Overview

The storage engine is the fundamental component of a database system that dictates how data is stored on disk and, critically, how efficiently that data can be retrieved or modified. Think of it as the engine of a car; it's the core mechanism that drives the entire system's performance. Different storage engines employ different techniques, each with its own strengths and weaknesses. Choosing the right storage engine for a specific application is crucial to achieving optimal performance and meeting the application's specific needs.

Core component determining data layout on disk and query performance.

At its heart, a storage engine determines how the database system organizes and manages data on physical storage (typically hard drives or solid-state drives). This organization profoundly impacts how quickly the database can locate and access specific pieces of data.

Consider a simple analogy: Imagine you have a library filled with books.

- **Scenario 1:** The books are arranged randomly on the shelves. Finding a specific book would require searching every shelf, one by one, until you locate it. This is analogous to a poorly designed storage engine. Query performance would be slow.
- **Scenario 2:** The books are arranged alphabetically by author. Finding a specific book becomes much faster because you can directly navigate to the relevant section of the library. This is analogous to a well-designed storage engine. Query performance is significantly improved.

The storage engine handles numerous low-level tasks, including:

- **Data storage format:** The specific format in which data is written to disk (e.g., row-oriented, column-oriented).
- **Indexing:** Creating data structures that speed up the process of finding specific data (we'll discuss indexing in more detail later).
- **Concurrency control:** Managing simultaneous access to data from multiple users or processes, ensuring data integrity.
- **Transaction management:** Ensuring that database operations are performed reliably, even in the face of errors or system failures (ACID properties: Atomicity, Consistency, Isolation, Durability).

Example:

Let's say we have a simple table representing users in a database:

```
CREATE TABLE users (
    id INT PRIMARY KEY,
    username VARCHAR(255),
    email VARCHAR(255)
);
```

The storage engine determines how this users table is physically stored on disk. A B-tree based storage engine might create a tree-like index on the id column, allowing the database to quickly find a user with a specific ID. Another storage engine might store the data in a log-structured format, optimized for high write throughput but potentially slower for reads.

Log-Structured Storage

Log-Structured Storage is a method for organizing and storing data, focused primarily on optimizing write operations.

- **Write-optimized, append-only approach; efficient for writes.**

At its core, Log-Structured Storage operates as an append-only system. This means that when new data is written, it's simply added to the end of a log file, rather than modifying existing data in place. Imagine a physical logbook where you always write new entries at the back, never erasing or overwriting previous entries. This append-only nature drastically speeds up write operations because it avoids the need to search for free space or modify existing blocks on the storage medium. Writing to the end of a file is a sequential operation, which is significantly faster than random writes. This makes Log-Structured Storage an excellent choice for applications that are write-intensive, such as logging systems, event tracking, and some types of databases. For example, in a system tracking website activity, each user action (page view, click, etc.) is written as a new entry in the log.

- **Compaction and garbage collection overhead.**

While the append-only approach provides fast writes, it introduces the need for compaction and garbage collection. As data is continuously appended, older versions of data, or data that has been deleted, accumulate in the log. This leads to wasted space and can slow down read operations. Compaction is the process of merging and rewriting segments of the log, discarding obsolete data and reorganizing the remaining valid data. Garbage collection identifies and reclaims space occupied by deleted or outdated data.

Think of it like this: over time, your logbook (append only) gets full of crossed-out entries and notes that are no longer relevant. Compaction is like creating a new, cleaner logbook, copying over only the important, up-to-date information. Garbage collection is like shredding the old, messy logbook to free up space. These operations are necessary to maintain performance and storage efficiency, but they introduce overhead. The system must periodically pause the usual write and read operations to perform compaction and garbage collection. The frequency and intensity of these operations must be carefully tuned to balance write performance with storage utilization and read latency.

Sorted String Tables (SSTables)

Sorted String Tables, often called SSTables, are a fundamental storage structure used in many modern databases and storage systems. They provide an efficient way to store and retrieve data, particularly when dealing with large datasets. The core idea behind an SSTable is that data is stored as key-value pairs, and these pairs are *sorted* by key. This sorting enables several performance optimizations.

Key-Value Pairs Sorted by Key: Facilitates Efficient Range Queries

The most crucial characteristic of SSTables is that the data is sorted by the key. Imagine you have a collection of names and associated phone numbers. In a traditional unsorted list, finding all names starting with "A" would require scanning the entire list. In an SSTable, because the names (keys) are sorted alphabetically, you can quickly locate the first name starting with "A" and then efficiently retrieve all subsequent names until you reach a name that does not start with "A".

This characteristic, the sorted nature, makes SSTables particularly well-suited for *range queries*. A range query asks for all data within a specified key range. For example, "Give me all customer records where customer ID is between 1000 and 2000". With an SSTable, you can efficiently locate the starting point (customer ID 1000), then sequentially read the records until you reach the end point (customer ID 2000). Without sorting, you would have to scan every single record to see if its ID falls within the range, a very slow process.

Example:

Imagine an SSTable containing website visit data, where the key is the timestamp of the visit, and the value is information about the visitor.

Let's represent this conceptually:

```
Key (Timestamp)  | Value (Visitor Data)
---------------------------------------
```

```
1678886400      | {user_id: 123, page: "/home"}
1678886460      | {user_id: 456, page: "/products"}
1678886520      | {user_id: 123, page: "/cart"}
1678886580      | {user_id: 789, page: "/contact"}
1678886640      | {user_id: 456, page: "/checkout"}
```

If you wanted to find all visits between timestamps 1678886400 and 1678886580, you could directly jump to the first relevant entry (1678886400) and then read sequentially until 1678886580 is reached. This direct access greatly improves query speed compared to scanning unsorted data.

Used in LevelDB, RocksDB, and Cassandra

SSTables are not just theoretical concepts; they are the foundation of several popular and widely used storage systems:

- **LevelDB:** A fast key-value storage library written at Google. It's used in Chrome browser and various other applications where fast, persistent storage is needed.
- **RocksDB:** Another high-performance key-value store, forked from LevelDB and heavily optimized by Facebook. It supports both disk-based and in-memory operation and is used in a wide variety of applications, including databases and distributed systems.
- **Cassandra:** A highly scalable, distributed NoSQL database designed for handling large amounts of data across many commodity servers. It uses SSTables as its primary storage format for data on disk.

The fact that these systems rely on SSTables is a testament to their efficiency and effectiveness in managing large-scale data. The specific implementations and optimizations vary across these systems, but the underlying principle of sorted, immutable data files remains the same.

B-Trees

Balanced tree structure; efficient for reads and writes.

B-Trees are a type of self-balancing tree data structure. The key characteristic of a B-Tree is that it maintains sorted data and allows searches, sequential access, insertions, and deletions in logarithmic time. This makes them highly efficient for both reading and writing data, a crucial feature for database systems and file systems.

Unlike binary search trees, B-Trees are designed to be shallow and wide. Each node in a B-Tree can have a large number of child nodes, allowing for fewer levels in the tree. This is especially beneficial when data is stored on disk, as it minimizes the number of disk accesses required to find a particular piece of data. Disk accesses are significantly slower than memory accesses, so reducing them is essential for performance.

Widely used in traditional relational databases (e.g., PostgreSQL, MySQL).

B-Trees are the workhorse of many traditional relational databases, including PostgreSQL and MySQL. Their efficiency in handling both reads and writes makes them ideal for these applications. Let's consider a few examples of how they are used:

- **Indexing in Databases:** Databases use B-Trees to create indexes on table columns. This allows the database to quickly locate rows that match a specific search criteria. For instance, imagine a table of customers with an index on the `customer_id` column. When a query searches for a customer with a specific `customer_id`, the database can use the B-Tree index to rapidly find the corresponding row without scanning the entire table.

- **Storage of Data:** In some databases, the actual data itself is stored within the B-Tree. Each leaf node in the B-Tree contains not only the index key but also the complete data record associated with that key.

Let's try to visualize a very basic B-Tree (with an order of 3, meaning each node can have up to 3 children):

```
[50]
    /    \
```

```
  [20, 30]  [70, 80]
  /  |  \  /  |  \
[10][25][35][60][75][90]
```

In this simplified example:

- The root node contains the key 50.
- The left child of the root contains the keys 20 and 30. All values in this subtree are less than 50.
- The right child of the root contains the keys 70 and 80. All values in this subtree are greater than 50.
- The leaf nodes contain the actual data (or pointers to the data).

Why B-Trees are efficient:

- **Balanced Structure:** The balanced nature of B-Trees ensures that all leaf nodes are at the same depth. This guarantees a predictable search time, regardless of the value being searched for.

- **Wide Nodes:** The ability of each node to hold multiple keys and children reduces the height of the tree. This is especially crucial when data is stored on disk because the disk access cost is greatly minimized as the height is reduced. Fewer levels to traverse means fewer disk I/O operations.

Code Example (Conceptual, Simplified):

While implementing a full B-Tree is complex, here's a very simplified illustration of searching in a B-Tree-like structure (not a complete B-Tree implementation, but it gives the flavor):

```python
class Node:
    def __init__(self, keys=[], children=[]):
        self.keys = keys
        self.children = children


def search_tree(node, key):
    """
    A simplified search function for a B-Tree like structure
    """

    i = 0
    while i < len(node.keys) and key > node.keys[i]:
        i += 1

    if i < len(node.keys) and key == node.keys[i]:
        return True  # Key found

    if not node.children:
        return False # Key not found (leaf node)

    return search_tree(node.children[i], key) # Recursive search

# Example usage (creating a very small example tree):
root = Node(keys=[50], children=[
    Node(keys=[20, 30], children=[
        Node(keys=[10]), Node(keys=[25]), Node(keys=[35])
    ]),
    Node(keys=[70, 80], children=[
        Node(keys=[60]), Node(keys=[75]), Node(keys=[90])
    ])
])
```

```
print(f"Searching for 25: {search_tree(root, 25)}") # Output: True
print(f"Searching for 40: {search_tree(root, 40)}") # Output: False
```

This Python code provides a conceptual view of how searching operates in a B-Tree. Keep in mind that the complexities surrounding node splitting, merging, and balancing operations during insertion and deletion are omitted for simplicity.

In summary, B-Trees are balanced, tree-based data structures fundamental to database systems and other applications requiring efficient storage and retrieval of data. Their key advantages lie in minimizing disk access and providing predictable performance for a wide range of operations.

Indexing

Creating secondary indexes enhances query performance but increases write overhead.

In Detail:

Imagine you have a large phone book. If you want to find someone's number, you usually look them up by their last name, which is how the phone book is sorted (indexed). This makes finding a specific name very fast. However, what if you wanted to find everyone who lived on a particular street? The phone book isn't sorted by street address, so you would have to go through *every single entry* to find those people. This would be very slow.

That's where indexes come in. In databases (and storage engines), an index is like creating a *second* phone book, but sorted in a different way. For example, you could create an index on the "street address" column of a database table. This extra index would be a separate data structure that makes it quick to find all the entries with a specific street address, *without* having to scan the entire main table.

How it works conceptually:

Let's say you have a table called users with the following columns: id, name, city.

Without an index, if you want to find all users in "London", the database has to look at every row in the users table and check if the city column is "London". This is called a full table scan, and it is very inefficient for large tables.

Now, let's create an index on the city column. The database might create a data structure something like this (a simplified example, real implementations are more sophisticated):

Index: city_index

```
London  ->  [1, 5, 10, 22]  (list of user IDs living in London)
Paris   ->  [2, 7, 15]      (list of user IDs living in Paris)
Tokyo   ->  [3, 8, 12]      (list of user IDs living in Tokyo)
```

When you search for users in "London", the database uses the city_index to quickly find the user IDs (1, 5, 10, 22) that match. Then, it only needs to retrieve the data for those specific users from the main users table. This is *much* faster than scanning the entire table.

Simplified Sketch:

```
+------------------------+      +------------------------------+
| users Table            |      | city_index (conceptual)      |
|------------------------|      |------------------------------|
| id | name | city       |      | city      | list of user IDs |
|------------------------|      |------------------------------|
| 1  | Alice| London     | -->  | London    | [1, 5, 10, 22]   |
| 2  | Bob  | Paris      | -->  | Paris     | [2, 7, 15]       |
| 3  | Carol| Tokyo      | -->  | Tokyo     | [3, 8, 12]       |
```

```
| 4  | David| New York |        | ...      | ...                    |
| 5  | Eve  | London   |        |----------------------------|
| ...| ...  | ...      |        |                            |
+----------------------+        +----------------------------+
```

Query: SELECT FROM users WHERE city = 'London';
Uses city_index to quickly find matching IDs.

Code example (SQL):

```sql
-- Create a table
CREATE TABLE users (
    id INT PRIMARY KEY,
    name VARCHAR(255),
    city VARCHAR(255)
);


-- Insert some data
INSERT INTO users (id, name, city) VALUES
(1, 'Alice', 'London'),
(2, 'Bob', 'Paris'),
(3, 'Carol', 'Tokyo'),
(4, 'David', 'New York'),
(5, 'Eve', 'London');


-- Create an index on the city column
CREATE INDEX idx_city ON users (city);


-- Query using the index
SELECT  FROM users WHERE city = 'London';
```

The Trade-off: Increased Write Overhead

Indexes aren't free. While they drastically improve the speed of certain SELECT queries, they also *increase* the time it takes to perform INSERT, UPDATE, and DELETE operations. This is because:

- **Insert:** When you add a new row to the users table, the database not only has to write the data to the main table, but it *also* has to update the city_index.
- **Update:** If you change a user's city (e.g., from "London" to "Berlin"), the database has to *remove* the user's ID from the "London" entry in the city_index and *add* it to the "Berlin" entry.
- **Delete:** When you delete a user, the database must remove their ID from *all* relevant indexes.

Therefore, every write operation now involves writing to multiple locations: the main table *and* all the relevant indexes. The more indexes you have, the slower your write operations will be.

When to use indexes:

- **Frequently queried columns:** Create indexes on columns that are often used in WHERE clauses, JOIN conditions, or ORDER BY clauses.
- **Read-heavy applications:** If your application performs many more reads than writes, the performance benefits of indexes will likely outweigh the write overhead.
- **Carefully consider the trade-offs:** Don't create indexes on *every* column. Analyze your query patterns and choose indexes strategically. Too many indexes can actually *hurt* performance.
- **Avoid Indexing Columns with Low Cardinality:** An index on a column with very few distinct values (e.g., a "gender" column with only "male" and "female") is often not beneficial. The database might still choose to perform a full table scan because the index doesn't significantly narrow down the search.

In summary, indexing is a powerful technique for optimizing query performance, but it's crucial to understand the trade-offs and use it judiciously to avoid negatively impacting write performance.

Chapter 4 Foundations of Data Systems-Data Encoding, Serialization, and Evolution

Here are 5 bullet points explaining Data Encoding, Serialization, and Evolution:

- **Data Encoding Formats:** Choosing appropriate formats (JSON, XML, binary) impacts efficiency, readability, and compatibility.

- **Serialization:** Transforms in-memory data into a byte stream for storage or transmission.

- **Backward Compatibility:** Newer code can read data written by older code.

- **Forward Compatibility:** Older code can read data written by newer code.

- **Schema Evolution:** Managing changes to data structure over time to maintain system integrity.

Data Encoding Formats

The choice of data encoding format is a foundational decision in software development, influencing application performance, interoperability, and maintainability. Selecting the *appropriate* format hinges on factors like data complexity, human readability requirements, and cross-platform compatibility needs. Broadly, encoding formats can be categorized as text-based (like JSON and XML) or binary.

Text-Based Formats: JSON and XML

Text-based formats, particularly JSON (JavaScript Object Notation) and XML (Extensible Markup Language), prioritize human readability and platform independence.

- **JSON:** JSON is a lightweight data-interchange format that is easy for humans to read and write. It's based on a subset of the JavaScript programming language, making it straightforward to parse and generate in many programming languages. JSON uses key-value pairs and arrays to represent data structures.

  Example:

  ```
  {
    "name": "John Doe",
    "age": 30,
    "city": "New York"
  }
  ```

  JSON's simplicity lends itself well to web APIs and configurations where readability is paramount. Most web applications use JSON to exchange data between client and server.

- **XML:** XML is a markup language designed for encoding documents in a format that is both human-readable and machine-readable. XML uses tags to define elements and attributes to provide additional information about those elements.

Example:

```
<person>
  <name>John Doe</name>
  <age>30</age>
  <city>New York</city>
</person>
```

While XML offers features like schema validation (using XSD) for enforcing data structure, its verbosity can lead to larger file sizes compared to JSON. Historically, XML saw widespread use in enterprise systems and document storage but has largely been superseded by JSON in modern web development, though it still maintains niches such as configuration files.

Binary Formats

Binary formats represent data in a compact, machine-readable format, sacrificing human readability for efficiency in storage and transmission. These formats are often more complex to work with directly but offer significant performance benefits, especially when dealing with large datasets or performance-critical applications. Examples include Protocol Buffers, Apache Avro, and MessagePack.

- **Protocol Buffers:** Developed by Google, Protocol Buffers are a language-neutral, platform-neutral, extensible mechanism for serializing structured data. They require defining a schema in a `.proto` file, which is then compiled into code for various languages.

Example `.proto` *definition:*

```
syntax = "proto3";
package example;

message Person {
  string name = 1;
  int32 age = 2;
  string city = 3;
}
```

Protocol Buffers excel in scenarios demanding high performance and data integrity. Their strong typing and schema evolution features are invaluable for building robust, scalable systems.

- **Apache Avro:** Avro is a data serialization system developed within the Apache Hadoop project. It provides rich data structures, a compact, fast binary data format, and schema evolution capabilities. Avro schemas are typically defined in JSON.

Example Avro Schema (JSON):

```
{
  "type": "record",
  "name": "Person",
  "fields": [
    {"name": "name", "type": "string"},
    {"name": "age", "type": "int"},
    {"name": "city", "type": "string"}
  ]
}
```

Avro is particularly well-suited for handling large volumes of data in distributed systems due to its efficient serialization and schema evolution features.

- **MessagePack:** MessagePack is another binary serialization format that aims to be efficient and simple. It's designed to be similar to JSON but in binary format, resulting in smaller message sizes and faster processing. MessagePack supports a variety of data types and is used in various applications, including gaming and messaging systems.

Comparing Encoding Formats: A Summary

Feature	JSON	XML	Protocol Buffers	Apache Avro	MessagePack
Readability	High	Medium	Low	Low	Low
Verbosity	Low	High	Low	Low	Low
Performance	Medium	Low	High	High	High
Schema Support	Implicit	Optional (XSD)	Required	Required	Implicit
Use Cases	Web APIs, Configuration	Documents, Enterprise	RPC, Data Storage	Data Pipelines	Messaging, Gaming

Sketch Visualization:

```
+------------------+        +-----------------+        +-----------------+
| Text-Based       |----->| JSON            |        | Binary          |----->| Protocol Buffers|
| (Human Readable) |        | (Simple, Web)   |        | (Efficient)     |        | (Strong Schema) |
+------------------+        +-----------------+        +-----------------+
        ^                                                       ^
        |                                                       |
        |                                                       |
        |        +-----------------+             +-----------------+
        ------| XML             |             | Apache Avro     |
                 | (Verbose, Legacy)|             | (Schema, Hadoop)|
                 +-----------------+             +-----------------+
                                                         ^
                                                         |
                                                         |
                                                 +-----------------+
                                                 | MessagePack     |
                                                 | (Simple Binary) |
                                                 +-----------------+
```

Choosing the right data encoding format requires careful consideration of the trade-offs between readability, efficiency, and compatibility. Text-based formats like JSON and XML are suitable for scenarios where human readability and interoperability are priorities, while binary formats such as Protocol Buffers, Apache Avro, and MessagePack are preferable for performance-critical applications and large-scale data processing.

Serialization

Serialization is the process of transforming data that exists in memory (like objects, data structures) into a format that can be stored or transmitted. Think of it as taking a snapshot of your data and converting it into a sequence of bytes. This byte stream can then be saved to a file, sent over a network, or stored in a database. Later, this byte stream can be deserialized (the reverse process) to reconstruct the original data in memory.

Why is Serialization Important?

Imagine you have a complex object in your program representing a customer, complete with their name, address, order history, etc. You want to save this customer's information to a file so you can retrieve it later. You can't simply copy the raw memory contents of the object because that memory address is only valid for the current execution of the program. Serialization provides a structured way to convert this complex object into a portable format that can be saved and loaded anywhere. Similarly, if you need to send this customer object to another service over a network, serialization provides the mechanism to convert it into a stream of bytes that can be transmitted.

A Simple Analogy:

Think of serialization like packing a suitcase. You have various items (data) that you need to transport. Serialization is like carefully arranging those items into a suitcase (byte stream) in a standardized way so that someone else (another program or system) can unpack the suitcase and reconstruct the original items. Deserialization is like unpacking the suitcase and putting all items back.

Examples:

Let's illustrate with a simple Python example:

```python
import json

# Our data object (a dictionary)
customer = {
    "name": "Alice Smith",
    "age": 30,
    "city": "New York"
}

# Serialization: Convert the dictionary to a JSON string
serialized_customer = json.dumps(customer)

print(serialized_customer)  # Output: {"name": "Alice Smith", "age": 30, "city": "New York"}

# Deserialization: Convert the JSON string back to a dictionary
deserialized_customer = json.loads(serialized_customer)

print(deserialized_customer)  # Output: {'name': 'Alice Smith', 'age': 30, 'city': 'New York'}
print(deserialized_customer["name"]) #Access a specific element, e.g. retriving name of the cust
```

In this example, the json.dumps() function serializes the Python dictionary into a JSON (JavaScript Object Notation) string. json.loads() performs the deserialization, converting the JSON string back into a Python dictionary. JSON is a text-based format, making it human-readable and widely supported across different programming languages.

Different Serialization Formats:

JSON is just one serialization format. Other popular formats include:

- **XML (Extensible Markup Language):** Another text-based format, but generally more verbose than JSON. It uses tags to define data elements.
- **Protocol Buffers (protobuf):** A binary serialization format developed by Google. It's efficient in terms of space and speed but requires a schema definition.
- **Apache Avro:** Another binary serialization format designed for data serialization and exchange, particularly within Apache Hadoop. It also relies on a schema.
- **MessagePack:** A binary serialization format that is efficient and lightweight, focusing on simplicity and speed.

Binary vs. Text-Based Formats:

- **Binary formats** (like Protocol Buffers, Avro, and MessagePack) are generally more compact and faster to serialize and deserialize than text-based formats. However, they are not human-readable, which can make debugging more difficult. They often require a schema to define the structure of the data.
- **Text-based formats** (like JSON and XML) are human-readable, making them easier to debug. They are also more readily interoperable between different systems. However, they tend to be larger and slower to process compared to binary formats.

Sketch example:

A simple diagram showing serialization and deserialization processes

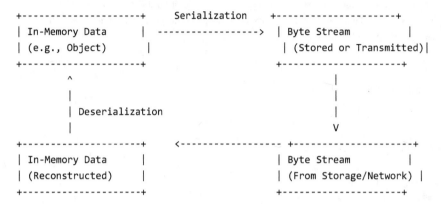

This diagram shows the flow of data from an in-memory representation to a byte stream (serialization) and back again (deserialization).

Serialization plays a vital role in various software development aspects such as data persistence, inter-process communication, and distributed systems. The appropriate serialization choice impacts performance, compatibility, and maintainability.

Backward Compatibility

Backward compatibility is a crucial aspect of software development, especially when dealing with data storage and transmission. It ensures that newer versions of your application or system can successfully read and process data created by older versions. Think of it as your new software speaking the same language as your old software's data.

Why is it important?

Imagine you have a database filled with customer information created by version 1.0 of your application. Now, you release version 2.0 with an updated data structure, perhaps adding new fields or changing data types. Without backward compatibility, version 2.0 would be unable to understand the data created by version 1.0, leading to data loss, errors, or complete system failure. Users would be unable to access their existing data, which would be unacceptable.

How to Achieve It

Achieving backward compatibility often involves careful planning and design during schema evolution. Here are some common strategies:

- **Adding New Fields as Optional:** When adding new fields to your data structure, make them optional. Older versions of the application, which don't know about these fields, can safely ignore them.

- **Providing Default Values:** If a new field is not present in older data, provide a reasonable default value. This prevents errors and ensures that the new application can function correctly.

- **Data Transformation:** Implement data transformation routines that can convert older data formats into the new format. This might involve reading the old data, applying a series of transformations, and then writing it out in the new format. This can be done "on-the-fly" when the older data is first accessed by the newer system, or as a batch migration.

- **Version Tagging**: Add version identifiers to data records to help newer code determine how to interpret the data. This is particularly useful for handling more complex evolutions.

Example

Let's consider a simple example using JSON, a common data encoding format. Suppose you have a user profile represented as follows in version 1.0:

```json
{
  "username": "john.doe",
  "email": "john.doe@example.com"
}
```

Now, in version 2.0, you want to add a new field for the user's profile picture:

```json
{
  "username": "john.doe",
  "email": "john.doe@example.com",
  "profile_picture": "john.doe.jpg"
}
```

To ensure backward compatibility, you can make the `profile_picture` field optional. Version 1.0 of your application can still read and process the data, ignoring the new field. When Version 2.0 processes data without `profile_picture`, it can use a default image, or display no image.

Code example (Python)

```python
import json

def process_user_data(json_data):
    """Processes user data, handling potential missing fields."""
    data = json.loads(json_data)

    username = data["username"]
    email = data["email"]
    profile_picture = data.get("profile_picture", "default_profile.jpg") # Provide a default value

    print(f"Username: {username}")
    print(f"Email: {email}")
    print(f"Profile Picture: {profile_picture}")


# Example usage with version 1.0 data
v1_data = '{"username": "jane.doe", "email": "jane.doe@example.com"}'
process_user_data(v1_data)

# Example usage with version 2.0 data
v2_data = '{"username": "peter.pan", "email": "peter.pan@example.com", "profile_picture": "peter
process_user_data(v2_data)
```

In this example, the `process_user_data` function uses the `get` method to retrieve the `profile_picture` field. If the field is not present in the JSON data (i.e., it's version 1.0 data), the `get` method returns a default value of "default_profile.jpg". This allows the function to handle both version 1.0 and version 2.0 data without errors.

Sketch

```
Data v1.0: [Username] [Email] --------------------> Application v2.0 (Reads Username, Email)
                                                  |
Data v2.0: [Username] [Email] [Profile Pic] --------> Application v2.0 (Reads Username, Email, F
```

The sketch above illustrates that the Application v2.0 can read both data from V1.0, and data from V2.0, therefore preserving backward compatibility. Even though Data v1.0 doesn't have "Profile Pic", V2.0 can still operate with the older format (perhaps by using a default image when the Profile Pic is missing).

Challenges

Maintaining backward compatibility can be challenging, especially as your application evolves significantly over time. Complex data transformations can become difficult to manage, and adding too many optional fields can clutter your data structure. It's essential to strike a balance between maintaining compatibility and introducing necessary changes to your system.

Conclusion

Backward compatibility is a critical aspect of software development. Without it, new versions of your software could render existing data unusable. Careful planning, design, and the use of appropriate techniques can help ensure that your application can evolve gracefully without disrupting your users or losing valuable data.

Forward Compatibility

Forward compatibility refers to the ability of older software or systems to correctly process data generated by newer versions of the same software or systems. In essence, it means that your old code can still understand and use data created by new code. This is crucial for maintaining system uptime and preventing data loss during upgrades or migrations.

To simplify forward compatibility, there are some techniques you can use, let us consider the following:

- **Data Encoding Formats:** Choosing appropriate formats (JSON, XML, binary) impacts efficiency, readability, and compatibility.

Selecting a suitable data encoding format is the foundation of forward compatibility. Formats like JSON (JavaScript Object Notation) and XML (Extensible Markup Language) are human-readable and offer flexibility because of their key-value pair structure. Binary formats are more compact, but often require strict schema definitions which can make forward compatibility difficult.

For example, in JSON, if an older system encounters a new field, it can often ignore it without crashing, provided it's designed to handle unknown fields.

Consider a simple JSON example:

Old Version Data:

```
{
  "user_id": 123,
  "username": "john.doe"
}
```

New Version Data:

```
{
  "user_id": 123,
  "username": "john.doe",
  "email": "john.doe@example.com"
}
```

An older system designed to only process `user_id` and `username` can still read the new version's data. It simply ignores the `email` field.

- **Serialization:** Transforms in-memory data into a byte stream for storage or transmission.

Serialization is the process of converting in-memory data structures into a format suitable for storage or transmission. The way data is serialized impacts its compatibility. Utilizing serialization libraries that support versioning or schema evolution features can greatly enhance forward compatibility. For instance, Google's Protocol Buffers or Apache Avro allow you to define schemas and evolve them over time, providing mechanisms for older versions to read data serialized by newer versions.

- **Backward Compatibility:** Newer code can read data written by older code.

Backward compatibility is related but distinct from forward compatibility. While forward compatibility ensures old systems can handle new data, backward compatibility ensures new systems can handle old data. Ideally, both should be maintained, but forward compatibility is often more challenging. Maintaining backward compatibility often simplifies achieving forward compatibility. If newer systems still understand old data formats, introducing new data formats that older systems need to handle is less problematic.

- **Schema Evolution:** Managing changes to data structure over time to maintain system integrity.

Schema evolution is the core of enabling forward compatibility. It involves carefully managing changes to your data structures (schemas) to ensure that older versions can still interpret the data. Strategies include:

```
Adding new fields: This is typically the safest and most common approach. Older systems can simp
    Making fields optional:  If a field might be removed in the future, making it optional from 1
    Using default values: When a new field is added, provide a default value that older systems (
    Renaming fields (with care): Renaming fields can break compatibility. If necessary, provide a
    Transformations: Sometimes, data needs to be transformed. For instance, a unit change (e.g.,
```

A sketch demonstrating schema evolution is as follows:

```
Old Schema:        [Field A] - [Field B]
                        |
                        | Adding Field C (Schema Evolution)
                        V
New Schema:        [Field A] - [Field B] - [Field C]
```

Consider a database schema change. Initially, you have a `users` table:

```
CREATE TABLE users (
  id INT PRIMARY KEY,
  name VARCHAR(255)
);
```

Later, you add an `email` column:

```
ALTER TABLE users ADD COLUMN email VARCHAR(255);
```

Older applications querying this table will still work fine because they will only select `id` and `name`. They are unaware of the `email` column, so they're not affected.

Forward compatibility allows gradual upgrades without forcing a simultaneous update of all systems. It ensures that older systems can continue functioning while newer systems take advantage of new features. Proper planning and a well-defined schema evolution strategy are crucial for achieving forward compatibility, minimizing disruptions, and maintaining system stability.

Schema Evolution

Schema evolution is the process of managing changes to the structure of data over time. This is crucial because data structures are rarely static; they evolve as applications grow, business requirements change, and new features are added. Without proper schema evolution strategies, systems can become brittle and prone to errors when encountering data in unexpected formats. This ensures that older and newer versions of the software can work together harmoniously.

Consider a simple example: imagine you have a system that stores user profiles. Initially, each profile might only contain a `name` and an `email` field.

```
// Version 1: User Profile Schema
{
  "name": "John Doe",
  "email": "john.doe@example.com"
}
```

Later, you decide to add an `age` field to the user profile. The schema has now evolved.

```
// Version 2: User Profile Schema (with age)
{
  "name": "John Doe",
  "email": "john.doe@example.com",
  "age": 30
}
```

The Problem:

What happens when your application (which now expects the `age` field) reads an older user profile that doesn't have the `age` field? Or, conversely, what if an older version of your application receives a user profile with the `age` field, which it doesn't understand? This is where schema evolution strategies come into play.

Strategies for Schema Evolution:

There are several techniques to handle schema evolution. The key is to ensure backward and forward compatibility, so let's explore these first.

Backward Compatibility

Backward compatibility means that newer code can read data written by older code. In our user profile example, the newer application that expects the `age` field should still be able to process older user profiles that don't have the `age` field.

- **Default Values:** A common approach is to assign a default value to the new field (`age` in this case) when it's missing in the older data.

  In code (illustrative Python example):

  ```python
  def process_user_profile(profile):
      name = profile.get("name")
      email = profile.get("email")
      age = profile.get("age", None)  # Default value is None

      print(f"Name: {name}, Email: {email}, Age: {age}")

  # Processing an older profile
  old_profile = {"name": "Jane Smith", "email": "jane.smith@example.com"}
  process_user_profile(old_profile)  # Output: Name: Jane Smith, Email: jane.smith@example.co

  # Processing a newer profile
  new_profile = {"name": "Peter Jones", "email": "peter.jones@example.com", "age": 40}
  process_user_profile(new_profile)  # Output: Name: Peter Jones, Email: peter.jones@example.
  ```

  Here the `.get()` method handles missing fields gracefully.

- **Optional Fields:** Design schemas with new fields as optional. This allows older data to be valid.

Forward Compatibility

Forward compatibility means that older code can read data written by newer code. This is often trickier to achieve than backward compatibility.

- **Ignoring Unknown Fields:** Older applications should be designed to gracefully ignore fields they don't understand. This requires that data encoding formats allow for extra data without throwing errors. JSON provides the feature to ignore unknown fields.

- **Schema Versioning:** Include a version number in the data. Older applications can then determine if they can handle the data or if they need to be upgraded.

```
// Example with versioning
{
  "version": 2,
  "name": "John Doe",
  "email": "john.doe@example.com",
  "age": 30
}
```

The older application can verify the version number before processing.

```
def process_user_profile(profile):
    version = profile.get("version", 1)  # Assume version 1 if not specified

    if version == 1:
        name = profile["name"]
        email = profile["email"]
        print(f"Version 1 Processing: Name: {name}, Email: {email}")
    elif version == 2:
        name = profile["name"]
        email = profile["email"]
        age = profile["age"]
        print(f"Version 2 Processing: Name: {name}, Email: {email}, Age: {age}")
    else:
        print("Unsupported version")
```

Importance of Data Encoding Formats

The choice of data encoding format plays a significant role in schema evolution.

- **JSON (JavaScript Object Notation):** JSON is flexible and human-readable. It naturally supports optional fields because parsers typically ignore unknown fields.

- **XML (Extensible Markup Language):** XML also allows for schema evolution, but it tends to be more verbose and complex than JSON.

- **Binary Formats (e.g., Protocol Buffers, Apache Avro):** These formats are highly efficient in terms of storage and transmission. They often come with built-in schema evolution support, including default values, optional fields, and schema versioning. They often require schema definition language and a compilation step.

Sketch Representation of Schema Evolution:

```
+---------+         +---------+         +---------+
| Old App |----->|  Data    |----->| New App |
|  (V1)   |        |  (V1)   |        |  (V2)   |
+---------+         +---------+         +---------+
```

```
        |
        | Reads Old Data OK (Backward Compatibility)
        v
+---------+
| Data    |
| (V2)    |
+---------+
        |
        | But can older app (V1) read new Data (Forward Comp)
        v
+---------+
| Schema  |---Versioning, Default Values, Optional Fields---> Evolution Management
+---------+
```

Real-World Example: Database Schema Changes

Consider a database table storing customer information.

- Initially, the table might have columns for customer_id, name, and address.
- Later, you might add a column for phone_number.

To handle this evolution:

- Provide a default value for the phone_number column for existing rows (e.g., NULL or an empty string).
- Update the application to handle cases where the phone_number is NULL (for older records).

Summary:

Schema evolution is a critical aspect of software development. Proper planning and the use of appropriate techniques (default values, optional fields, schema versioning) are essential for maintaining system integrity and ensuring that applications can gracefully handle changes in data structures over time. Selecting the right data encoding format (JSON, XML, Protocol Buffers, Avro) also contributes significantly to the ease and robustness of schema evolution.

Chapter 5 Building Scalable and Reliable Systems-Distributed Systems Foundations: CAP Theorem and Beyond

- **CAP Theorem:** Consistency, Availability, Partition Tolerance; only two can be guaranteed simultaneously in a distributed system.

- **Consistency Trade-offs:** Explore different consistency models (strong, eventual) and their impact on application behavior.

- **Availability Considerations:** Understand strategies for maintaining uptime despite failures, including replication and failover.

- **Partition Tolerance is Mandatory:** Distributed systems *must* tolerate network partitions, forcing a choice between consistency and availability.

- **Beyond CAP (PACELC):** PACELC extends CAP, highlighting the latency/consistency trade-off even when there are no partitions.

CAP Theorem

The CAP Theorem is a fundamental principle in distributed system design. It states that a distributed system can only guarantee two out of the following three properties simultaneously: **Consistency**, **Availability**, and **Partition Tolerance**. Understanding this trade-off is crucial when building any distributed application.

Let's break down each property:

- **Consistency:** Every read receives the most recent write or an error. Essentially, all nodes in the system see the same data at the same time. Think of it like a highly synchronized database. If one part of the system updates a piece of data, all other parts of the system instantly reflect that change. Imagine a banking application. If you transfer $100 from your savings account to your checking account, consistency means that immediately after the transfer, all ATMs, mobile apps, and bank tellers will see the updated balances in both accounts. A sketch might look like this:

```
[User] --(Transfer $100)--> [System (Node A)]
   |
   | Updates Data
   V
[System (Node B)] --(Read Balance)--> [User Sees Correct Balance]
```

In this case, even if the user connects to a different node (Node B) after the transfer, they will still see the accurate, updated balance because the system guarantees consistency.

- **Availability:** Every request receives a non-error response – without guarantee that it contains the most recent write. In simpler terms, the system is always "up" and responding to requests. Even if some parts of the system are down, the remaining parts should still be able to serve requests. Consider an e-commerce website. Even if some servers are experiencing issues, the website should still allow users to browse products and place orders. It may not be perfect (e.g., inventory counts might be slightly off for a short period), but the core functionality remains available. A simple sketch:

```
[User] --(Request)--> [Load Balancer]
                         |
                         +--> [Node A (Down)]
                         |
                         +--> [Node B (Serving Request)]
                         |
                         V
                    [User Receives Response]
```

Even though Node A is down, the load balancer directs the request to Node B, and the user receives a response, maintaining availability.

- **Partition Tolerance:** The system continues to operate despite arbitrary partitioning due to network failures. Network partitions are unavoidable in distributed systems. They occur when communication between different parts of the system is disrupted, essentially creating isolated "islands." A system is partition-tolerant if it can continue to function correctly even when these partitions occur. Consider a system with two data centers. If the network connection between the data centers is severed, creating a partition, a partition-tolerant system will continue to operate in both data centers independently. This might mean that some data becomes temporarily inconsistent between the two data centers, but the system remains functional. A sketch:

```
[Data Center A] --------X-------- [Data Center B]  (Network Partition)
        |                           |
      +--> [Nodes Operating]      +--> [Nodes Operating]
```

Despite the network partition, both data centers continue to process requests and operate independently.

The CAP Theorem tells us we can only pick two. This means we can have:

- **CA (Consistency and Availability):** Suitable for systems where partitions are rare and the cost of inconsistency is high. For example, a single, strongly consistent database on a reliable network.
- **CP (Consistency and Partition Tolerance):** Suitable for systems where data consistency is critical, even at the expense of availability during partitions. Examples include banking systems where transaction accuracy is paramount.
- **AP (Availability and Partition Tolerance):** Suitable for systems where high availability is critical, and some data inconsistency can be tolerated during partitions. Examples include social media platforms where it's more important to keep the service running than to guarantee absolute consistency of every post or like count in real-time.

The choice of which two properties to prioritize depends entirely on the specific requirements and use case of the distributed system.

Consistency Trade-offs

Consistency isn't a binary concept; there are different consistency models that offer various guarantees. Understanding these models is crucial for designing distributed systems that meet specific application requirements. Here are two common consistency models:

- **Strong Consistency:** This is the most intuitive form of consistency. It guarantees that after an update is made, all subsequent reads will see that update. This is often achieved through techniques like distributed transactions and consensus algorithms. With strong consistency, the system behaves as if there's only a single copy of the data. This simplifies application development, as developers don't need to worry about dealing with stale data. However, strong consistency can come at the cost of lower availability and higher latency, especially during network partitions. Example: Database transaction.

  Imagine a financial transaction where you're transferring money between accounts. Strong consistency would guarantee that once the money is debited from one account, it's immediately visible when reading the balance of the other account. This is critical to prevent overspending or lost funds.

- **Eventual Consistency:** This model guarantees that if no new updates are made to a given data item, eventually all accesses to that item will return the last updated value. In other words, the system will eventually become consistent, but there might be a period of time where different parts of the system see different values. Eventual consistency is often used in systems where high availability and low latency are more important than immediate consistency. Techniques like replication and asynchronous updates are commonly used to achieve eventual consistency. Example: DNS Consider a Domain Name System (DNS). When you update the IP address associated with a domain name, it takes time for the changes to propagate across all DNS servers worldwide. During this propagation period, some users might still be directed to the old IP address. Eventually, all DNS servers will be updated, and everyone will be directed to the new IP address.

The choice between strong and eventual consistency depends on the specific needs of the application. If data accuracy and immediate consistency are paramount, strong consistency is the way to go. If high availability and low latency are more important, and some temporary inconsistency can be tolerated, eventual consistency is a better choice.

Availability Considerations

Maintaining uptime in a distributed system requires careful consideration of potential failure scenarios. Here are two key strategies for ensuring availability:

- **Replication:** This involves creating multiple copies of data and storing them on different nodes in the system. If one node fails, the other nodes can continue to serve requests, ensuring that the data remains available. Replication can be synchronous (where updates are applied to all replicas before the transaction is considered complete) or asynchronous (where updates are applied to replicas after the transaction is complete). Imagine a database with multiple replicas. If the primary database server fails, one of the replicas can be automatically promoted to become the new primary, ensuring that the database remains available.

```
[User] --(Request)--> [Load Balancer]
                            |
                            +--> [Primary DB (Failed)]
                            |
                            +--> [Replica DB (Promoted to Primary)]
                            |
                            V
                      [User Receives Response]
```

- **Failover:** This is the process of automatically switching to a backup system when the primary system fails. Failover can be implemented in various ways, such as using a hot standby (where the backup system is constantly running and ready to take over) or a cold standby (where the backup system is only started when the primary system fails). Consider a web server cluster with a load balancer. If one of the web servers fails, the load balancer automatically redirects traffic to the remaining healthy servers, ensuring that the website remains available. A sketch might look something like this:

```
[User] --(Request)--> [Load Balancer]
                            |
                            +--> [Web Server 1 (Failed)]
                            |
                            +--> [Web Server 2 (Healthy)]
                            |
                            V
                      [User Receives Response]
```

Here, the load balancer detects the failure of Web Server 1 and automatically routes traffic to the available Web Server 2.

By implementing replication and failover strategies, distributed systems can significantly improve their availability and resilience to failures.

Partition Tolerance is Mandatory

In a distributed system, network partitions *must* be tolerated. Network failures are inevitable, and a system that cannot handle them is inherently unreliable. This means that when a partition occurs, you are forced to choose between consistency and availability. When a partition occurs, you have two basic options:

1. **Choose Consistency (CP):** In this scenario, the system prioritizes data consistency over availability. When a partition occurs, the system might choose to become unavailable in one or more partitions to ensure that data remains consistent across all partitions. This is typically achieved by preventing updates to data in the unavailable partitions.
2. **Choose Availability (AP):** In this scenario, the system prioritizes availability over data consistency. When a partition occurs, the system will continue to serve requests in all partitions, even if it means that data becomes

temporarily inconsistent between the partitions. This is often achieved by allowing updates to data in all partitions, even if those updates cannot be immediately synchronized with other partitions.

The decision of whether to choose consistency or availability during a partition depends on the specific requirements of the application. If data consistency is critical, then CP is the better choice. If high availability is more important, then AP is the better choice.

Beyond CAP (PACELC)

While the CAP Theorem is a valuable tool for understanding the trade-offs in distributed system design, it only focuses on the scenario where a network partition occurs. The PACELC theorem extends CAP by highlighting the latency/consistency trade-off that exists even when there are no partitions.

PACELC stands for:

- **If there is a Partition (P), choose between Availability (A) and Consistency (C)** (This is the CAP Theorem restated).
- **Else (E), when the system is running normally, choose between Latency (L) and Consistency (C)**

PACELC acknowledges that even in the absence of partitions, there's a trade-off between latency and consistency. Achieving strong consistency often involves additional communication and coordination between nodes, which can increase latency. On the other hand, relaxing consistency requirements can allow for lower latency operations.

For example, a system that prioritizes low latency might choose to use eventual consistency even when there are no partitions. This allows updates to be applied quickly without requiring immediate synchronization across all nodes. However, it also means that there might be a small window of time where different parts of the system see different values. In summary, CAP highlights the choice between availability and consistency during partitions, while PACELC emphasizes that the latency/consistency trade-off exists even under normal operating conditions. Both theorems provide valuable insights for designing robust and performant distributed systems.

Consistency Trade-offs

When building a distributed system, you face choices about how "consistent" your data needs to be. Consistency refers to the guarantee that all users see the same, up-to-date view of the data at the same time. There are different levels of consistency, each with its own advantages and disadvantages. These are called consistency models. Two important consistency models are strong consistency and eventual consistency.

Strong Consistency:

With strong consistency, after an update, all subsequent reads will see that update. Imagine a bank account. If you deposit $100, and then immediately check your balance from another computer, you expect to see the $100 reflected right away. This is strong consistency in action.

Strong consistency simplifies application development. You don't need to worry about stale data. However, achieving it in a distributed system can be challenging. It typically involves coordinating updates across multiple servers, which can slow things down.

Here's a basic example to illustrate the concept:

Let's say we have two servers, Server A and Server B, and a database that stores a value x.

1. Client writes $x = 5$ to Server A.
2. Server A replicates the update to Server B *before* acknowledging the write to the client.
3. Client reads x from Server B. The client *must* read $x = 5$.

If Server B returned $x = 0$ (the old value) after the update, this would *not* be strong consistency. To better visualize the same example, let's try to do a visual sketch.

```
Client -> Server A (Write x=5)
        |
        v
   Server A <-> Server B (Replication of x=5)
        |
        v
Client -> Server B (Read x) -> Returns x=5 (Consistent!)
```

Achieving strong consistency often relies on techniques like two-phase commit or Paxos/Raft, which can increase latency.

Eventual Consistency:

In contrast, eventual consistency allows for some delay in propagating updates. After an update, reads *eventually* reflect that update. Think of a social media post. You might post a status update, and it might not appear to all your friends instantly. It might take a few seconds or even minutes to show up for everyone. This delay is the essence of eventual consistency.

Eventual consistency is easier to achieve in a distributed system and typically offers better performance and availability. Updates can be applied quickly to one server, and then propagated to other servers in the background.

Here's how eventual consistency might work:

1. Client writes $x = 5$ to Server A.
2. Server A immediately acknowledges the write to the client.
3. Server A *asynchronously* replicates the update to Server B.
4. Client reads x from Server B. It *might* read $x = 0$ (the old value) for a short period, before it eventually reads $x = 5$.

Visual sketch for eventual consistency:

```
Client -> Server A (Write x=5) -> Acknowledges Write
        |
        v
   Server A --> Server B (Asynchronous Replication of x=5)
        |
        v
Client -> Server B (Read x) -> Might return x=0 (Temporarily Inconsistent) -> Eventually return:
```

The drawback of eventual consistency is that your application must be able to handle potentially stale data. This requires more careful design and can introduce complexity. For example, if two users edit the same document concurrently, you need a mechanism to resolve conflicts.

Impact on Application Behavior:

The choice of consistency model has a significant impact on how your application behaves.

- **Strong consistency:** Offers a simpler programming model but can lead to higher latency and reduced availability, especially during network partitions. Suitable for applications where data accuracy is paramount, such as financial transactions.

- **Eventual consistency:** Provides better performance and availability but requires more complex application logic to handle potential data inconsistencies. Suitable for applications where eventual data convergence is acceptable, such as social media feeds or content distribution networks.

Choosing the right consistency model involves balancing these trade-offs based on the specific requirements of your application. Consider the importance of data accuracy versus performance and availability, and choose the model that best meets your needs.

Availability Considerations

Maintaining uptime, or *availability*, is a critical concern when designing distributed systems. If a system is down or unresponsive, users cannot access its services, leading to frustration and potential loss of revenue. Several strategies can be employed to maximize availability, even in the face of failures. Two key techniques are replication and failover.

Replication:

Replication involves creating multiple copies of data and services across different nodes in the distributed system. These replicas act as backups, ensuring that if one node fails, others can take over. This redundancy helps to maintain availability.

Let's consider a simple example using a key-value store, a common component in distributed systems. Imagine you have three servers (Server A, Server B, and Server C) all holding the same data.

```
Server A: { key1: "value1", key2: "value2" }
Server B: { key1: "value1", key2: "value2" }
Server C: { key1: "value1", key2: "value2" }
```

If Server A fails, clients can still retrieve the data from Server B or Server C. This is a basic form of replication. There are several replication strategies, each with its own consistency and performance trade-offs:

- **Synchronous Replication:** All replicas are updated before a transaction is considered complete. This guarantees strong consistency but can impact performance, as updates require coordination between all replicas. If one replica is down, updates can stall.

```
Client -> Server A (write key3: "value3")
    Server A -> Server B (replicate)
    Server A -> Server C (replicate)
    Server A -> Client (ack only after B and C confirm)
```

- **Asynchronous Replication:** Updates are applied to the primary replica first, and then propagated to the other replicas asynchronously. This improves performance but introduces the possibility of data inconsistency, as some replicas may be out of date.

```
Client -> Server A (write key3: "value3")
    Server A -> Client (ack immediately)
    Server A -> Server B (replicate, but not immediately)
    Server A -> Server C (replicate, but not immediately)
```

The choice between synchronous and asynchronous replication depends on the specific requirements of the application. For applications that require strong consistency, synchronous replication may be necessary. For applications that can tolerate some degree of inconsistency, asynchronous replication may be a better choice.

Failover:

Failover is the process of automatically switching to a backup system when the primary system fails. This ensures that services remain available even if a server crashes or becomes unavailable. Failover mechanisms typically involve monitoring the primary system and detecting failures. Upon detection of a failure, a backup system is activated and takes over the responsibilities of the primary system.

Consider the following sketch to understand failover concept.

```
+----------+        +----------+
| Primary  |------->|  Backup  |
| Server   |        | Server   |
+----------+        +----------+
```

```
        ^                   |
        | Monitoring        | Takeover
        -----------------
        Failure Detection
```

In this sketch, the Primary Server is actively serving requests. The Backup Server is in standby mode, constantly monitoring the Primary Server's health. If the monitoring system detects a failure in the Primary Server, it triggers a failover process. The Backup Server then takes over the Primary Server's IP address and starts serving requests.

There are two main types of failover:

- **Automatic Failover:** The failover process is automated, without requiring human intervention. This is typically achieved using a cluster management system that monitors the health of the nodes in the cluster and automatically switches to a backup node when a failure is detected. This is ideal for minimizing downtime.

- **Manual Failover:** The failover process requires manual intervention. This is typically used in situations where automatic failover is not possible, such as when the failure is complex and requires human judgment. This is less desirable because it can lead to longer downtimes.

To illustrate with a code example, here's a simplified Python code snippet that represents a basic failover mechanism using a heartbeat check (though real-world systems are significantly more complex):

```python
import time
import socket

def is_server_alive(host, port):
    """Checks if a server is alive by attempting a connection."""
    try:
        sock = socket.socket(socket.AF_INET, socket.SOCK_STREAM)
        sock.settimeout(2) # Timeout after 2 seconds
        sock.connect((host, port))
        sock.close()
        return True
    except (socket.error, socket.timeout):
        return False

primary_host = "primary.example.com"
primary_port = 8080
backup_host = "backup.example.com"
backup_port = 8080

while True:
    if is_server_alive(primary_host, primary_port):
        print("Primary server is alive.")
    else:
        print("Primary server is down! Initiating failover to backup server.")
        # Here you would implement the logic to switch DNS, load balancer, etc.
        # In this example, we'll just print a message.
        print(f"Switching traffic to backup server: {backup_host}:{backup_port}")
        break # Exit the loop after "failover"

    time.sleep(5) # Check every 5 seconds
```

This simple code demonstrates a basic heartbeat check. A real-world failover implementation would involve significantly more complex logic, including updating DNS records, reconfiguring load balancers, and ensuring data consistency.

In conclusion, replication and failover are essential strategies for ensuring high availability in distributed systems. Careful consideration of the consistency and performance trade-offs associated with each approach is crucial for building robust and reliable applications.

Partition Tolerance is Mandatory

Distributed systems, by their very nature, consist of multiple nodes communicating over a network. This introduces the unavoidable reality that network partitions *will* occur. A network partition is simply a break in the connection between parts of the system. Nodes in different partitions can't communicate with each other, even though each part is still running. It's like having two separate, functioning computers that can no longer "see" each other over the network.

Because network failures are inevitable, a distributed system *must* be designed to tolerate them. This is what we mean when we say partition tolerance is mandatory. It's not a feature you can opt out of; it's a fundamental requirement for any system spread across multiple machines.

The implication of mandatory partition tolerance is a crucial trade-off, forcing us to choose between consistency and availability when a partition occurs. Let's break this down:

- **Consistency:** Every read receives the most recent write or an error. In essence, all nodes see the same data at the same time.
- **Availability:** Every request receives a response, without a guarantee that it contains the most recent write. The system remains operational even if some nodes are down or unreachable.

During a partition, you have two choices:

1. **Prioritize Consistency:** You can choose to make the system consistent. This means that if a node cannot reach other nodes to verify that it has the most up-to-date data, it will refuse to respond to requests. The system remains consistent but becomes unavailable for some users.

2. **Prioritize Availability:** You can choose to make the system available. This means that even if a node cannot reach other nodes, it will continue to respond to requests based on the data it has. The system remains available but may return stale or inconsistent data.

To illustrate with a simple code analogy, consider a distributed key-value store.

```
# Simplified example, not production-ready
class KeyValueStore:
    def __init__(self, nodes):
        self.nodes = nodes
        self.data = {} # Simulate data storage

    def get(self, key):
        # Scenario 1: Prioritize Consistency
        # Require majority of nodes to agree on value
        if not self.can_reach_majority():
            raise Exception("Cannot guarantee consistency during partition") # System becomes ur

        # Get values from nodes, find the most recent
        values = [node.get_value(key) for node in self.nodes]
        most_recent_value = self.find_most_recent(values)
        return most_recent_value

    def put(self, key, value):
        # Scenario 2: Prioritize Availability
        # Write to the local node, replicate asynchronously later (eventual consistency)
        self.data[key] = value
```

```
        # Attempt to replicate, but don't fail if it can't
        self.replicate_to_others(key, value)
        return True # System remains available
```

In the `get` example, if the system cannot reach a majority of nodes (indicating a partition), it refuses to return a value, thus prioritizing consistency. In the `put` example, the system accepts the write and attempts to replicate later, prioritizing availability even if some writes are lost during a partition.

Choosing between consistency and availability depends heavily on the specific application requirements. For example:

- **Banking applications** usually prioritize consistency. It's better for a transaction to fail than for money to be incorrectly transferred.
- **Social media applications** may prioritize availability. It's acceptable for a post to take a few seconds to appear everywhere than for the entire platform to be unavailable.

In short, partition tolerance *must* be addressed. The critical design question then becomes: When a partition occurs, do we favor consistency or availability?

Beyond CAP (PACELC)

CAP theorem states that in a distributed system, we can only guarantee two out of three properties: Consistency, Availability, and Partition Tolerance. However, CAP primarily focuses on scenarios where network partitions occur. PACELC extends CAP by addressing the latency and consistency trade-offs even when there *aren't* any network partitions.

Understanding PACELC

PACELC essentially asks two questions:

- **PA:** *If* a partition occurs, *then* should we choose Availability (A) or Consistency (C)?
- **EL:** *Else* (if no partition occurs), *then* should we choose Latency (L) or Consistency (C)?

This framework highlights that even in the absence of network failures, there's still a crucial trade-off between latency and consistency. Every distributed system has to make this trade-off.

Explaining the Components

- **Partition (P):** This refers to a situation where the network is broken, and parts of the system can't communicate with each other. This is the same "P" from CAP.

- **Availability (A):** The system remains operational and returns a response for every request, even if the response might not be the most up-to-date.

- **Consistency (C):** All reads receive the most recent write or an error. Everyone sees the same data at the same time.

- **Latency (L):** The time it takes for a request to be processed and a response to be returned.

PACELC in Action: Examples

Let's look at how different systems might apply PACELC.

1. **Cassandra (AP/EL):** Cassandra is often configured to prioritize availability and low latency. *If* a partition occurs, Cassandra chooses Availability (AP). *Else*, even without a partition, it opts for lower Latency (EL) over strong consistency. This means reads might sometimes return slightly stale data, but the system remains highly responsive.

   Here's a simplified code example demonstrating eventual consistency:

```
# Simplified illustration - not actual Cassandra code
data = {} # Represents the distributed database

def write_data(key, value):
    # Write to a local node first (fast)
    data[key] = value
    # Asynchronously replicate to other nodes

def read_data(key):
    # Read from a local node (fast)
    return data.get(key)
```

In this example, `write_data` quickly writes to the local node and replicates asynchronously. `read_data` simply reads from the local node. This provides low latency but sacrifices immediate consistency. If a read happens before replication is complete, it might return an older value.

2. **MongoDB (CP/EC):** MongoDB can be configured for strong consistency at the cost of availability (CP). *If* a partition occurs, MongoDB chooses Consistency (CP), meaning it might refuse writes until the partition is resolved. *Else*, it defaults to strong consistency (EC), which can increase latency.

Here's a basic illustration of how this might work with write acknowledgements:

```
# Simplified illustration - not actual MongoDB code
data = {}

def write_data(key, value):
    # Write to a primary node
    data[key] = value
    # Wait for confirmation from a majority of replicas
    replication_success = confirm_replication()
    if replication_success:
        return "Write acknowledged"
    else:
        return "Write failed - consistency not guaranteed"

def read_data(key):
    return data[key]
```

Here, `write_data` waits for confirmation from replicas before acknowledging the write. This ensures consistency but adds latency. If replication fails (due to a partition or other issue), the write is rejected to maintain consistency.

Sketch to illustrate Latency vs Consistency tradeoff

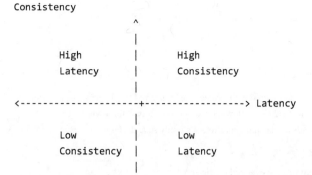

```
Consistency
                        ^
                        |
        High            |       High
        Latency         |       Consistency
                        |
<----------------------+------------------> Latency
                        |
        Low             |       Low
        Consistency     |       Latency
                        |
```

```
------------------
```
Availability

Key Differences between CAP and PACELC

- **CAP focuses on partitions; PACELC focuses on partitions *and* non-partitioned scenarios.** CAP helps us decide what to do *when* a network split occurs. PACELC extends this by saying that there's always a trade-off, even when everything is working perfectly.
- **PACELC highlights the latency/consistency trade-off.** CAP doesn't directly address latency. PACELC makes it explicit that choosing consistency often comes at the cost of increased latency, and vice versa.

Why PACELC Matters

PACELC provides a more complete picture of the trade-offs involved in designing distributed systems. It forces us to consider not just what happens when things go wrong (partitions), but also what the normal operating characteristics (latency vs. consistency) will be. By understanding PACELC, we can make more informed decisions about how to architect our systems to meet specific application requirements. Understanding these considerations lets you think in terms of if things go wrong, what should i consider. In absence of any failure what should i consider.

Chapter 6 Building Scalable and Reliable Systems-Replication Strategies: Leader-Follower, Multi-Leader, and Consensus Protocols

Here's a concise, 5-bullet-point breakdown of replication strategies suitable for a single slide:

- **Leader-Follower Replication:** Single leader for writes, followers replicate data.
  - Asynchronous Replication: Potential data loss, higher availability.
  - Synchronous Replication: Strong consistency, lower availability.
- **Multi-Leader Replication:** Multiple leaders accept writes, resolving conflicts.
- **Trade-offs and Conflicts:** Conflict Resolution strategies needed for multi-leader, potential for data inconsistencies.
- **Use Cases:** Leader-Follower fits read-heavy workloads; Multi-Leader for multi-datacenter operation.
- **Consensus Protocols:** Achieving agreement among nodes using algorithms like Paxos or Raft ensuring fault tolerance.

Leader-Follower Replication

Single leader for writes, followers replicate data.

In Leader-Follower replication, one node is designated as the "leader." This leader is the single point of entry for all write operations. Any time data needs to be added, updated, or deleted, the request is sent to the leader node. The leader then replicates these changes to one or more "follower" nodes. These followers maintain copies of the data, staying synchronized with the leader.

Think of it like a school classroom. The teacher (leader) is the only one who writes on the whiteboard (database). The students (followers) copy down everything the teacher writes, ensuring they have the same information.

Asynchronous Replication: Potential data loss, higher availability.

Asynchronous replication means the leader doesn't wait for confirmation from the followers before acknowledging the write operation as successful. The leader writes to its local storage and *then* sends the update to the followers. Because the leader doesn't wait, it can process write requests very quickly, leading to higher availability. Even if a follower is temporarily unavailable, the leader continues to operate.

However, this speed comes at a cost: potential data loss. If the leader fails *before* it has replicated the data to all followers, those changes are lost.

Sketch:

```
Leader --> Write Ack (Immediate)
    |
    -----> Follower 1 (Replication happens later)
    |
    -----> Follower 2 (Replication happens later)
```

In this sketch, "Write Ack" happens quickly, *before* the replication lines reach the followers.

Synchronous Replication: Strong consistency, lower availability.

In synchronous replication, the leader *waits* for confirmation from one or more followers that the data has been successfully replicated before acknowledging the write operation. This ensures a higher level of data consistency. If the leader fails, the replicated data on the followers is guaranteed to be up-to-date (at least on the followers that acknowledged the write).

However, synchronous replication reduces availability. If a follower is unavailable or slow to respond, the leader must wait, which can slow down write operations. If too many followers are unavailable, the leader might become blocked completely, reducing overall system availability.

Sketch:

```
Leader --> Follower 1 (Replication & Ack) --> Write Ack
    |
    -----> Follower 2 (Replication & Ack)
```

Here, "Write Ack" is delayed until *after* replication and acknowledgements are received from the followers.

Use Cases: Leader-Follower fits read-heavy workloads.

Leader-Follower replication is well-suited for read-heavy workloads. Since followers are exact copies of the leader's data, read requests can be distributed among them, reducing the load on the leader. This allows the system to handle a large number of concurrent read operations efficiently. Think of a news website: many more people read articles than write them. Leader-follower is very effective for this scenario

Example: Imagine you're building a social media platform. Users primarily read posts, comments, and profiles, but only occasionally create or update content. You can set up a Leader-Follower architecture where the leader handles write operations (new posts, edits) and the followers handle the vast majority of read operations (displaying feeds, profiles). This drastically improves response times for users browsing the platform.

Asynchronous Replication

Asynchronous replication, within the context of Leader-Follower replication, involves a single leader node handling all write operations. These write operations are then replicated to one or more follower nodes. The key characteristic of asynchronous replication is that the leader does *not* wait for confirmation from the followers that the data has been successfully replicated before acknowledging the write operation to the client.

The following point explain potential for data loss.

Potential Data Loss: A primary consequence of asynchronous replication is the potential for data loss. If the leader node fails after acknowledging a write but *before* all followers have received and applied the replicated data, that data is lost.

Sketch:

```
Client --> Leader (Write Ack)
        Leader --> Follower 1 (Data Replicated)
        Leader --> Follower 2 (Data Replicated)
        (Leader fails BEFORE all replication complete)
```

In the above sketch, consider a scenario where the Leader acknowledges the write to the Client. The leader starts replicating the data to Follower 1 and Follower 2. If the Leader fails before both followers complete replication, the data is lost.

Higher Availability: Despite the risk of data loss, asynchronous replication offers higher availability compared to synchronous replication. Because the leader doesn't need to wait for follower confirmation, it can continue serving write requests even if one or more followers are unavailable or experiencing network issues. This improves the overall system's resilience to failures.

Sketch:

```
Client --> Leader (Write Ack - No Follower Check)
        Leader --> Follower 1 (Down)
        Leader --> Follower 2 (Data Replicated)
```

In this scenario, even if Follower 1 is down, the Leader continues to serve writes and replicate to available followers like Follower 2. This keeps the system operational for clients, albeit with a potential for data inconsistency if Follower 1 remains unavailable for an extended period.

Code Example (Conceptual - Python):

```python
import time
import threading

class Database:
    def __init__(self, name, is_leader=False, followers=None):
        self.name = name
        self.data = {}
        self.is_leader = is_leader
        self.followers = followers if followers else []

    def write(self, key, value):
        self.data[key] = value
        print(f"{self.name}: Wrote {key}:{value}")
        if self.is_leader:
            self.replicate(key, value)

    def replicate(self, key, value):
        for follower in self.followers:
```

```
            # Simulate asynchronous replication
            threading.Thread(target=self._async_replicate, args=(follower, key, value)).start()

    def _async_replicate(self, follower, key, value):
        time.sleep(0.1)  # Simulate network latency
        follower.write(key, value) # Write data to follower

    def read(self, key):
        return self.data.get(key)

# Example Usage:
db_leader = Database("Leader", is_leader=True)
db_follower1 = Database("Follower1", followers=[])
db_follower2 = Database("Follower2", followers=[])

db_leader.followers = [db_follower1, db_follower2]

db_leader.write("item1", "value1")
db_leader.write("item2", "value2")

time.sleep(0.5) # Simulate some work before reading

print(f"Leader Data: {db_leader.read('item1')}")
print(f"Follower1 Data: {db_follower1.read('item1')}")
print(f"Follower2 Data: {db_follower2.read('item1')}")
```

This simplified Python example illustrates the concept. The Database class represents a node. The leader replicates writes to followers asynchronously using threads. The time.sleep() call simulates network latency, highlighting the asynchronous nature. Note that the leader immediately returns after initiating replication, even if the followers haven't finished writing the data. There is no error-handling or acknowledgement logic included for simplicity's sake. Real-world implementations involve considerably more complex mechanisms.

Synchronous Replication

Definition: In synchronous replication, every write operation to the primary server (leader) must be successfully replicated to one or more secondary servers (followers) *before* the primary server acknowledges the write to the client. This ensures that the data is consistently updated across all replicas at the cost of potentially slower write performance.

Guarantees and Trade-offs: Synchronous replication prioritizes strong consistency. This means that if a client successfully receives a write acknowledgement, it's guaranteed that the data is present on at least two servers (the leader and at least one follower). The major trade-off is availability. If a follower is unavailable or slow, the primary server might be blocked, impacting write performance and potentially application availability.

Availability Considerations: If the synchronous replica becomes unavailable, the primary server cannot acknowledge write operations, effectively stalling the system. In practice, a combination of synchronous and asynchronous replication is often used for greater resilience. For instance, one synchronous replica guarantees consistency, while other replicas update asynchronously to maintain higher availability.

Illustrative Example (Conceptual Sketch):

```
Client --> Write Request --> Primary Server

Primary Server --> Write to Disk
Primary Server --> Send Write to Secondary Server
```

```
Secondary Server --> Write to Disk
Secondary Server --> Acknowledge to Primary Server

Primary Server --> Acknowledge to Client
```

In the diagram above, a write request is sent to the Primary server. It writes to the disk. Than Primary server sends the write to Secondary server. Than Secondary server after writing to disk, than acknowledge to primary server and than primary server acknowledge to client.

Code Snippet Example (Conceptual, simplified):

Although the actual implementation of synchronous replication happens within the database/distributed system itself, this Python example illustrates the *concept* of waiting for confirmation from a replica before confirming to the client:

```python
import time
import threading

class Database:
    def __init__(self):
        self.data = {}
        self.replica = None
        self.replica_ack = False

    def set_replica(self, replica):
        self.replica = replica

    def write_to_replica(self, key, value):
        time.sleep(0.1) #Simulate writing data to replica and disk
        self.replica.data[key] = value
        print (f"Data written to replica : {key} : {value}")
        self.replica_ack = True


    def write_data(self, key, value):
        # 1. Write to primary
        self.data[key] = value
        print(f"Write to primary complete {key} : {value}")

        # 2. Replicate synchronously
        if self.replica:
            replica_thread = threading.Thread(target=self.write_to_replica, args=(key, value))
            replica_thread.start()
            replica_thread.join() # Wait for the thread to finish
        else:
            print ("No replica present, continue without replicating")


            #while not self.replica_ack:  # Wait for replica to acknowledge
            #    time.sleep(0.01)  # Avoid busy-waiting

        # 3. Acknowledge to client
        print("Write acknowledged to client")
        self.replica_ack = False #resetting after sending acknowledged
```

```
class Replica:
    def __init__(self):
        self.data = {}

# Example Usage
primary = Database()
secondary = Replica()
primary.set_replica(secondary)


primary.write_data("item", "apple")
print(f"Primary Data: {primary.data}")
print(f"Secondary Data: {secondary.data}")
```

Explanation:

1. `Database` class represents primary database
2. `Replica` class represents the replica
3. `write_data` function perform write operations
4. `write_to_replica` function perform replica write operations.

Important Considerations:

- **Network Latency:** Synchronous replication is sensitive to network latency. Higher latency directly translates to slower write times.
- **Fault Tolerance:** Careful monitoring and failover mechanisms are crucial. If the synchronous replica fails, the system must have a way to either switch to an asynchronous mode (potentially sacrificing consistency temporarily) or promote another replica quickly.
- **Quorum:** While the example shows a single synchronous replica, more sophisticated systems can employ quorums. For instance, a write might need to be acknowledged by a majority of replicas before being considered successful, increasing resilience.
- **Performance Tuning:** Optimizations at the network, storage, and database levels are often necessary to mitigate the performance impact of synchronous replication.

When to Use:

Synchronous replication is ideal for applications where data consistency is paramount. Examples include financial transactions, critical business records, or systems requiring strict compliance with regulations that mandate data durability and immediate availability across replicas. If data loss is unacceptable and can be handled gracefully even with a potential short-term performance hit, synchronous replication is an important consideration.

Multi-Leader Replication

In a multi-leader replication setup, the database system allows writes (updates, insertions, deletions) to be accepted by multiple nodes, each acting as a *leader*. This differs from the leader-follower approach, where only one node acts as the leader and the others are followers, replicating data from the leader.

Multiple leaders accept writes, resolving conflicts.

The key benefit is improved write availability and reduced latency, especially in geographically distributed systems. If one leader fails, other leaders can continue accepting writes. Users close to a particular leader can experience lower latency because their writes don't need to traverse a network to a single central leader. However, this architecture introduces complexity in managing data consistency. Imagine that you have a system to manage a global retail store. If you have a single master data, if it goes down, the entire global retail store will stop writing data and be completely down. So, to avoid that we have a multi-leader replicated system.

Consider an e-commerce application with users across different regions.

- **Scenario:** You have servers in the US, Europe, and Asia.
- **Multi-Leader Setup:** Each server can accept writes from users in its region. For example, a user in Europe updating their address writes directly to the European server, while a user in the US updating their credit card writes to the US server.

This reduces latency for users in different regions and ensures that even if one data center goes down, the others can continue to function.

```
# Example demonstrating conceptual write operations to multiple leaders

# Leader Nodes (simulated)
leader_us = {}
leader_europe = {}
leader_asia = {}

def update_user_address(user_id, address, leader_node):
    """Simulates updating a user's address on a leader node."""
    leader_node[user_id] = {"address": address}
    print(f"User {user_id}'s address updated on {leader_node}")

# Simulate updates from different regions
update_user_address("user123", "123 Main St, USA", leader_us)
update_user_address("user456", "456 Oxford St, UK", leader_europe)
update_user_address("user789", "789 Ginza, Japan", leader_asia)

# Print the data on each leader
print("US Leader Data:", leader_us)
print("Europe Leader Data:", leader_europe)
print("Asia Leader Data:", leader_asia)
```

This simplified Python code illustrates how updates can be directed to different leader nodes, each responsible for a particular region. While this code doesn't address conflict resolution (which is a critical part of multi-leader replication), it demonstrates the basic concept of multiple leaders independently accepting write operations.

Trade-offs and Conflicts: Conflict Resolution strategies needed for multi-leader, potential for data inconsistencies.

The biggest challenge with multi-leader replication is managing *conflicts*. Since multiple leaders can accept writes concurrently, it's possible for conflicting updates to occur. For instance:

1. **User Profile Update:** Two different administrators update the same user's profile at almost the same time, but on different leaders. One admin changes the user's name, and the other changes the user's email.
2. **Inventory Management:** Two simultaneous orders reduce the inventory count for the same product on different leader nodes.

These conflicts must be resolved to maintain data consistency. Various conflict resolution strategies exist:

- **Last Write Wins (LWW):** The update with the latest timestamp wins. This is simple but can lead to data loss if timestamps are not perfectly synchronized or if a later update isn't necessarily the "correct" one. This approach often leads to unwanted data loss

  - **Example:** If Leader A updates a user's phone number at 10:00:00, and Leader B updates the same user's phone number at 10:00:01, the update from Leader B wins.

- **Conflict-Free Replicated Data Types (CRDTs):** Data types designed to automatically resolve conflicts in a deterministic way. These can be more complex to implement but guarantee eventual consistency without data loss.

  - **Example:** A counter CRDT ensures that even if two leaders increment a counter concurrently, the final value will be the sum of all increments.

- **Custom Conflict Resolution Logic:** Applications can implement custom logic to resolve conflicts based on specific business rules. This offers the most flexibility but requires careful design and implementation.

  - **Example:** For an inventory system, a custom conflict resolution might prioritize the order from a premium customer.

- **Version Vectors:** Used to track the history of updates to a data item. When conflicts arise, the version vectors are compared to determine which updates are causally related and can be merged or resolved accordingly.

  - **Example:** Consider an item x. Leader A updates x to $x1$, resulting in version vector VA. Leader B, without seeing the update from A, updates x to $x2$, resulting in version vector VB. When these updates are replicated, the system compares VA and VB. Since they are divergent (neither is a descendant of the other), a conflict is detected, and resolution is triggered.

-

  ```
  Sketch Depiction

  Initial State:   x (version vector: {})

  Leader A:  Updates x to x1 (version vector: {A:1})
             x --(Update A)--> x1

  Leader B:  Updates x to x2 (version vector: {B:1}) - without seeing A's update
             x --(Update B)--> x2

  Conflict Detected upon Replication.
  ```

- **Detecting and Manual Resolution:** The system detects the conflict but requires human intervention to resolve it.

Use Cases: Multi-Leader for multi-datacenter operation.

Multi-leader replication is most appropriate for systems with the following characteristics:

- **Multi-Datacenter Operation:** As highlighted earlier, geographically distributed systems benefit from each data center having its own leader node.
- **High Write Availability:** When continuous write availability is critical, even at the cost of temporary inconsistencies, multi-leader is a good choice.
- **Tolerance for Eventual Consistency:** If the application can tolerate data inconsistencies for a short period until conflicts are resolved, multi-leader is viable.

Example scenarios include:

- **Collaborative Applications:** Where multiple users can edit the same document concurrently from different locations.
- **Content Delivery Networks (CDNs):** Where content updates need to be rapidly propagated across multiple edge servers.
- **IoT Platforms:** Where devices in different regions are constantly sending data, and immediate write availability is essential.

By understanding the trade-offs and carefully choosing appropriate conflict resolution strategies, multi-leader replication can provide significant benefits in terms of availability, latency, and scalability. However, you must consider all design considerations before implemenation of this feature, this is very complect design and you can make a very bad impact to your business, if you chose the incorrect conflict resolution system.

Trade-offs and Conflicts

The multi-leader replication strategy introduces significant trade-offs, primarily centered around managing conflicting writes and potential data inconsistencies. Unlike leader-follower replication where a single source of truth simplifies data management, multi-leader systems inherently require sophisticated conflict resolution mechanisms.

Conflict Resolution Strategies Needed for Multi-Leader

When multiple leaders can accept writes simultaneously, conflicts are inevitable. Imagine two users editing the same record (e.g., a user profile) on different leaders at almost the same time. These changes will propagate to other leaders, but which change should "win"? Several strategies exist to resolve these conflicts:

- **Last Write Wins (LWW):** This is the simplest approach. Each write is timestamped, and the write with the latest timestamp is applied, overwriting any previous conflicting write.

    - **Trade-off:** Data loss is possible. If the timestamp isn't perfectly synchronized across all leaders, the *logical* order of updates might not match the *timestamp* order, leading to the incorrect update being applied.
    - **Example:** Suppose two leaders A and B update a user's name. A changes "John Doe" to "Jonathan Doe" at timestamp 10:00:01, and B changes "John Doe" to "John D. Doe" at timestamp 10:00:02. LWW will apply B's change ("John D. Doe"), regardless of which leader the user preferred.

- **Conflict-Free Replicated Data Types (CRDTs):** CRDTs are data structures designed to resolve conflicts automatically in a way that guarantees eventual consistency. Different types of CRDTs exist, each suited for different operations.

    - **Trade-off:** CRDTs can be more complex to implement than LWW and might not be suitable for all data types.
    - **Example:** Consider an increment-only counter. Each leader increments its local counter independently. When the counters are synchronized, they are simply added together. There's no conflict because the order of increment operations doesn't matter. For more complex data types, specialized CRDTs like observed-remove sets exist.

- **Custom Conflict Resolution Logic:** This approach allows developers to define their own rules for resolving conflicts based on the application's specific needs.

    - **Trade-off:** Requires more development effort and careful consideration to ensure the conflict resolution logic is correct and prevents data corruption.
    - **Example:** In a collaborative document editing application, you might implement a three-way merge algorithm (similar to Git) to resolve conflicting edits. The system compares the current version on each leader with a common ancestor version to determine the best way to combine the changes.

- **Version Vectors:** These track the history of updates at each leader. Conflicts are detected when the version vectors are not comparable (i.e., neither is a descendant of the other). Applications then need to resolve these conflicts.

    - **Trade-off:** More complex than LWW. Application needs to implement the conflict resolution.

Potential for Data Inconsistencies

Regardless of the conflict resolution strategy employed, multi-leader replication inherently introduces the potential for temporary data inconsistencies. It takes time for changes to propagate between leaders, creating a window where different leaders might have different views of the data.

- **Eventual Consistency:** Multi-leader systems typically provide eventual consistency, meaning that if no new updates are made to the data, all replicas will eventually converge to the same value. However, there's no guarantee of immediate consistency.

- **Read-Your-Writes Problem:** A user might write data to one leader and then immediately read that data from a different leader *before* the write has been replicated. This can lead to a frustrating experience where the user doesn't see their own changes.

  - **Mitigation:** Sticky sessions (routing a user's requests to the same leader) or read-after-write consistency (guaranteeing that reads after a write will see the updated value, possibly by reading from the same leader that handled the write) can mitigate this problem, but increase complexity.

- **Non-Monotonic Reads:** A user might read data and then, at a later time, read older data.

  - **Example:** A user reads a comment on a blog post. Later, due to replication delays, they read the same blog post from a different replica and the comment is missing.

Sketch of a Multi-Leader Conflict:

```
+----------+
          | Leader A |
          +----------+
              |      ^
              |      | Write 1: Update User Profile: Name = "Alice"
              v      |
          +----------+        +----------+
          |          | <--> |          |
          | Replicas |        | Replicas |
          |          | <--> |          |
          +----------+        +----------+
              |      ^
              |      | Write 2: Update User Profile: City = "New York"
              v      |
          +----------+
          | Leader B |
          +----------+


          (Replication happens asynchronously)

          Potential Conflict: Which update "wins" if both update the same user profile?
```

In this scenario, Leader A receives an update to the user's name, and Leader B receives an update to the user's city. Both updates eventually need to be replicated to all replicas. The conflict arises if both leaders try to update the same base data simultaneously, leading to the need for a defined strategy to resolve which update is applied and in what order.

```python
# Example of Last Write Wins conflict resolution in Python (simplified)

class DataRecord:
    def __init__(self, key, value, timestamp):
        self.key = key
        self.value = value
        self.timestamp = timestamp


def resolve_conflict_lww(existing_record, new_record):
    """Resolves conflicts using Last Write Wins (LWW)."""
```

```
    if new_record.timestamp > existing_record.timestamp:
        return new_record
    else:
        return existing_record

# Example usage
record1 = DataRecord("user1", "John Doe", 1678886400)  # Timestamp: March 15, 2023
record2 = DataRecord("user1", "Jonathan Doe", 1678886460) # Timestamp: March 15, 2023 + 1 minute

resolved_record = resolve_conflict_lww(record1, record2)
print(f"Resolved value for user1: {resolved_record.value}") # Output: Jonathan Doe
```

This python code provides a simple example of how a last-write-wins policy might be implemented.

Use Cases

Leader-Follower replication and Multi-Leader replication strategies are chosen based on the specific requirements of the application and its environment. Each approach excels in different situations.

Leader-Follower Fits Read-Heavy Workloads:

Leader-Follower replication is an excellent choice when your application primarily involves reading data much more frequently than writing. In this model, one node acts as the "leader," handling all write operations. The other nodes, known as "followers," replicate the data from the leader. Since all write operations are centralized to the leader, reads can be distributed across all followers, increasing the system's read capacity.

Consider an e-commerce website's product catalog. Product information is updated relatively infrequently (e.g., when a new product is added or the price changes). However, customers browse the catalog constantly, resulting in a high volume of read requests. Leader-Follower replication is well-suited for this scenario: the leader handles product updates, and the followers handle the numerous read requests from customers browsing the website.

```
# Simple illustration (conceptual - doesn't represent actual database interaction)

# Leader (handles writes)
def update_product_price(product_id, new_price):
    # Code to update the product price in the leader's database
    print(f"Leader: Updated price for product {product_id} to {new_price}")
    # (Implementation to replicate this change to followers would be here)

# Follower (handles reads)
def get_product_details(product_id):
    # Code to retrieve product details from the follower's database
    print(f"Follower: Retrieved details for product {product_id}")
    # Returns product details
    return {"product_id": product_id, "price": 100}  # Dummy data

# Example Usage:
update_product_price(123, 110) # Write happens on leader
product = get_product_details(123) # Read happens on follower
print(product)
```

In the code example, you can see that update_product_price happens on the leader. get_product_details happens on the follower. Leader node will replicate the data to follower node to make data consistent.

Multi-Leader for Multi-Datacenter Operation:

Multi-Leader replication shines in scenarios involving multiple data centers, especially when low latency and high availability are paramount. In this configuration, each data center has its own leader node that can accept write operations. This allows users in different geographical regions to write to the database with minimal latency, as their requests are processed by the nearest leader.

Imagine a global social media platform with users spread across the world. Instead of directing all write requests to a single data center, the platform can deploy leader nodes in multiple data centers (e.g., one in North America, one in Europe, and one in Asia). Users in each region can then write to their local leader, reducing latency and improving the overall user experience.

```python
# Conceptual example (multi-datacenter writes)
# Data Center A (Leader A)
def update_user_profile_A(user_id, new_data):
    # Update user profile data in Data Center A
    print(f"Data Center A: Updated profile for user {user_id}")
    # (Replication logic to other leaders)


# Data Center B (Leader B)
def update_user_profile_B(user_id, new_data):
    # Update user profile data in Data Center B
    print(f"Data Center B: Updated profile for user {user_id}")
    # (Replication logic to other leaders)


# Example Usage:
update_user_profile_A(1, {"name": "Alice", "location": "New York"}) # Write to Leader A
update_user_profile_B(1, {"name": "Alice", "location": "London"}) # Write to Leader B
```

In the above example, both Data Center A and Data Center B leaders are able to update the user's profile at the same time. The most important part of this approach is the conflict resolution strategy that will be used to solve conflicts as the data is replicated between the nodes.

In the above code examples replication logic part will be done using Consensus protocols.

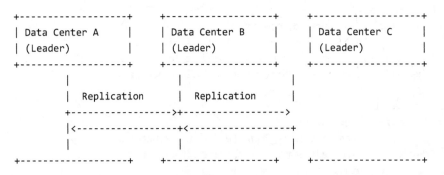

The above sketch shows replication between Data Center A,B, and C using Multi-Leader architecture.

Chapter 7 Building Scalable and Reliable Systems- Partitioning and Sharding: Strategies for Horizontal Scaling

- **Partitioning Introduction**: Dividing a large dataset into smaller, manageable partitions for distributed storage and processing.

- **Key-Based Partitioning**:

  - Partitioning data based on a key, enabling efficient retrieval and distribution.

- **Range Partitioning**: Assigning keys within a specific range to a partition, suitable for ordered data access.

- **Hash Partitioning**: Using a hash function to distribute keys evenly across partitions, ensuring load balance.

- **Partitioning Considerations**: Rebalancing, hot spots, and strategies for minimizing cross-partition queries are crucial for performance and reliability.

Partitioning Introduction

Dividing a large dataset into smaller, manageable partitions is a fundamental concept in distributed systems, known as partitioning. This is necessary when a dataset becomes too large to be stored and processed efficiently on a single machine. Think of it like organizing a massive library: instead of keeping all the books in one giant pile, you divide them into smaller, more manageable sections based on genre, author, or subject.

The Problem: Imagine you have a database with billions of customer records. A single server might struggle to handle the storage, querying, and processing of this data. Queries become slow, and the system becomes difficult to scale.

The Solution: Partitioning breaks this large dataset into smaller, independent units called partitions or shards. Each partition contains a subset of the overall data and can be stored on a separate machine or node in a distributed system.

Benefits of Partitioning:

- **Scalability:** Partitioning allows you to scale your system horizontally by adding more machines to handle the increased load. As your data grows, you can simply add more partitions to accommodate the growth.
- **Performance:** By distributing the data across multiple machines, you can improve query performance. Queries can be processed in parallel across multiple partitions, significantly reducing response times.
- **Availability:** If one partition becomes unavailable due to a hardware failure, the other partitions remain accessible, ensuring that the entire system doesn't go down.
- **Manageability:** Smaller partitions are easier to manage, back up, and restore than a single large dataset.

Analogy:

Imagine you have a single checkout counter in a grocery store handling a long line of customers. This is like a single server handling a large dataset. Partitioning is like adding more checkout counters to handle the customers more efficiently. Each counter handles a subset of the customers, reducing the waiting time and improving the overall throughput.

Simple Illustration:

Let's say we have customer data with customer IDs ranging from 1 to 1000. We can partition this data into two partitions:

- Partition 1: Customer IDs 1 to 500

- Partition 2: Customer IDs 501 to 1000

Each partition can be stored on a separate server. When a query for a customer with ID 300 arrives, it is routed to Partition 1. A query for customer with ID 700 will be routed to Partition 2.

Key-Based Partitioning

Key-based partitioning is a strategy where you divide your data into different partitions based on the value of a specific key. Think of it as sorting items into different boxes, where each box is labeled with a specific key value or range of key values. This approach is fundamental for efficient data retrieval and distribution in distributed systems.

The core idea is to use a key – a specific attribute or set of attributes – within your data to determine which partition a particular data record should reside in. This key is chosen based on how your data is most commonly accessed and queried.

Enabling Efficient Retrieval and Distribution

The primary advantage of key-based partitioning is that it allows for highly efficient data retrieval. When you need to access a specific data record, you can directly target the partition that contains the record based on its key value. This avoids the need to search through all partitions, significantly reducing the time it takes to retrieve the data.

Consider a database of customer information. You might choose the customer ID as the key for partitioning. If you need to retrieve information about customer with ID 12345, you can directly query the partition that stores data for customer IDs.

Here's an analogy: imagine a library where books are shelved based on their genre (e.g., fiction, science, history). If you're looking for a science book, you know to go directly to the science section, rather than searching the entire library.

Furthermore, key-based partitioning facilitates efficient data distribution. Since data is divided based on a key, you can distribute these partitions across multiple servers or nodes in a distributed system. This parallelizes both storage and processing, allowing you to handle larger datasets and higher query loads.

Example

Let's illustrate with a simplified example using Python-like pseudocode to insert data into partitions. Suppose you have user data with user_id as the key and you want to partition data across three servers.

```
def get_partition(user_id, num_partitions=3):
    """Determines the partition number for a given user_id."""
    return user_id % num_partitions


def insert_user_data(user_data, partitions):
    """Inserts user data into the appropriate partition based on user_id."""
    user_id = user_data['user_id']
    partition_number = get_partition(user_id)
    partitions[partition_number].append(user_data)


# Example Usage
partitions = [[], [], []] # Representing three partitions (lists) on different servers.
user_data1 = {'user_id': 1, 'name': 'Alice'}
user_data2 = {'user_id': 2, 'name': 'Bob'}
user_data3 = {'user_id': 3, 'name': 'Charlie'}
user_data4 = {'user_id': 4, 'name': 'David'}


insert_user_data(user_data1, partitions) # user_id 1 goes to partition 1 (1 % 3 = 1)
insert_user_data(user_data2, partitions) # user_id 2 goes to partition 2 (2 % 3 = 2)
```

```
insert_user_data(user_data3, partitions) # user_id 3 goes to partition 0 (3 % 3 = 0)
insert_user_data(user_data4, partitions) # user_id 4 goes to partition 1 (4 % 3 = 1)

print(partitions)
# Output (conceptually):
# Partition 0: [{'user_id': 3, 'name': 'Charlie'}]
# Partition 1: [{'user_id': 1, 'name': 'Alice'}, {'user_id': 4, 'name': 'David'}]
# Partition 2: [{'user_id': 2, 'name': 'Bob'}]
```

In this simplified example:

1. get_partition(user_id, num_partitions): determines the partition number based on the user_id modulo the number of partitions (servers). This ensures that each user_id is consistently assigned to the same partition.
2. insert_user_data(user_data, partitions): Inserts the user data into the appropriate partition based on the user_id.

This example shows how data is distributed across partitions based on a key. When you need to retrieve Alice's data, you know to look at partition 1.

Sketch of Key-Based Partitioning

```
+---------------------+      +---------------------+      +---------------------+
|    Server/Node 1    |      |    Server/Node 2    |      |    Server/Node 3    |
+---------------------+      +---------------------+      +---------------------+
| Partition 1         |      | Partition 2         |      | Partition 0         |
| User_ID: 1, 4, ...  |      | User_ID: 2, 5, ...  |      | User_ID: 3, 6, ...  |
+---------------------+      +---------------------+      +---------------------+

Data Ingestion --> [Partitioning Logic based on User_ID] --> Distributes data to servers
```

This sketch illustrates how data is partitioned and distributed across multiple servers based on the User_ID key. Each server holds a specific partition containing data for a specific set of user IDs.

Range Partitioning

Assigning keys within a specific range to a partition, suitable for ordered data access. This means you divide your data into sections based on where the key falls within a defined range. Think of it like organizing books on a shelf by the author's last name: each shelf represents a range of names (e.g., A-F, G-L, M-R, S-Z).

Range partitioning is especially useful when you need to access data in a specific order. Because data within a partition is likely stored together physically, retrieving a range of data is efficient.

Example:

Imagine you have a database of user accounts, and each account has a unique user ID (an integer). You could partition this data based on user ID ranges:

- Partition 1: User IDs 1 to 1000
- Partition 2: User IDs 1001 to 2000
- Partition 3: User IDs 2001 to 3000
- And so on...

If you need to retrieve all users with IDs between 1500 and 2500, you know immediately that you only need to query Partition 2 and Partition 3.

Code Example (Python - Illustrative):

While this isn't a direct code example for a distributed database system, it illustrates the logic:

```python
class Partition:
    def __init__(self, start_id, end_id, data=None):
        self.start_id = start_id
        self.end_id = end_id
        self.data = {} if data is None else data

    def insert(self, user_id, user_data):
        if self.start_id <= user_id <= self.end_id:
            self.data[user_id] = user_data
            return True
        return False

    def get_user(self, user_id):
        if user_id in self.data:
            return self.data[user_id]
        return None


# Create partitions
partition1 = Partition(1, 1000)
partition2 = Partition(1001, 2000)
partition3 = Partition(2001, 3000)

# Simulate inserting data
partition2.insert(1500, {"name": "Alice", "city": "New York"})
partition3.insert(2500, {"name": "Bob", "city": "London"})

# Simulate retrieving data
alice = partition2.get_user(1500)
print(alice) # Output: {'name': 'Alice', 'city': 'New York'}
```

This Python code demonstrates how data can be assigned and retrieved to a partition based on the range of user IDs. In a real distributed database, this logic would be handled by the database system itself.

Sketch to Visualize:

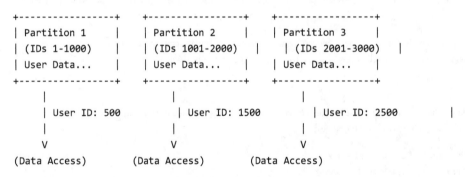

Considerations:

While range partitioning is beneficial for ordered data access, it has potential drawbacks:

- **Uneven Distribution:** If the data is not uniformly distributed across the key range, some partitions may become much larger than others, leading to an imbalance in storage and processing load. For example, if many users sign up with IDs in the range 1001-1200, partition 2 will be much busier.

- **Hotspots:** A "hotspot" occurs when a specific range of keys is accessed much more frequently than others. This can overload a single partition and reduce overall system performance. Consider a scenario where user IDs 1001-1010 are extremely active; Partition 2 will be under significant load.

Hash Partitioning

Hash Partitioning involves using a hash function to determine which partition a particular piece of data belongs to. The primary goal is to distribute data as evenly as possible across all available partitions, leading to a balanced workload and improved performance.

How it Works

1. **Hash Function:** A hash function takes the partition key as input and produces an integer output. This output is typically a large number.

2. **Modulo Operation:** The result of the hash function is then subjected to a modulo operation (%). The modulo is performed with the number of partitions as the divisor. For example, if you have 10 partitions, you would calculate `hash(key) % 10`.

3. **Partition Assignment:** The result of the modulo operation gives you the partition number where the data will be stored. This ensures that the data is distributed across all partitions, minimizing hot spots.

Example

Imagine you have a system with 4 partitions (numbered 0, 1, 2, and 3) and you're partitioning customer data based on their customer ID.

1. Customer ID = 12345
2. Hash Function (Simplified): Let's assume the hash function simply returns the customer ID itself for simplicity. `hash(12345) = 12345`
3. Modulo Operation: `12345 % 4 = 1`
4. Partition Assignment: This customer's data will be stored in partition 1.

Let's try another example

1. Customer ID = 6789
2. Hash Function (Simplified): `hash(6789) = 6789`
3. Modulo Operation: `6789 % 4 = 1`
4. Partition Assignment: This customer's data will be stored in partition 1.

Code Example (Python)

```python
import hashlib

def hash_partition(key, num_partitions):
    """
    Hashes the key and returns the partition number.
    """
    key_bytes = str(key).encode('utf-8')  # Encode key to bytes
    hash_object = hashlib.md5(key_bytes)  # Use MD5 hash (can be another hash function)
    hash_value = int(hash_object.hexdigest(), 16)  # Convert hex digest to integer
    partition_number = hash_value % num_partitions
    return partition_number

# Example usage:
customer_id = "user123"
num_partitions = 10
partition = hash_partition(customer_id, num_partitions)
```

```
print(f"Customer {customer_id} will be stored in partition: {partition}")

customer_id = "user456"
num_partitions = 10
partition = hash_partition(customer_id, num_partitions)
print(f"Customer {customer_id} will be stored in partition: {partition}")
```

In this Python example, we use the `hashlib` library to generate an MD5 hash of the key. MD5 is a common hashing algorithm. The resulting hexadecimal hash is converted to an integer, and then the modulo operation is performed to determine the partition number.

Diagrammatic representation:

```
+---------+    Hash Function  +-------------+   Modulo (%)   +------------+
|   Key   |------------------>|  Hash Value |--------------->|  Partition |
+---------+                   +-------------+    Number of    +------------+
                                                 Partitions
```

Ensuring Load Balance

The effectiveness of hash partitioning relies heavily on the choice of the hash function. A good hash function should:

- **Be uniform:** Distribute keys evenly across the output range.
- **Be consistent:** The same key should always map to the same partition.

Common hash functions used in practice include MD5, SHA-1, and MurmurHash. The `hashlib` library in python has these implementations.

Benefits

- **Even Data Distribution:** Hash partitioning, when used with a suitable hash function, helps prevent data skew and hot spots.
- **Scalability:** It's relatively straightforward to add or remove partitions, although rebalancing might be necessary.
- **Simplicity:** The concept is easy to understand and implement.

Considerations

- **Range Queries:** Hash partitioning is not ideal for range queries. For example, if you need to retrieve all customers with IDs between 1000 and 2000, you might have to query all partitions.
- **Rebalancing:** When the number of partitions changes (e.g., when scaling the system), data needs to be redistributed. This process, called rebalancing, can be resource-intensive.
- **Choosing the Right Hash Function:** The choice of the hash function is critical. Poorly designed hash function will result in uneven data distribution. It is recommended to test a few hashing algorithms to find the one that best distributes the keys.

Partitioning Considerations

When you break your big dataset into smaller pieces (partitions), you need to think about a few important things to make sure everything runs smoothly and efficiently. These considerations include:

- **Rebalancing**:

Imagine you have divided your work among several people, but suddenly, one person gets overloaded while others have very little to do. Rebalancing is like redistributing the work so that everyone has a fair share.

In the context of partitioning, data might not be evenly distributed initially, or the amount of data in each partition might change over time. Rebalancing involves moving data between partitions to ensure each partition has roughly the same amount of data. This helps prevent overload on any single server and maintains overall system performance.

Example:

Let's say you initially partition user data based on the first letter of their last name, with each letter assigned to a separate partition. Over time, you find that users with last names starting with 'S' create significantly more data than users with last names starting with 'Z'. Rebalancing would involve moving some users from the 'S' partition to other less loaded partitions to even out the workload.

Sketch:

```
Initial State:

[Partition A (A-M)] ------ (Light Load)
[Partition B (N-Z)] ------ (Heavy Load due to more data from N-S names)

After Rebalancing:

[Partition A (A-L)] ------ (Medium Load)
[Partition B (M-S)] ------ (Medium Load)
[Partition C (T-Z)] ------ (Medium Load)
```

- **Hot Spots**:

A hot spot is like a popular restaurant where everyone wants to go at the same time. In partitioning, it's a partition that receives a disproportionately high number of requests compared to other partitions. This can happen if a small subset of keys is accessed much more frequently than others. Hot spots lead to performance bottlenecks because the server hosting that partition becomes overloaded.

Example:

Consider an e-commerce system partitioned by product ID. If there's a sudden viral trend for a particular product (e.g., product ID 123), the partition containing that product's data will experience a massive spike in requests, creating a hot spot.

Mitigation Strategies:

```
Sharding Hot Keys: Split up hot keys to more than one partition.
    Caching: Cache frequently accessed data to reduce the load on the database.
```

Sketch:

```
[Partition 1] -------- (Normal Load)
[Partition 2] -------- (EXTREME LOAD - Hot Spot)
[Partition 3] -------- (Normal Load)
```

- **Strategies for Minimizing Cross-Partition Queries**:

Cross-partition queries are queries that require data from multiple partitions. They are generally slower and more expensive than queries that can be satisfied from a single partition because they involve network communication and data aggregation across multiple servers.

Example:

Suppose you have an online store partitioned by user ID. If you want to generate a report that shows the total sales for a specific product across all users, this would require querying all partitions, as users and their purchases are spread across different partitions.

Data Colocation: Try to store related data together in the same partition.
   Denormalization: Duplicate frequently accessed data across multiple partitions.

Here is a python code example:

```python
import hashlib

def hash_partition(key, num_partitions):
    """
    Hashes the key and returns the partition number.
    """
    hashed_key = int(hashlib.md5(key.encode('utf-8')).hexdigest(), 16)
    return hashed_key % num_partitions

# Example Usage:
num_partitions = 4
key1 = "user123"
key2 = "product456"

partition1 = hash_partition(key1, num_partitions)
partition2 = hash_partition(key2, num_partitions)

print(f"Key '{key1}' belongs to partition: {partition1}")
print(f"Key '{key2}' belongs to partition: {partition2}")
```

This code will help to use hash partitioning. So, ensure that the cross-partition queries must be minimized.

These considerations - rebalancing, hot spots, and minimizing cross-partition queries - are crucial for ensuring that your partitioned system remains performant, reliable, and scalable as your data grows and your application evolves. Failing to address these issues can lead to performance bottlenecks, system instability, and increased operational costs.

Chapter 8 Building Scalable and Reliable Systems-Consistency Models: Strong vs. Eventual Consistency

Here are 5 bullet points explaining strong vs. eventual consistency, suitable for a single slide:

- **Consistency Spectrum:** Data consistency models range from strong to eventual, impacting system behavior and complexity.

- **Strong Consistency:**

- Guarantees all reads see the most recent write, providing linearizability.
  - Often achieved through techniques like consensus algorithms (e.g., Paxos, Raft) or atomic commits.

- **Eventual Consistency:**

  - Guarantees that if no new updates are made to a data item, eventually all accesses will return the last updated value.
  - Simpler to implement but can lead to read-your-writes and other anomalies if not handled carefully.

- **Trade-offs:** Strong consistency sacrifices availability and latency; eventual consistency prioritizes them.

- **Choosing a Model:** Depends on application requirements; consider data criticality, user expectations, and fault tolerance needs.

Consistency Spectrum

Data consistency models occupy a spectrum, ranging from strong consistency at one end to eventual consistency at the other. This spectrum represents the different guarantees provided by distributed systems regarding the visibility and order of data updates. The choice of consistency model significantly impacts the behavior of the system, its complexity, and its ability to handle failures.

Think of it like the volume control on a radio. On one end (strong consistency), you have crystal-clear audio but potentially lower volume (availability). On the other end (eventual consistency), you might have higher volume (availability) but some occasional static or fuzziness in the audio (data inconsistencies).

```
Strong Consistency <--------------------> Eventual Consistency
       (High Consistency, Low Availability)    (Low Consistency, High Availability)
```

The position you choose on this spectrum depends entirely on the specific requirements of your application.

Strong Consistency

Let's explore the concept of strong consistency in distributed systems.

Guarantees all reads see the most recent write, providing linearizability.

Strong consistency means that after a write operation (an update to the data), any subsequent read operation from any client will always return the most recent written value. Think of it as a single, globally consistent view of the data, as if there's only one copy of the data. This property is also referred to as *linearizability*. Linearizability implies that operations appear to happen in a single, total order, consistent with the real-time ordering of the operations. This makes reasoning about the system much easier.

For example, imagine you have a bank account balance represented as data in a distributed system.

1. You deposit $100 into your account.
2. Immediately after, you check your balance from a different computer or phone.

With strong consistency, you are *guaranteed* to see the updated balance reflecting the $100 deposit. If another person checks the balance at the same time, they *also* will *guaranteed* to see the updated balance. There is no possibility of seeing the old, pre-deposit balance.

Often achieved through techniques like consensus algorithms (e.g. Paxos, Raft) or atomic commits.

Achieving strong consistency in a distributed system is complex because of the potential for network delays and failures. To ensure that *all* nodes agree on the state of the data, consensus algorithms are often used.

- **Consensus Algorithms:** These algorithms allow a distributed system to agree on a single value, even in the presence of failures. Examples include Paxos, Raft, and Zab (used by ZooKeeper). These algorithms ensure that only one node is the "leader" at a time, responsible for writing data, and that changes are replicated to other nodes in a consistent manner before a write is considered complete.

- **Atomic Commits:** Another approach involves atomic commits, which ensure that a transaction is either fully completed across all involved nodes or rolled back entirely. Two-Phase Commit (2PC) is a common protocol for achieving atomic commits.

To illustrate Raft in a simplified way:

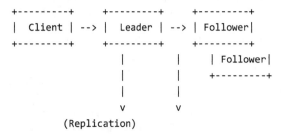

```
+---------+      +---------+      +---------+
| Client  | -->  | Leader  | -->  | Follower|
+---------+      +---------+      +---------+
                     |      |     | Follower|
                     |      |     +---------+
                     |      |
                     v      v
          (Replication)
```

The client sends a write request to the Leader. The Leader replicates the update to the Followers. Once a majority of Followers have acknowledged the update, the Leader commits the change and informs the Client of success.

A code example using a hypothetical Raft library:

```python
class RaftNode:
    def __init__(self):
        self.data = None
        self.log = []

    def write(self, value):
        # 1. Append to local log
        self.log.append(value)

        # 2. Replicate to followers (simplified)
        success = self.replicate_to_followers(value)

        if success:
            # 3. Commit to state
            self.data = value
            return True
        else:
            # Handle failure (rollback log, elect new leader)
            return False

    def replicate_to_followers(self, value):
        # Hypothetical replication logic. In real raft implementation, it will be handled intern
        # In real life followers will reply to leader and than decision is made.
        print("Replicating value {0} to followers".format(value))
        return True #Assume Replicated succesfully

# In a distributed environment, nodes elect leader and do write operations.
# Simplified example, for illustration purpose.
node = RaftNode()
result = node.write("Initial value")
print("Write success {0}".format(result))
print("Data: ", node.data)
```

This example shows a simplified representation. In a real Raft implementation, the 'replicate_to_followers' function would involve complex network communication, election mechanisms, and handling of failures.

Simpler to implement but can lead to read-your-writes and other anomalies if not handled carefully.

While strong consistency provides guarantees that are easy to understand and reason about, it comes at a cost. It typically involves more complex and heavyweight mechanisms (like the consensus algorithms discussed above) to maintain consistency across the distributed system.

Guarantees All Reads See The Most Recent Write: A Deep Dive

This aspect is central to understanding *strong consistency*. It means that the moment data is written or updated, every subsequent attempt to read that data, no matter where it originates, will return the most up-to-date version. There is no delay, no possibility of seeing stale data. This provides a high degree of predictability and simplifies application development, as developers don't need to worry about managing different versions of data.

To illustrate, consider a simple banking application. When a customer transfers $100 from their savings account to their checking account, a strongly consistent system *guarantees* that if the customer (or the bank itself) immediately checks the balances, the savings account will show $100 less, and the checking account will show $100 more. No one can see the old balances, even for a fleeting moment.

Imagine two clerks, Alice and Bob, processing the same customer's transaction concurrently. Alice initiates a withdrawal of $50 from the customer's account. Simultaneously, Bob tries to deposit $100 into the same account. With strong consistency, one of these transactions will be processed first (let's say Alice's withdrawal). Once that withdrawal is complete and the database is updated, Bob's deposit will *see* the effect of Alice's transaction and correctly update the balance *after* the withdrawal.

Here's a simplified analogy: Think of a shared whiteboard. When someone writes on the whiteboard, everyone looking at it immediately sees the new writing. There's no lag, no chance of seeing the whiteboard *before* the writing appeared.

```
// Example of Strong Consistency (Conceptual)

// Assume a strongly consistent database 'db'

function transferFunds(accountFrom, accountTo, amount) {
  // Start a transaction to ensure atomicity
  db.beginTransaction();

  try {
    // Read current balances
    const balanceFrom = db.read(accountFrom);
    const balanceTo = db.read(accountTo);

    // Check if sufficient funds are available
    if (balanceFrom < amount) {
      db.rollbackTransaction();
      throw new Error("Insufficient funds");
    }

    // Update balances
    db.write(accountFrom, balanceFrom - amount);
    db.write(accountTo, balanceTo + amount);

    // Commit the transaction
    db.commitTransaction();
```

```
  } catch (error) {
    // Rollback transaction in case of errors
    db.rollbackTransaction();
    throw error;
  }
}


//Alice trying to withdraw
transferFunds("savings", "checking", 50);

//Bob trying to deposit
transferFunds("checking", "savings", 100);

//After complete transaction, all reads to balance must be updated.
```

In this code (which only serves as an example), the `beginTransaction`, `read`, `write`, `commitTransaction`, and `rollbackTransaction` functions are provided by the strongly consistent database and it will ensure that the operations happen in an all-or-nothing fashion and that all reads reflect the latest writes.

Achieving Strong Consistency: The Role of Consensus Algorithms

The pursuit of strong consistency, where every read operation reflects the most recent write, often relies on sophisticated techniques, primarily *consensus algorithms*. These algorithms ensure that a distributed system agrees on a single, consistent state, even in the presence of failures.

Understanding Consensus:

Imagine you and a group of friends are trying to decide on a restaurant for dinner. Everyone has their preferences, and sometimes people change their minds. A consensus algorithm is like a protocol that helps you all agree on a restaurant, even if some friends are indecisive or unavailable.

In a distributed system, instead of friends, we have multiple servers (nodes) that need to agree on the next state of the data. Instead of restaurants, we have data updates or operations. The goal is to ensure that all servers agree on the order of these updates, preventing inconsistencies.

How Consensus Algorithms Work (Simplified):

Consensus algorithms generally involve a process where nodes propose values, and then a mechanism is used to reach an agreement on a single value. Common elements include:

- **Leader Election:** Many algorithms designate a leader node, responsible for proposing updates. If the leader fails, a new leader is elected.
- **Proposal and Acceptance:** The leader proposes an update to the other nodes. These nodes then vote to accept or reject the proposal.
- **Commitment:** Once a quorum (a majority) of nodes has accepted the proposal, the update is considered committed and applied to the system's state.

Popular Consensus Algorithms:

Two widely used consensus algorithms are Paxos and Raft.

- **Paxos:** One of the earliest and most influential consensus algorithms. It is known for its complexity but provides a robust solution for achieving consensus in distributed systems.

- **Raft:** Designed to be more understandable than Paxos. It achieves consensus through leader election, log replication, and safety mechanisms. Raft is often preferred for its relative simplicity and ease of implementation.

Example Scenario (Simplified Raft):

Consider a simple key-value store replicated across three servers (A, B, and C). We want to update the value associated with a key.

1. **Leader Election:** Let's say server A is elected as the leader.

2. **Proposal:** A client sends a request to update the value. Server A proposes this update to servers B and C.

3. **Voting:** Servers B and C, if they agree, append the update to their local logs and vote to accept the proposal.

4. **Commitment:** Once server A receives a majority of votes (in this case, one vote from either B or C), it commits the update to its local store and informs B and C to commit as well.

5. **Client Response:** Server A then responds to the client, confirming the successful update.

Code Example (Conceptual - Go):

This is a simplified representation and not a complete implementation.

```go
// Assume we have a struct to represent a log entry
type LogEntry struct {
        Term  int // Term number
        Value string
}


//Function to propose a log entry
func ProposeValue(value string) {
        //Simplified:  The leader proposes the value
    //and waits for majority acknowledgement.
        //Error handling and retries are skipped for brevity.
        logEntry := LogEntry{Term: currentTerm, Value: value}
    broadcast(logEntry) // Send to followers

}


//Function to broadcast value
func broadcast(logEntry LogEntry) {
        // Logic to send log entry to followers
}
```

Sketch:

```
+----------+      +----------+      +----------+
| Server A |  --> | Server B |  --> | Server C |
| (Leader) |      | (Follower)|      | (Follower)|
+----------+      +----------+      +----------+
     |                 ^                 ^
     | Proposal        | Vote            | Vote
     | ---------->  |  ---------->  |  ---------->
     |                 |                 |
     | Commit          | Commit          | Commit
     | ---------->  |  ---------->  |  ---------->
     V                 V                 V
  Key-Value        Key-Value        Key-Value
  Store            Store            Store
```

The sketch illustrates the flow of a proposal from the leader (Server A) to the followers (Server B and C), the voting process, and the subsequent commitment of the update to each server's key-value store.

Consequences and Considerations:

Using consensus algorithms to achieve strong consistency has implications:

- **Performance Overhead:** Consensus algorithms involve communication and coordination, which can introduce latency.
- **Availability Trade-offs:** If a sufficient number of nodes fail, the system might be unable to reach a consensus, leading to temporary unavailability.
- **Complexity:** Implementing and managing consensus algorithms requires expertise and careful consideration of fault tolerance and recovery mechanisms.

In summary, consensus algorithms like Paxos and Raft provide a robust way to achieve strong consistency in distributed systems. While they introduce complexity and potential performance overhead, they are essential for applications where data integrity and correctness are paramount.

Eventual Consistency

Eventual consistency is a data consistency model that stands in contrast to strong consistency. It is crucial for understanding distributed systems and their trade-offs.

Guarantees: Eventual consistency guarantees that if no new updates are made to a data item, eventually all accesses to that item will return the last updated value. The "eventually" part is key. It doesn't promise immediate consistency across all replicas; rather, it assures that consistency will be achieved over time. This time window is referred to as "convergence."

Think of it like this sketch:

```
Time ---->

Server A: [Initial Value] --Update--> [New Value]

Server B: [Initial Value] --------------------> [New Value] (Eventually)

Server C: [Initial Value] --------> [New Value] (Sooner)
```

Server A receives the update first. Servers B and C eventually receive the update, but not necessarily at the same time, nor immediately after Server A.

Implementation & Challenges: Eventual consistency is simpler to implement than strong consistency, making it appealing for systems that prioritize availability and scalability. However, it introduces the possibility of reading stale data, leading to anomalies if not carefully managed. The main issues stem from potential temporary inconsistencies.

A potential problem can be **Read-Your-Writes** anomaly which mean, you can read an older version immediately after writing. This means your write has not propagated yet.

Example: Imagine you update your profile picture on a social media platform.

1. You upload the new picture (write operation).

2. You immediately refresh your profile page (read operation).

With eventual consistency, it's possible that you might still see your old profile picture temporarily. Why? Because the update might not have propagated to all the servers serving your profile yet. Eventually, all servers will be updated, and you will see the new picture, but there might be a brief period where you see the old one.

Programming Code Example:

Here's a simplified conceptual illustration using Python to demonstrate eventual consistency in a distributed cache scenario. Note: This is a drastically simplified example and lacks the complexities of real-world distributed caching.

```python
import time
import threading

class DistributedCache:
    def __init__(self):
        self.data = {}
        self.locks = {} # to simulate per key locking which is very very important
    def get(self, key):
        # Simulate a delay to represent network latency and eventual consistency
        time.sleep(0.1)
        with self.locks.get(key,threading.Lock()):
            return self.data.get(key)

    def put(self, key, value):
        with self.locks.setdefault(key,threading.Lock()):
            self.data[key] = value
            # Simulate asynchronous propagation to other nodes (not implemented here)
            # In reality, this would involve message queues, replication strategies, etc.
            print(f"Key '{key}' updated to '{value}'")

# Example Usage
cache = DistributedCache()

# Thread 1: Update a value
def update_value(cache, key, value):
    cache.put(key, value)

# Thread 2: Read the value
def read_value(cache, key):
    print(f"Reading key '{key}': {cache.get(key)}")

# Start threads
t1 = threading.Thread(target=update_value, args=(cache, "mykey", "newvalue"))
t2 = threading.Thread(target=read_value, args=(cache, "mykey"))

t1.start()
time.sleep(0.05)  # Simulate a slight delay before the read
t2.start()

t1.join()
t2.join()

print(f"Final value of 'mykey': {cache.get('mykey')}")
```

In this example:

- `DistributedCache` simulates a simple distributed cache.
- `put` updates the value and prints a message, representing an update.
- `get` simulates a delay to illustrate the potential for reading stale data before the update propagates (in a real-world system, this delay would be network latency and the time it takes for updates to replicate).

- The threads represent different clients accessing the cache.
- The delay before the `read_value` is called creates a chance for Thread 2 to read an older version. The final print statement should print the last written value.
- The use of per key locking ensures that writes do not conflict and that updates are atomic with respect to a given key.

This example shows how reading shortly after writing might return an older value, demonstrating eventual consistency in a simplified manner. A real distributed system will have more complex mechanism for replicating data, and handling conflicts.

Trade-offs: Eventual consistency is often chosen over strong consistency when availability and low latency are paramount. This trade-off is fundamental:

- **Advantages:** Higher availability (the system can still serve requests even if some nodes are down or unreachable). Lower latency (reads can be served from the nearest replica, even if it's not fully up-to-date). Greater scalability (easier to distribute data and handle high loads).

- **Disadvantages:** Potential for reading stale data. Increased complexity in application logic to handle inconsistencies. Requires careful design to minimize the impact of inconsistencies on the user experience.

Choosing the Right Model: The selection of a consistency model depends heavily on the specific application requirements. Consider:

- **Data criticality:** How important is it that the data is always up-to-date? For financial transactions, strong consistency is typically essential. For less critical data, like social media post counts, eventual consistency might suffice.

- **User expectations:** What do users expect in terms of data consistency? If users expect immediate consistency, eventual consistency might lead to a poor user experience.

- **Fault tolerance needs:** How resilient does the system need to be to failures? Eventual consistency typically offers better fault tolerance than strong consistency.

Ultimately, understanding the trade-offs between strong and eventual consistency is crucial for designing robust and scalable distributed systems. Careful consideration of application needs and user expectations is essential when choosing the appropriate consistency model.

Eventual Consistency: "If No New Updates Are Made..."

The core idea of eventual consistency centers around what happens to your data *over time* when things stop changing. Specifically, it *guarantees that if no new updates are made to a data item, eventually all accesses will return the last updated value.* Let's unpack this statement.

Imagine a simple key-value store. You put the value "1" against the key "counter." Over time, you update the counter; let's say it becomes "5." In an eventually consistent system, that value might not immediately be visible to *everyone* who asks for it. Some users might temporarily see "1", "2", or even an older value. The system is working on updating all copies of the data in the background. *Eventually*, however, if you stop updating the "counter," the system *guarantees* that *eventually*, *every* read request will return the value "5."

Think of it like this. You have multiple copies of the same file spread across different servers. When you update the file on one server, the system starts a process to copy this change to the other servers. It takes time for the update to reach all the servers. During that brief period, some users querying some servers might get the old version of the file. But if you *stop* making any changes to the file, the system guarantees that *eventually* all servers will have the same, latest version of the file. All users querying any server will see the most up-to-date file.

Analogy: Spreading News

Think of spreading news across a network of people. You tell one person something. That person tells two others, and they, in turn, tell more people. It takes time for the news to spread to *everyone*. Some people will hear the initial version of the news, while others might hear a slightly updated version later on. However, *if the news stops changing*, eventually *everyone* in the network will hear the exact same, final version of the news. This eventual agreement on the same information is analogous to eventual consistency.

Code Illustration (Conceptual - simplified):

This is a simplified illustration. Actual implementations are more complex.

```python
import time
import threading

# Shared Data (in a real system, this would be distributed)
shared_data = {"counter": 0}
lock = threading.Lock()  # To prevent race conditions in this example

def read_counter():
    with lock:
        return shared_data["counter"]

def update_counter(new_value):
    with lock:
        shared_data["counter"] = new_value
    # In a distributed system, this is where propagation to other nodes
    # would happen asynchronously (in the background).  We're skipping
    # that part for simplicity.

# Simulate reading from different "nodes" at different times
def simulate_read(node_id):
    time.sleep(node_id  0.5)  # Simulate network latency differences
    value = read_counter()
    print(f"Node {node_id}: Read counter value: {value}")

# Main Execution
update_counter(5) # First update

threads = []
for i in range(3):  # Simulate 3 different nodes reading
    thread = threading.Thread(target=simulate_read, args=(i,))
    threads.append(thread)
    thread.start()

for thread in threads:
    thread.join()  # Wait for all readers to finish
print ("No other threads accessing data now. Eventually Consistent")
```

In this example, even with thread sleeps simulating latency, the output shows different "nodes" might read the counter at slightly different times. This highlights how, after updates stop, these value converges to the actual expected updated value. In a true distributed system, the time difference and potential inconsistencies would be much more pronounced during the propagation phase.

Important Considerations:

This "eventual" aspect is critical. It doesn't specify *when* consistency will be achieved, only that it *will* happen. The time it takes to reach consistency is called the "convergence window." This window can vary based on network conditions, system load, and the specific consistency algorithm used.

Chapter 9 Building Scalable and Reliable Systems- Transactions and Concurrency Control in Distributed Databases

- **ACID Properties in Distributed Systems:**
  - Challenges implementing Atomicity, Consistency, Isolation, Durability across multiple nodes.
- **Distributed Transactions:**
  - Atomic commits using protocols like two-phase commit (2PC).
- **Concurrency Control:**
  - Techniques such as distributed locking, optimistic concurrency control.
- **Linearizability and Total Order Broadcast:**
  - Ensuring operations appear to happen in a single, consistent order.
- **Fault Tolerance and Recovery:**
  - Handling node failures and ensuring data consistency during recovery.

ACID Properties in Distributed Systems

Implementing ACID (Atomicity, Consistency, Isolation, and Durability) properties in a distributed system presents significant challenges compared to a single-node database. The inherent nature of distributed systems – involving multiple interconnected computers – introduces complexities that require careful consideration to maintain data integrity and reliability.

Challenges implementing Atomicity, Consistency, Isolation, Durability across multiple nodes.

- **Atomicity:** In a single database, atomicity means a transaction is treated as a single, indivisible unit of work. Either all operations within the transaction are applied successfully, or none are. In a distributed system, this becomes complex. A single transaction might involve updates across several nodes. If one node fails midway through the transaction, some nodes might have applied the changes while others have not, violating atomicity.

  - **Example:** Consider a banking application where transferring funds from account A to account B involves two operations: debiting account A on Node 1 and crediting account B on Node 2. If Node 2 fails after the debit on Node 1 succeeds, the system is left in an inconsistent state.

    - **Sketch of Atomicity Problem:**

      ```
      Transaction: Transfer $100 from A to B

      Node 1 (Account A): Debit $100   --> Success
      Node 2 (Account B): Credit $100  --> FAILURE!
      ```

```
Result:  $100 disappears!
```

- **Consistency:** Consistency ensures that a transaction brings the system from one valid state to another. It maintains database invariants and rules. In a distributed system, achieving consistency is harder because data is spread across multiple locations. Ensuring all replicas of data remain consistent after a transaction requires special protocols.

  - **Example:** Suppose you have multiple copies of a user's profile data stored on different servers. If a user updates their email address, all copies need to be updated consistently. If some updates fail, the system ends up with inconsistent versions of the user's profile.

    - **Sketch of Consistency Problem:**

      ```
      User Profile (Email): john.doe@oldemail.com  (Replicated on 3 Nodes)

      User Updates Email: john.doe@newemail.com

      Node 1: Updated Successfully
      Node 2: Update Fails!
      Node 3: Updated Successfully

      Result: Nodes 1 & 3 show new email, Node 2 shows old email. INCONSISTENT!
      ```

- **Isolation:** Isolation guarantees that concurrent transactions do not interfere with each other. In a single database, this is usually achieved with locking mechanisms. In a distributed system, providing isolation becomes more challenging due to network latency and the need for distributed locking or other concurrency control mechanisms.

  - **Example:** Imagine two transactions trying to update the same product's inventory count on different nodes. Without proper isolation, one transaction might read an outdated inventory count, leading to an incorrect update when both transactions commit.

    - **Sketch of Isolation Problem:**

      ```
      Inventory Count (Product X): 100 (Replicated on 2 Nodes)

      Transaction 1 (Node 1):
          Read Inventory: 100
          Deduct 10
          Write Inventory: 90

      Transaction 2 (Node 2):  (Occurs concurrently)
          Read Inventory: 100  (Reads stale data)
          Deduct 5
          Write Inventory: 95

      Result: Should be 85 (100 - 10 - 5), but one transaction overwrites the other.
      ```

- **Durability:** Durability ensures that once a transaction is committed, the changes are permanent and will survive even system failures. In a distributed system, achieving durability requires replicating data across multiple nodes and using robust recovery mechanisms.

  - **Example:** After a customer completes an order, the order details must be stored persistently across multiple servers. If one server crashes, the order information should still be recoverable from other replicas.

- **Sketch of Durability Problem:**

  ```
  Order Details: Stored on Node 1 (Primary) and Node 2 (Backup)

  Order Placed:  Transaction commits, data written to Node 1

  Node 1 Crashes BEFORE data replicates to Node 2!

  Result: Order information LOST if Node 1 is unrecoverable.
  ```

Implementing ACID properties in distributed systems is not a simple task; it requires careful planning, a deep understanding of trade-offs, and the use of appropriate technologies and protocols.

Distributed Transactions

Distributed transactions address the challenge of ensuring that a series of operations, spread across multiple computers (nodes) in a distributed system, are treated as a single, indivisible unit of work. This means either all operations succeed (the transaction commits), or all operations fail (the transaction aborts), maintaining data consistency across the system. Imagine you're transferring money from one bank account to another, where the accounts reside on different servers. A distributed transaction ensures that either the money is deducted from the first account *and* credited to the second, or neither operation occurs, preventing money from disappearing or being created.

- **Atomic commits using protocols like two-phase commit (2PC).**

To achieve this atomicity in distributed systems, protocols like Two-Phase Commit (2PC) are crucial. Let's break down how 2PC works:

Two-Phase Commit (2PC):

2PC is a distributed algorithm that guarantees all participants in a distributed transaction either commit or abort the transaction. It involves a coordinator and multiple participants.

Phase 1: Prepare Phase

1. **Coordinator's Request:** The coordinator initiates the transaction and asks each participant (e.g., database servers) if they're ready to commit their part of the transaction.
2. **Participants' Response:** Each participant performs its portion of the transaction and then replies to the coordinator. A participant can respond with either:
   - "Vote Commit": The participant is ready to commit and has prepared its resources (e.g., logged changes to disk).
   - "Vote Abort": The participant cannot commit due to some error (e.g., insufficient resources, constraint violation).

Phase 2: Commit/Abort Phase

The coordinator collects the votes from all participants. Based on the votes, it decides whether to commit or abort the transaction.

1. **Commit Decision:** If all participants voted "Commit", the coordinator sends a "Commit" message to all participants. Each participant then permanently applies the changes and acknowledges the commit.

   ```
   Sketch: Commit Decision
   ------------------------------------------------------------------
   | Coordinator                                                    |
   | (Received all "Vote Commit") -> Send "Commit" to Participants  |
   ------------------------------------------------------------------
                       /        |        \
   ```

```
                        /          |          \
    ---------------------   ---------------------   ---------------------
    | Participant 1         | Participant 2         | Participant 3         |
    | Apply changes         | Apply changes          | Apply changes        |
    | Acknowledge Commit    | Acknowledge Commit    | Acknowledge Commit    |
    ---------------------   ---------------------   ---------------------
```

2. **Abort Decision:** If even one participant voted "Abort", or if the coordinator doesn't receive a response from a participant within a timeout period, the coordinator sends an "Abort" message to all participants. Each participant then rolls back any changes it made and acknowledges the abort.

```
Sketch: Abort Decision
----------------------------------------------------------------
| Coordinator                                                  |
| (Received "Vote Abort" or Timeout) -> Send "Abort" to Participants|
----------------------------------------------------------------
                        /          |          \
                       /           |           \
    ---------------------   ---------------------   ---------------------
    | Participant 1         | Participant 2         | Participant 3         |
    | Rollback changes      | Rollback changes       | Rollback changes     |
    | Acknowledge Abort     | Acknowledge Abort     | Acknowledge Abort     |
    ---------------------   ---------------------   ---------------------
```

Example Code (Conceptual - illustrating the process):

```python
class Participant:
    def __init__(self, name):
        self.name = name
        self.prepared = False
        self.committed = False

    def prepare(self):
        # Simulate preparing the transaction (e.g., logging changes)
        print(f"{self.name}: Preparing transaction...")
        # If preparation fails (e.g., resource unavailable), return False
        self.prepared = True
        return True  # Simulate successful preparation

    def commit(self):
        if self.prepared:
            print(f"{self.name}: Committing transaction...")
            # Apply changes permanently
            self.committed = True
        else:
            print(f"{self.name}: Cannot commit, not prepared.")

    def abort(self):
        print(f"{self.name}: Aborting transaction...")
        # Rollback any changes
        self.prepared = False
        self.committed = False

class Coordinator:
    def __init__(self, participants):
```

```
        self.participants = participants

    def execute_transaction(self):
        # Phase 1: Prepare
        votes = {}
        for participant in self.participants:
            votes[participant] = participant.prepare()

        # Check if all participants voted to commit
        if all(votes.values()):
            print("Coordinator: All participants voted to commit.")
            # Phase 2: Commit
            for participant in self.participants:
                participant.commit()
            print("Coordinator: Transaction committed successfully.")
        else:
            print("Coordinator: At least one participant voted to abort.")
            # Phase 2: Abort
            for participant in self.participants:
                participant.abort()
            print("Coordinator: Transaction aborted.")


# Example Usage
participant1 = Participant("Database Server 1")
participant2 = Participant("Database Server 2")
coordinator = Coordinator([participant1, participant2])
coordinator.execute_transaction()
```

Limitations of 2PC:

While 2PC guarantees atomicity, it has some drawbacks:

- **Blocking:** If the coordinator fails after participants have prepared but before they've committed or aborted, the participants remain blocked, holding resources until the coordinator recovers. This can severely impact system availability.
- **Complexity:** Implementing 2PC can be complex, requiring careful coordination and error handling.
- **Performance Overhead:** The multiple rounds of communication can introduce latency, especially in geographically distributed systems.

Despite these limitations, 2PC remains a fundamental protocol for achieving atomic commits in many distributed systems. Other protocols like Paxos and Raft address some of 2PC's drawbacks, particularly the blocking problem, by employing consensus mechanisms.

Concurrency Control

In distributed systems, multiple processes or threads might try to access and modify the same data simultaneously. Concurrency control mechanisms are essential to ensure that these concurrent operations don't lead to inconsistencies or data corruption. Essentially, it's about managing the order and access rights to shared resources in a way that guarantees data integrity.

Techniques such as distributed locking, optimistic concurrency control

We will explore two main categories of concurrency control: distributed locking and optimistic concurrency control. Each has its own strengths and weaknesses, making them suitable for different scenarios.

Distributed Locking:

Distributed locking operates much like locking in a single-machine system, but with the added complexity of coordinating locks across multiple machines. When a process needs to modify data, it first requests a lock on that data. If the lock is available, the process acquires it and can proceed with the modification. Other processes attempting to access the same data will be blocked until the lock is released.

- **How it works:** A centralized or decentralized lock manager coordinates the granting and releasing of locks.

  - *Centralized Lock Manager:* A single server is responsible for managing all locks. This is simpler to implement but can become a bottleneck and a single point of failure.
  - *Decentralized Lock Manager:* Lock management is distributed across multiple nodes, typically using a consensus algorithm. This provides better fault tolerance but is more complex to implement.

- **Example:**

  Assume we have a distributed database storing user account balances. Imagine two concurrent transactions:

  - Transaction A: Transfers $100 from User X to User Y.
  - Transaction B: Transfers $50 from User X to User Z.

  Without locking, these transactions could interleave in a way that leads to an incorrect final balance for User X.

  Here's a simplified Python-like pseudocode example of how distributed locking might be used to prevent this:

```
class DistributedLock:
    def __init__(self, resource_id):
        self.resource_id = resource_id

    def acquire(self):
        # Code to request and acquire a lock from the lock manager
        # (Implementation details depend on the lock manager)
        print(f"Lock acquired for {self.resource_id}")
        return True #Simulating lock acquisition

    def release(self):
        # Code to release the lock
        print(f"Lock released for {self.resource_id}")

def transfer_funds(user_from, user_to, amount):
    lock_user_from = DistributedLock(user_from)
    lock_user_to = DistributedLock(user_to)

    try:
        #Acquire both locks to prevent deadlock
        if lock_user_from.acquire() and lock_user_to.acquire():
            # Read balances
            balance_from = get_balance(user_from)
            balance_to = get_balance(user_to)

            # Check if sufficient funds
            if balance_from >= amount:
                # Update balances (atomically)
                new_balance_from = balance_from - amount
                new_balance_to = balance_to + amount

                set_balance(user_from, new_balance_from)
```

```
                    set_balance(user_to, new_balance_to)
                    print(f"Transfer of {amount} from {user_from} to {user_to} successful.")

                else:
                    print(f"Insufficient funds in {user_from}'s account.")
            else:
                print("Failed to acquire locks. Transaction aborted.")

        finally:
            # Ensure locks are released, even if an error occurs
            lock_user_from.release()
            lock_user_to.release()


# Example Usage
transfer_funds("UserX", "UserY", 100)
```

In this example, `DistributedLock` represents a lock that is managed across the distributed system. Before transferring funds, the code attempts to acquire locks for both the sender and receiver accounts. The `acquire()` and `release()` methods are placeholders for the actual implementation of communication with a lock manager. The 'Try Finally' block ensures that locks are released even if the transaction fails.

- **Advantages:** Ensures serializability, preventing conflicting updates. Simple to understand.

- **Disadvantages:** Can lead to bottlenecks if the lock manager is centralized. Risk of deadlocks if not implemented carefully. Performance overhead of acquiring and releasing locks.

Optimistic Concurrency Control (OCC):

Unlike locking, optimistic concurrency control assumes that conflicts are rare. Instead of acquiring locks, processes read data, perform their computations, and then attempt to write the changes back. Before writing, the system checks if the data has been modified by another process since it was read. If a conflict is detected (i.e., the data has changed), the write is rejected, and the process typically retries the operation.

- **How it works:** Processes maintain a version number or timestamp of the data they read. When writing, they check if the current version number matches the version they read. If they match, the write succeeds, and the version number is incremented. If they don't match, the write fails.

- **Example:**

  Consider a distributed inventory management system. Multiple processes might be trying to update the quantity of a product simultaneously.

  Here's a simplified pseudocode example:

```
class InventoryItem:
    def __init__(self, product_id, quantity, version):
        self.product_id = product_id
        self.quantity = quantity
        self.version = version


def get_inventory_item(product_id):
    #Simulate fetching the data
    version = 1 #Initial Version
    quantity = 100
    return InventoryItem(product_id, quantity, version)


def update_inventory(item, new_quantity):
```

```
        #Check the version before updating the quantity
        current_item = get_inventory_item(item.product_id) #Fetching current Item

        if item.version == current_item.version:
            # Simulate writing the data with an incremented version
            new_version = current_item.version + 1
            #Write the changes to DB
            print("Updating the Inventory")
            return True #Successful update
        else:
            print("Conflict: Inventory item has been updated by another transaction. Please ret
            return False #Conflict - Update failed


    # Example usage
    item = get_inventory_item("ProductA") #Item with Version 1
    #item.quantity is 100

    #Process 1 reduces item
    new_quantity1 = item.quantity - 20 #80
    #item.version is 1

    #Process 2 reduces item
    new_quantity2 = item.quantity - 10 #90
    #item.version is 1


    #Process 1 updates
    update1 = update_inventory(item, new_quantity1) #Successful
    if update1:
        print("Item quantity is now 80, version has been updated")


    #Process 2 updates
    update2 = update_inventory(item, new_quantity2) #Fails

    if update2:
        print("Item quantity is now 90, version has been updated")
    else:
        print("Process 2 to retry")
```

In this scenario, two processes attempt to update the inventory of "ProductA". Process 1 successfully updates the inventory because its version number matches the current version in the database. Process 2's update fails because the version number it read is no longer current (Process 1 already incremented it). Process 2 would need to retry the operation, re-reading the current data and re-applying its changes.

- **Advantages:** Higher concurrency than locking, as processes don't block each other. Suitable for systems with low contention.

- **Disadvantages:** Requires a retry mechanism, which can be complex to implement. Can lead to wasted work if conflicts are frequent.

Choosing between distributed locking and optimistic concurrency control depends on the specific characteristics of your application. If conflicts are common and you need strong consistency guarantees, distributed locking might be the better choice. If conflicts are rare and you prioritize high concurrency, optimistic concurrency control might be more suitable.

Linearizability and Total Order Broadcast

This section explores how to make sure that operations in a distributed system appear to happen in a single, consistent order. This is crucial for maintaining the illusion that your distributed system is behaving like a single, powerful computer, even when it's actually composed of many separate machines. Two key concepts help achieve this: Linearizability and Total Order Broadcast.

Ensuring operations appear to happen in a single, consistent order.

Imagine you have several bank servers scattered across the globe. Alice wants to transfer $100 from her account to Bob's. Without a consistent order of operations, the following scenario could occur:

1. Alice's server deducts $100 from her account.
2. Bob's server receives the instruction to add $100 to his account.
3. Before Bob's server completes the addition, a failure occurs, and the operation is rolled back on Alice's server due to a perceived timeout.
4. Now, Alice has her $100 back, and Bob never received it!

A system guaranteeing a single, consistent order of operations prevents such anomalies. It ensures that all operations appear to have happened in a specific sequence, agreed upon by all nodes in the system.

Linearizability

Linearizability is a strong consistency model for shared memory or data stores. It means that each operation appears to execute atomically at some point between its invocation and its response. Furthermore, this execution order must be consistent with the real-time order of operations. In simpler terms, if operation A completes before operation B starts, then A must appear to happen before B in the system's history.

It guarantees each read returns the most recent write.

Consider a distributed key-value store. Suppose we have two clients, Client 1 and Client 2.

1. Client 1 writes the value "foo" to key "X".
2. Client 2 then reads the value of key "X".

With Linearizability, Client 2 *must* read "foo". There's no possibility of reading an older value, as the write from Client 1 is guaranteed to have taken effect before Client 2's read.

To illustrate with a simplified code example, let's assume a simple key-value store API:

```
class KeyValueStore:
    def __init__(self):
        self.data = {}

    def write(self, key, value):
        # Imagine this write is happening atomically
        self.data[key] = value

    def read(self, key):
        # Imagine this read is retrieving the most recent write
        return self.data.get(key)
```

A linearizable system makes sure that the `write` operation is instantly available before the `read` operation happens. The code itself doesn't *guarantee* linearizability; it's just a simplified representation. Achieving it requires specific distributed consensus mechanisms.

If several operations execute concurrently on different machines, they may appear in different orders on different machines. Linearizability requires that there is a single global ordering of these operations that respects the real-time order of events.

Consider three operations A, B, and C.

- A starts at time t1 and completes at time t2.
- B starts at time t3 and completes at time t4.
- C starts at time t5 and completes at time t6.

If t2 < t3, then A must appear to happen before B. If t4 < t5, then B must appear to happen before C. But, if the periods (t1,t2), (t3,t4) and (t5, t6) all overlap, then A, B and C could happen in any order, yet the order must be the same for all observers.

Total Order Broadcast

Total Order Broadcast (TOB), also known as Atomic Broadcast, is a different but related concept. It's a communication primitive that guarantees that all messages are delivered to all nodes in the *same* order. This is a fundamental building block for constructing distributed systems with strong consistency guarantees.

It ensures every node sees the same operations in the same order.

Imagine a group of nodes that need to reach a consensus on a series of events. With Total Order Broadcast, if node A broadcasts message M1 and then message M2, and node B receives M1 and M2, it's guaranteed that node B will receive M1 before M2. Furthermore, all other nodes receiving M1 and M2 will also see them in that order.

TOB can be visualized like this:

```
Node 1:  M1 --> M2 --> M3
                              \
Node 2:  M1 --> M2 --> M3      \
                               \
                                \
Node 3:  M1 --> M2 --> M3       \
                                 \
Node 4:  M1 --> M2 --> M3
```

All nodes receive the messages in the same total order (M1, M2, M3).

While it may seem similar to Linearizability, TOB is a message-passing concept, while Linearizability applies to operations on a shared data store. However, TOB is often used as a building block to implement Linearizable data stores. By using TOB to agree on the order of operations, you can then apply those operations in the agreed-upon order at each node, achieving Linearizability.

Here's a conceptual Python example illustrating the basic principle. This isn't a working implementation, but it showcases the idea:

```python
class TotalOrderBroadcast:
    def __init__(self):
        self.messages = []  # Global list to store messages in order
        self.listeners = [] # List of nodes listening to broadcast

    def broadcast(self, message, sender_node):
        # (In a real system, a consensus algorithm like Paxos or Raft
        # would determine the order of messages)

        # Simulate adding message to a globally agreed-upon list:
        self.messages.append((message, sender_node))
        self.notify_listeners(message, sender_node)
```

```python
    def register_listener(self, node):
      self.listeners.append(node)
      # Send all previous messages to node
      for message, sender_node in self.messages:
        node.receive(message, sender_node)


    def notify_listeners(self, message, sender_node):
      for node in self.listeners:
        node.receive(message, sender_node)

class Node:
  def __init__(self, tob):
    self.tob = tob
    self.received_messages = []
    tob.register_listener(self)

  def send(self, message):
    self.tob.broadcast(message, self)

  def receive(self, message, sender_node):
    self.received_messages.append((message, sender_node))
    print(f"Node received message: {message} from {sender_node}")
```

In this simplified example, the `TotalOrderBroadcast` class maintains a global list of messages in the agreed-upon order. The `broadcast` method adds the message to this list (in a real system, a consensus algorithm would determine the order). The `Node` class represents a node in the system that can send and receive messages via the `TotalOrderBroadcast`. This is a very basic idea, in reality TOB requires robust consensus algorithms.

In summary, Linearizability and Total Order Broadcast are vital for building consistent and reliable distributed systems. Linearizability provides strong guarantees about the order in which operations appear to happen, while Total Order Broadcast ensures that messages are delivered to all nodes in the same order. While distinct concepts, they are often used together to create powerful and robust distributed applications.

Fault Tolerance and Recovery

In distributed systems, "Fault Tolerance and Recovery" refers to the system's ability to continue operating correctly even when some of its components fail and the processes involved in restoring the system to a consistent state after such failures. This is a crucial aspect because node failures are inevitable in distributed environments.

Handling node failures and ensuring data consistency during recovery.

Node failures are a common occurrence in distributed systems. These failures can range from simple software crashes to complete hardware breakdowns. The system needs mechanisms to detect these failures and react appropriately to minimize disruption. Furthermore, data consistency must be maintained throughout these failures and during the recovery process.

Example of Node Failure and Recovery

Imagine a distributed database with three nodes, A, B, and C. Each node holds a replica of the data.

```
+---+       +---+       +---+
| A |------| B |------| C |
+---+       +---+       +---+
(Master)  (Replica)  (Replica)
```

If node A (the master) fails, the system should:

1. **Detect the Failure:** Use heartbeat mechanisms (periodic signals sent between nodes) or timeout-based detection.
2. **Failover:** Promote one of the replicas (B or C) to be the new master. This election process can use algorithms like Raft or Paxos.
3. **Data Recovery:** The new master (say B) might be slightly behind A. It needs to catch up by replaying logs of operations that A had processed but B hadn't yet received. This is often achieved using write-ahead logging.
4. **Reintegration:** When the failed node A recovers, it needs to synchronize its data with the current master (B) before rejoining the cluster.

Ensuring Data Consistency During Recovery

Data consistency is paramount during failure and recovery. Various techniques are used:

- **Write-Ahead Logging (WAL):** Before applying a change to the database, the operation is first recorded in a durable log. This log can be used to replay operations and bring a node back to a consistent state after a crash.

```
// Example (Conceptual)
log.append("Transaction X: Update account A's balance to $100"); // Write to log
apply_update("Account A", 100);                                   // Apply update
```

If the system crashes between these two steps, on recovery, the log is replayed to ensure the update is applied.

- **Checkpoints:** Periodically, a snapshot of the database's state is taken. This reduces the amount of log that needs to be replayed during recovery.

- **Data Replication:** Multiple copies of the data are maintained across different nodes. If one node fails, the other replicas can continue to serve requests.

- **Quorum-Based Systems:** Operations require acknowledgement from a majority (quorum) of the nodes. This ensures that even if some nodes are unavailable, the system can still make progress and maintain consistency.

Sketch illustrating quorum

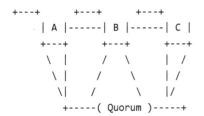

```
+---+        +---+        +---+
| A |------| B |------| C |
+---+        +---+        +---+
 \ |       /  \     | /
  \ |     /    \    | /
   \|    /      \   |/
    +-----( Quorum )-----+
```

In this sketch, if a write operation needs to succeed, it must be acknowledged by at least two nodes (a quorum). This ensures that even if one node is unavailable, the write operation can still be considered successful if the other two nodes agree.

Considerations for Fault Tolerance and Recovery

- **Detection Time:** How quickly can the system detect a failure? Faster detection allows for quicker failover and reduces downtime.
- **Recovery Time:** How long does it take to recover from a failure and restore the system to a consistent state? Shorter recovery times minimize the impact of failures.
- **Consistency Guarantees:** What level of consistency does the system provide during and after failures? Stronger consistency guarantees come at a higher performance cost.
- **Complexity:** Implementing robust fault tolerance and recovery mechanisms can be complex and require careful design and testing.

By implementing robust fault tolerance and recovery mechanisms, distributed systems can provide high availability and reliability, ensuring that they can continue to operate correctly even in the face of failures.

Chapter 10 Data Processing and Analytics-Batch Processing: Hadoop, Spark, and Distributed File Systems

- **Batch Processing:** Processes large datasets in bulk, ideal for historical analysis and reporting.

- **Hadoop & MapReduce:**

  - **MapReduce:** Programming model dividing tasks into "map" (data transformation) and "reduce" (data aggregation) phases.
  - **HDFS:** Hadoop Distributed File System; stores large files across commodity hardware, providing fault tolerance.

- **Spark:**

  - **In-Memory Processing:** Speeds up computations by caching data in memory, suitable for iterative algorithms.
  - **Resilient Distributed Datasets (RDDs):** Immutable, partitioned collections enabling parallel processing and fault tolerance.

- **Distributed File Systems:** Underlying storage foundation for batch processing frameworks.

- **Trade-offs:** Latency (high) vs. throughput (high); suitable when immediate results aren't critical.

Batch Processing

Batch processing is a method of handling data by collecting it over a period of time and then processing it all at once as a batch. Think of it like this: instead of dealing with each piece of data individually as it arrives, you gather them together and process them in a group.

- **Processes large datasets in bulk:** This is the core idea of batch processing. It's designed to handle huge amounts of data efficiently. Imagine you have a file containing millions of customer transactions from an entire year. Batch processing is well-suited for tasks like analyzing all those transactions to generate yearly sales reports. It's not designed to show live updates of each transaction.

  - **Example:** A bank processing all the day's transactions overnight, or a company generating monthly reports based on sales data collected throughout the month.

- **Ideal for historical analysis and reporting:** Because batch processing handles data in large chunks, it's excellent for looking at data from the past. This is called historical analysis.

- **Example:** Looking at five years of sales data to find trends, or analyzing website traffic patterns over the last year to understand user behavior.

- **Trade-offs: Latency (high) vs. throughput (high); suitable when immediate results aren't critical:**

  - **Latency (high):** Latency refers to the delay between when data is submitted and when the results are available. In batch processing, there's a significant delay because the system waits until a sufficient amount of data has been collected before processing. Think of waiting for a weekly payroll run compared to getting paid instantly for each hour you work.

  - **Throughput (high):** Throughput is the amount of data that can be processed in a given time. Batch processing is designed to handle very large datasets, so it has high throughput.

  - **Suitable when immediate results aren't critical:** Batch processing is appropriate when you don't need results immediately. For example, generating monthly sales reports doesn't require real-time updates; waiting until the end of the month to process all the data is acceptable. However, it's unsuitable for applications where real-time data is critical.

    - **Example:** If you are building a system for fraud detection where you need to flag suspicious transactions immediately, batch processing would not be a good fit. An online transaction processing system would be better.

- **Distributed File Systems:** Batch processing frameworks rely heavily on distributed file systems for the actual storage of the data on which they are processing.

Hadoop & MapReduce

Hadoop and MapReduce are fundamental technologies for processing extremely large datasets that won't fit on a single computer. They work together: Hadoop provides the storage and resource management, while MapReduce is a programming model for processing the data.

MapReduce:

MapReduce is a programming model that breaks down data processing into two key phases: the "map" phase and the "reduce" phase. Think of it like a well-organized factory assembly line.

- **Map Phase (Data Transformation):** The "map" phase takes the input data and transforms it into key-value pairs. It's like taking raw materials and preparing them for further processing. The 'map' function is applied to each input record, and the function can perform filtering, sorting, or any other kind of transformation, like a manufacturing production line where initial data is processed for final products.

Example: Suppose you have a large text file and you want to count the frequency of each word. The "map" phase would read each line, split it into words, and output key-value pairs where the key is the word and the value is 1 (representing one occurrence).

Code Example(Python):

```python
def mapper(line):
    words = line.split()
    for word in words:
        yield (word, 1)
```

Explanation: In this simplified mapper function, each line of text is split into words. For each word, a key-value pair (word, 1) is generated.

- **Reduce Phase (Data Aggregation):** The "reduce" phase takes the output from the "map" phase, groups the data by key, and performs an aggregation or summarization operation. The MapReduce framework ensures that all key-value pairs with the same key are sent to the same "reducer." This is like consolidating parts and assemble into final products after some processing.

Example: Continuing the word count example, the "reduce" phase would take the output from the "map" phase (which would be many pairs of the same word with a value of 1) and sum the values for each word. The final output would be a list of words and their total counts.

Code Example(Python):

```python
def reducer(word, counts):
    total_count = sum(counts)
    yield (word, total_count)
```

Explanation: The reducer function receives a word and a list of counts (all 1s in this case, from the mapper). It sums these counts to determine the total occurrence of that word. **Diagram: MapReduce Data Flow**

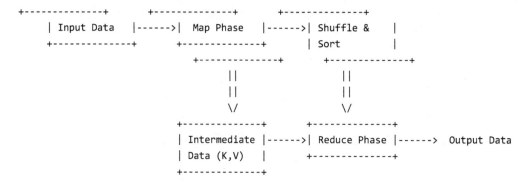

HDFS (Hadoop Distributed File System):

HDFS is the storage layer of Hadoop. It is a distributed file system designed to store extremely large files across a cluster of commodity hardware. This means you can use relatively inexpensive computers to store and process massive amounts of data.

- **Distributed Storage:** HDFS splits the large input file into smaller blocks and distributes these blocks across multiple machines in the cluster.
- **Fault Tolerance:** HDFS replicates each block multiple times (typically 3 times) across different machines. This ensures that if one machine fails, the data is still available on other machines. In HDFS you can think the fault tolerance concept as a data blocks (assume you want to store 128 MB data in HDFS and block size is 32 MB than 4 blocks are created) than each of the four data blocks are replicated with default number 3(this number can be altered) on different machines across the cluster of machines.
- **Scalability:** HDFS can scale to store petabytes or even exabytes of data by adding more machines to the cluster.

Example: Imagine storing a library of millions of books. Instead of trying to fit all the books into one giant room (a single hard drive), you distribute the books across many smaller rooms (multiple machines in a cluster). If one room is damaged (a machine fails), there are copies of those books in other rooms. This system ensures that you can find any book (data) even if there are problems.

Relationship between MapReduce and HDFS:

MapReduce relies on HDFS for data storage and retrieval. The MapReduce framework reads the input data from HDFS, processes it using the "map" and "reduce" phases, and writes the output data back to HDFS. They are tightly integrated.

How it works:

1. A large dataset is stored in HDFS, split into blocks across multiple machines.
2. The MapReduce job is submitted to the Hadoop cluster.
3. The MapReduce framework distributes the "map" tasks to the machines where the data blocks are located (or nearby). This is called "data locality," and it reduces network traffic.

4. Each "map" task processes its local data block and outputs key-value pairs.
5. The MapReduce framework shuffles and sorts the intermediate data, grouping it by key.
6. The "reduce" tasks are distributed to the machines that will perform the aggregation.
7. Each "reduce" task processes its assigned keys and outputs the final results.
8. The final results are stored in HDFS.

In Summary, Hadoop and MapReduce are powerful tools for processing large datasets in a distributed and fault-tolerant manner. They are well-suited for tasks like data warehousing, log analysis, and machine learning.

MapReduce

MapReduce is a programming model designed for processing vast amounts of data in parallel across a distributed computing environment. It breaks down complex tasks into two primary phases: the "map" phase and the "reduce" phase. This paradigm simplifies large-scale data processing, making it accessible even to those without extensive distributed systems expertise.

The Map Phase: Transforming the Data

The map phase takes raw input data and transforms it into key-value pairs. Think of it like sorting a deck of cards. Each card is like a piece of input data, and you're sorting them into piles based on their suit (hearts, diamonds, clubs, spades). The suit is the "key," and the pile of cards for each suit is the "value."

Imagine you have a large text file containing web server logs, and you want to count how many times each unique IP address appears. The map phase would read each line of the log file (each line being a record in our dataset) and extract the IP address. This IP address becomes the "key," and an initial count of '1' becomes the "value."

So, if a line in your log file is:

```
192.168.1.1 - - [01/Jan/2024:00:00:00] "GET /index.html"
```

The map function would output:

```
(192.168.1.1, 1)
```

This process happens in parallel across multiple machines in the cluster, each processing a subset of the data.

The Reduce Phase: Aggregating the Results

The reduce phase takes the key-value pairs generated by the map phase and aggregates the values for each unique key. This is like counting the number of cards in each suit pile after you've sorted them. The input is the "key" (the suit), and the output is the total count of cards for that suit.

Continuing with the IP address example, the reduce phase receives all the key-value pairs with the same IP address (the key). It sums up all the values (the counts) for that IP address.

So, if the reduce phase receives these inputs:

```
(192.168.1.1, 1) (192.168.1.1, 1) (192.168.1.1, 1)
```

It would output:

```
(192.168.1.1, 3)
```

This indicates that the IP address 192.168.1.1 appeared three times in the log file. The reduce phase also operates in parallel, combining the results from multiple map tasks.

A Simple Analogy

Imagine you have a very large library, and you want to count the number of times each word appears in all the books.

- **Map Phase:** You give each book to a different person. Each person reads their book and creates a list of (word, 1) for every word they find.

- **Reduce Phase:** You gather all the lists from each person. For each unique word, you add up all the "1"s to get the total count for that word.

Code Example (Conceptual Python-like Pseudocode)

While the actual implementation varies based on the MapReduce framework (like Hadoop), the concept remains the same. Here's a simplified example to illustrate the logic:

```
def map_function(document):
    """
    Processes a single document (e.g., a line in a file)
    and emits key-value pairs.
    """
    words = document.split() #splitting the document into individual words
    for word in words:
      yield (word, 1) # output as word, count


def reduce_function(key, values):
    """
    Aggregates the values for a given key.
    """
    total_count = sum(values) # summing the values in the list.
    return (key, total_count) #outputs as word, count.
```

HDFS: The Storage Backbone for MapReduce

MapReduce often works in conjunction with the Hadoop Distributed File System (HDFS). HDFS is designed to store massive datasets across a cluster of commodity hardware. It splits the data into blocks and replicates those blocks across multiple machines, providing fault tolerance. If one machine fails, the data is still available from other machines in the cluster.

HDFS provides a reliable and scalable storage layer for MapReduce. The MapReduce framework can access the data directly from HDFS, minimizing data movement and maximizing processing speed.

In essence: MapReduce provides a robust and scalable way to process huge datasets by dividing the work into smaller, manageable tasks that can be executed in parallel.

In-Memory Processing

In-memory processing is a technique that significantly speeds up computations by storing data in a computer's main memory (RAM) rather than on slower storage devices like hard drives or solid-state drives. This approach is particularly well-suited for iterative algorithms, where the same data needs to be accessed and processed repeatedly.

Speeding up Computations:

The key advantage of in-memory processing lies in its speed. Accessing data from RAM is orders of magnitude faster than accessing data from disk. Imagine having a frequently used recipe.

- **Disk-based Processing (Traditional):** Every time you need an ingredient list, you have to walk to the library, find the cookbook, locate the recipe, and write down the ingredients. This is analogous to reading data from a disk.

- **In-Memory Processing:** You copy the entire recipe onto a sheet of paper and keep it on your kitchen counter. Now, when you need the ingredient list, you can instantly read it off the paper. This represents accessing data from RAM.

The decreased latency dramatically improves performance, especially in scenarios involving complex calculations or repeated data access.

Suitable for Iterative Algorithms:

Iterative algorithms are those that repeatedly apply a set of operations to data until a desired result is achieved. Machine learning algorithms, such as gradient descent or k-means clustering, are excellent examples. These algorithms require multiple passes through the data, making in-memory processing extremely beneficial.

Example:

Consider a simple iterative algorithm: calculating the average of a large dataset multiple times to observe convergence.

Pseudo-code (Conceptual):

```
data = [1, 2, 3, ..., 1000] // Large dataset
iterations = 10

// Traditional (Disk-based - Slower)
for i in range(iterations):
    sum = 0
    for value in data:
        sum += value  // Read from disk each time
    average = sum / len(data)
    print(f"Iteration {i+1}: Average = {average}")

// In-Memory (Faster)
data_in_memory = load_data_into_memory(data) // Load data into RAM once
for i in range(iterations):
    sum = 0
    for value in data_in_memory:
        sum += value  // Read from RAM each time
    average = sum / len(data_in_memory)
    print(f"Iteration {i+1}: Average = {average}")
```

In the traditional approach, the data is read from disk in each iteration. In the in-memory approach, the data is loaded into RAM once, and subsequent iterations access the data directly from memory. This eliminates the overhead of disk I/O, resulting in a significant speedup.

Sketch Analogy

Sketch 1: (Disk based processing is like reading data from a file one at a time with disk symbol showing each read from data storage). Sketch 2: (In-memory processing is like pre-loading the data into memory and processing on that, with RAM symbol showing all processing on the data)

Resilient Distributed Datasets (RDDs)

Resilient Distributed Datasets (RDDs) are a fundamental concept in Apache Spark that enable parallel processing and fault tolerance. They form the backbone of Spark's ability to handle large datasets efficiently.

Immutable, Partitioned Collections:

At their core, RDDs are immutable, partitioned collections of data. Let's break down what that means:

- **Immutable:** Once an RDD is created, its contents cannot be changed. Instead, transformations create *new* RDDs. This immutability is crucial for fault tolerance, as it allows Spark to easily recompute lost partitions.

Think of it like creating a copy of a document instead of directly editing the original. If something goes wrong during the copy process, you still have the original, unchanged document.

- **Partitioned:** An RDD is divided into partitions, which are logical chunks of data. Each partition resides on a different node (machine) in the cluster. This partitioning is what allows Spark to distribute the processing of the data across multiple machines in parallel. Imagine splitting a large book into chapters and assigning each chapter to a different person to read simultaneously.

- **Collections:** RDDs can hold any type of data that can be represented in a programming language like Python, Java, or Scala. This could be numbers, text, objects, or anything else. They serve as a container for your data.

Parallel Processing:

Because RDDs are partitioned across a cluster, Spark can perform operations on each partition in parallel. This is the key to Spark's speed and scalability. Instead of processing all the data on a single machine, Spark distributes the workload across many machines, significantly reducing processing time. Let's suppose, we have an RDD representing log data from a website. Each partition might contain log entries for a specific time period. Spark can then analyze the log entries in each partition independently and simultaneously.

Fault Tolerance:

The "Resilient" part of "Resilient Distributed Datasets" means that RDDs are fault-tolerant. If a node in the cluster fails, the partitions of the RDD that were stored on that node are automatically recomputed on other nodes. Spark achieves this fault tolerance through a concept called lineage.

Lineage:

Lineage is a graph that tracks the sequence of transformations that were applied to create an RDD. Each RDD knows how it was derived from its parent RDDs. If a partition is lost, Spark can use the lineage to recompute that partition from the original data or from its parent RDDs. Imagine it like baking a cake. If a step is messed up the baker knows exactly where to restart from because they have the recipe. **Example:**

Consider the following simple example of how you might create and transform an RDD in Python using PySpark:

```python
from pyspark import SparkContext

# Create a SparkContext
sc = SparkContext("local", "RDD Example")

# Create an RDD from a list of numbers
data = [1, 2, 3, 4, 5]
rdd = sc.parallelize(data)

# Transform the RDD by squaring each number
squared_rdd = rdd.map(lambda x: x  x)

# Collect the results and print them
results = squared_rdd.collect()
print(results) # Output: [1, 4, 9, 16, 25]

# Stop the SparkContext
sc.stop()
```

In this example:

1. `sc.parallelize(data)` creates an RDD from the list `data`. The data will be partitioned across the available cores on your machine (or across the cluster if you're running in distributed mode).

2. `rdd.map(lambda x: x x)` transforms the RDD by applying the `lambda` function (which squares each number) to each element in the RDD. This `map` operation is performed in parallel on each partition.
3. `squared_rdd.collect()` retrieves all the elements from the `squared_rdd` and returns them as a list. This is generally only used for small RDDs, as it brings all the data back to the driver program.

Sketch: Imagine you have a box of Lego bricks. Each brick is data.

1. **Partitioning:** You divide the bricks into smaller piles (partitions).

```
[Pile 1]   [Pile 2]   [Pile 3]  ...  [Pile N]
```

2. **Distribution:** You give each pile to a different friend (node in the cluster).

```
Friend A   Friend B   Friend C  ...  Friend N
[Pile 1]   [Pile 2]   [Pile 3]  ...  [Pile N]
```

3. **Transformation:** Each friend follows the same instructions to build a mini-structure (transformation).

```
Friend A builds:  Mini-Structure 1
Friend B builds:  Mini-Structure 2
Friend C builds:  Mini-Structure 3
...
```

4. **Resilience:** If one friend loses some bricks (node failure), they can rebuild their mini-structure using the original instructions (lineage) and maybe some of the original bricks if available.

RDDs are a powerful abstraction that simplifies distributed data processing. Their immutability, partitioning, and lineage-based fault tolerance make them a cornerstone of the Spark framework. The operations on RDDs are inherently parallel and can handle large amount of data.

Distributed File Systems

Distributed file systems are the foundational storage layer upon which large-scale batch processing frameworks are built. Think of them as the digital equivalent of a vast warehouse, specifically designed for storing massive amounts of data across a network of computers.

Imagine you have a huge book, so big that no single bookshelf can hold it. Instead of trying to build a giant bookshelf, you break the book into smaller parts and put each part on a different bookshelf in different rooms. A distributed file system does something similar with data: it splits large files into smaller pieces (called blocks) and stores these blocks across many computers.

Key Characteristics:

- **Large-Scale Storage:** Designed to handle petabytes or even exabytes of data (a petabyte is a million gigabytes).
- **Fault Tolerance:** If one computer fails, the data is still accessible because the blocks are replicated (copied) across multiple machines. In our bookshelf example, it's like having multiple copies of each chapter in different rooms, so if one room is damaged, you can still find the chapter in another room.

```
+-------+   +-------+   +-------+
| Block |---| Block |---| Block |--- ...
+-------+   +-------+   +-------+
    |           |           |
    v           v           v
+-------+   +-------+   +-------+
| Node 1|   | Node 2|   | Node 3|--- ...
+-------+   +-------+   +-------+
(Computer) (Computer) (Computer)
```

Sketch illustrating data blocks distributed across multiple nodes (computers).

- **Data Locality:** Frameworks like Hadoop and Spark try to process data on the same computer where the data is stored. This reduces the need to move data across the network, which can be slow. In our bookshelf example, it's like having someone read the chapter in the same room where it's stored instead of carrying it to another room.

HDFS (Hadoop Distributed File System):

HDFS is a specific implementation of a distributed file system widely used with Hadoop. Let's look at it in more detail.

- **Stores large files across commodity hardware:** HDFS is designed to run on inexpensive, readily available computer hardware. It doesn't require specialized or high-end servers.

- **Provides fault tolerance:** HDFS achieves fault tolerance by replicating data blocks across multiple machines. By default, each block is replicated three times. This means that even if two machines fail, the data is still accessible from the third replica.

For example, say we have a file named `my_data.txt` that is split into three blocks: `block_1`, `block_2`, and `block_3`. With a replication factor of 3, HDFS would store these blocks as follows:

- `block_1`: Stored on Node A, Node B, and Node C
- `block_2`: Stored on Node B, Node C, and Node D
- `block_3`: Stored on Node C, Node D, and Node A

If Node A fails, the data in `block_1` and `block_3` is still available on Node B and Node C, and Node C and Node D respectively.

Sketch illustrating HDFS data replication. Each block is stored on multiple nodes for fault tolerance.

```
File: my_data.txt
Blocks: block_1, block_2, block_3

Node A: block_1, block_3
Node B: block_1, block_2
Node C: block_1, block_2, block_3
Node D: block_2, block_3

(If Node A fails...)

Node B: block_1, block_2
Node C: block_1, block_2, block_3
Node D: block_2, block_3

Data is still accessible!
```

Important Considerations:

While distributed file systems provide excellent scalability and fault tolerance for large datasets, they come with certain trade-offs.

- **Latency vs. Throughput:** These systems are designed for high throughput (processing a large amount of data) rather than low latency (fast response times for individual requests). Retrieving a small piece of data might take longer compared to a traditional file system.
- **Batch Processing Focus:** They are well-suited for batch processing tasks where you need to process large datasets in bulk, but not for real-time applications that require immediate responses. They work best when immediate results aren't critical, and speed of reading/writing is not too important.

Chapter 11 Data Processing and Analytics-Stream Processing: Apache Kafka, Flink, and Real-Time Pipelines

Here are 5 bullet points explaining stream processing in the context of "Designing Data-Intensive Applications":

- **Real-Time Data Processing:** Handles continuous data streams for immediate insights and actions.

    o Addresses limitations of batch processing for low-latency requirements.

- **Stream Processing Principles:** Focuses on event-time processing, windowing, and state management.

- **Apache Kafka:** A distributed, fault-tolerant streaming platform.

    o Provides a durable message queue for ingesting and buffering data streams.

- **Apache Flink:** A distributed stream processing engine.

    o Supports stateful computations, fault tolerance, and exactly-once semantics.

- **Real-Time Data Pipelines:** Architecting end-to-end systems with ingestion, processing, and storage.

Real-Time Data Processing

Real-Time Data Processing is about handling continuous streams of data the moment they arrive. The goal is to get immediate insights and take actions right away, instead of waiting for data to accumulate. Think of it like monitoring a patient's vital signs in a hospital. You need to know about any changes instantly to react appropriately.

- **Handles continuous data streams for immediate insights and actions.**

    Imagine a sensor on a machine in a factory continuously sending temperature readings. Real-time processing analyzes this stream of data as it comes in. If the temperature rises above a certain threshold, the system can automatically shut down the machine to prevent damage. This immediate action is the core of real-time data processing.

    Another example is fraud detection in online transactions. As transactions occur, they are analyzed instantly. Suspicious patterns, like unusually large purchases or transactions from unusual locations, can trigger an immediate alert, preventing fraudulent activity.

- **Addresses limitations of batch processing for low-latency requirements.**

    Traditional *batch processing* involves collecting data over a period (e.g., a day or an hour) and processing it all at once. This works well for tasks like generating daily sales reports. However, batch processing is not suitable when you need immediate results.

Consider this example of the limitations of Batch processing versus the advantages of Real-Time Processing:

Batch Processing Scenario: A social media company wants to identify trending topics. Using batch processing, they collect all posts from the past hour, analyze them overnight, and generate a report of trending topics in the morning. By then, the trends might have already changed!

Real-Time Processing Scenario: The same social media company uses real-time processing. As posts are created, they are immediately analyzed. The system identifies trending topics within seconds and displays them on a live dashboard. This allows users and advertisers to react to trends as they happen.

Batch Processing

```
Data Collection --> Processing (delayed) --> Insights (delayed)
```

Real-Time Processing:

```
Data Stream --> Immediate Processing --> Immediate Insights
```

The key difference is *latency* – the delay between data arrival and insight generation. Batch processing has high latency, while real-time processing aims for very low latency (seconds or even milliseconds).

Here is sketch that explains the scenario:

```
[Data Source] --(Stream of data)--> [Real-Time Processing Engine] --(Analyzed data)--> [Immediat
```

In essence, Real-Time Data Processing empowers applications to react to changing conditions instantly, enabling timely decision-making and automated responses that are simply not possible with batch-oriented approaches.

Stream Processing Principles

Stream processing isn't just about handling data quickly; it's built on specific principles that ensure correctness and efficiency when dealing with continuous data flows. The main principles revolve around event-time processing, windowing, and state management.

Event-Time Processing:

Imagine you are tracking website clicks. Each click is an *event*. Each event has a *timestamp* indicating *when* the click occurred. Now, what if some clicks arrive late? Maybe the user had a poor internet connection. *Event-time processing* means that we analyze the clicks based on their timestamps, *regardless* of when they arrive at our processing system.

Why is this important? Without event-time processing, your analyses would be wrong if events arrived out of order. You'd be analyzing the clicks in the *order you received them*, not in the *order they actually happened*. This is usually incorrect.

Think about calculating the number of clicks per hour. With event-time processing, a late-arriving click for 10:59 AM will still be counted in the 10:00-11:00 AM hour, even if it doesn't arrive until 11:15 AM. Without event-time, it would be incorrectly counted in the 11:00 AM - 12:00 PM hour.

In summary, event-time processing ensures accuracy by basing calculations on when events actually occurred, rather than when they were processed.

Windowing:

Since streams are continuous, we often need to divide them into smaller chunks for analysis. *Windowing* is the process of grouping events into finite sets based on time or other criteria.

Consider the clickstream example again. You might want to know:

- How many clicks occurred *per minute*?

- What was the *average time* spent on a page in the last *5 minutes*?
- Which pages were most popular in the last *hour*?

Windowing allows you to perform these types of calculations.

There are several types of windows:

- **Tumbling Windows:** These are fixed-size, non-overlapping windows. For example, one-minute tumbling windows would divide the stream into distinct one-minute intervals (0:00-0:59, 1:00-1:59, etc.).

```
# Simplified example (conceptual)
window_size = 60 # seconds
for event in stream:
  window_id = event.timestamp // window_size # Integer division gives window ID
  window[window_id].append(event)
```

- **Sliding Windows:** These windows have a fixed size but slide over the stream by a specified interval. For example, a five-minute sliding window that slides every minute would create windows like 0:00-5:00, 1:00-6:00, 2:00-7:00, and so on. This results in overlapping windows, where events can belong to multiple windows.

```
# Simplified example (conceptual)
window_size = 300 # seconds (5 minutes)
slide_interval = 60 # seconds (1 minute)

for event in stream:
  for i in range(window_size // slide_interval):
    window_start = event.timestamp - (i  slide_interval)
    if window_start >= 0: #Check to ensure it's not a negative timestamp
      window[window_start, window_start + window_size].append(event) #Append to all the relevar
```

- **Session Windows:** These windows are dynamic and based on the *activity* of a user or entity. A session window starts when a user first interacts with a system and ends after a period of inactivity. Session windows are useful for analyzing user behavior and identifying patterns within a single session.

```
# Simplified example (conceptual)
#Assumes that the session window is initialized with the first event
session_window = [event] #Initialize with first event
inactivity_gap = 300 #5 minutes (example)

for event in stream:
    if event.timestamp <= session_window[-1].timestamp + inactivity_gap:
        session_window.append(event)
    else:
        #Process old session and start a new session with the current event
        process_session(session_window) #Function to be defined to process the session data
        session_window = [event]
```

- **Count-based windows:** Trigger processing after a specific number of events.

```
#Simplified example (conceptual)
window = []
count_threshold = 10 #Process after 10 events

for event in stream:
    window.append(event)
    if len(window) >= count_threshold:
```

```
        process_window(window)
        window = []
```

State Management:

Many stream processing applications require maintaining *state*. State refers to the information a stream processing job remembers over time.

Examples of state include:

- **Aggregates:** Running totals, counts, or averages. If you're calculating the number of clicks per user, you need to store a count for each user.
- **Caches:** Storing frequently accessed data for faster retrieval. For example, caching user profiles.
- **Machine Learning Models:** Storing model parameters for real-time predictions.

State management is complex because stream processing systems need to be *fault-tolerant*. If a processing node fails, its state must be recovered to prevent data loss and ensure accurate results. This requires techniques like:

- **Checkpointing:** Periodically saving the state to durable storage (e.g., a distributed file system).
- **Replication:** Maintaining multiple copies of the state across different nodes.
- **Exactly-Once Semantics:** Guaranteeing that each event affects the state exactly once, even in the presence of failures.

Imagine you are counting the number of times each word appears in a stream of text. The *state* is the count for each word.

```
# Simplified example (conceptual)
word_counts = {} # This is the "state"

for event in stream:
  words = event.text.split()
  for word in words:
    if word in word_counts:
      word_counts[word] += 1
    else:
      word_counts[word] = 1


# The word_counts dictionary now holds the state
```

If the system crashes, you need to restore the word_counts dictionary to its last known correct state. This is what checkpointing is for. *Exactly-once semantics* ensures that even if you process some events twice due to a failure, the word counts are still accurate.

In essence, event-time processing, windowing, and state management are essential pillars in building robust and reliable stream processing applications. These principles ensure your processing is accurate, insightful, and fault-tolerant.

Apache Kafka: A Distributed Streaming Platform

Apache Kafka is a core component in modern data-intensive applications, especially those dealing with real-time data. It serves as a robust, fault-tolerant streaming platform designed to handle high volumes of data with low latency. Essentially, Kafka acts as the central nervous system for your data streams.

A Durable Message Queue for Ingesting and Buffering Data Streams

At its heart, Kafka is a distributed message queue. But it's more than just a queue; it's designed for durability, high throughput, and fault tolerance, making it ideal for ingesting and buffering data streams.

Let's break this down:

- **Message Queue:** Imagine a physical queue where messages (pieces of data) are placed and consumed in order. Kafka does this digitally, allowing applications to produce (write) data to the queue and other applications to consume (read) data from the queue.

- **Durable:** Kafka is built to persist data. This means that even if a server fails, the data is not lost. Kafka replicates data across multiple servers (brokers) to ensure that it can survive failures. Think of it as having multiple copies of the same message stored on different computers. If one computer crashes, the other computers still have the message.

- **Ingesting Data Streams:** Kafka excels at taking in a continuous flow of data from various sources. These sources could be anything: website activity, sensor data, financial transactions, or application logs. Kafka efficiently captures this stream of data.

- **Buffering Data Streams:** Once ingested, Kafka buffers the data. This means it temporarily stores the data before it's processed. This buffering capability is crucial for handling bursts of data and decoupling producers (applications sending data) from consumers (applications processing data). Consumers can process data at their own pace without overwhelming the producers.

Kafka Architecture Sketch

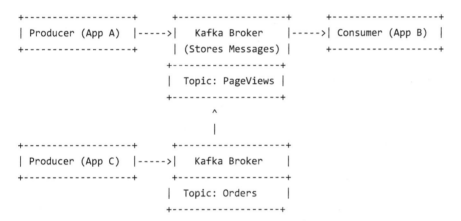

In the above sketch:

- **Producers:** Applications like App A and App C send data to Kafka.
- **Kafka Broker:** This is the core of Kafka, where messages are stored in topics.
- **Topics:** A category or feed name to which records are published. In this example, PageViews and Orders are topics.
- **Consumers:** Applications like App B read and process data from Kafka topics.

Example: Website Activity Tracking

Imagine you are building a system to track website activity in real-time. Every time a user visits a page, clicks a button, or performs any action on your website, an event is generated.

1. **Producers (Website Servers):** Your website servers act as producers. They send these events (e.g., "user X visited page Y at time Z") to Kafka.

2. **Kafka Broker:** Kafka receives these events and stores them in a topic called, for instance, "website_activity."

3. **Consumers (Analytics Applications):** Your analytics applications act as consumers. They subscribe to the "website_activity" topic and process the events to generate reports, dashboards, or personalized recommendations.

Code Example (Producer - Python):

```python
from kafka import KafkaProducer
import json
import time

producer = KafkaProducer(
    bootstrap_servers='localhost:9092', # Kafka broker address
    value_serializer=lambda v: json.dumps(v).encode('utf-8') # Serialize data to JSON
)

for i in range(10):
    data = {'user_id': i, 'page': '/home', 'timestamp': time.time()}
    producer.send('website_activity', data)  # Send data to the 'website_activity' topic
    print(f"Sent: {data}")
    time.sleep(1)

producer.flush() # Ensure all messages are sent
producer.close()
```

Code Example (Consumer - Python):

```python
from kafka import KafkaConsumer
import json

consumer = KafkaConsumer(
    'website_activity', # Topic to consume from
    bootstrap_servers='localhost:9092', # Kafka broker address
    auto_offset_reset='earliest', # Start consuming from the beginning if no offset is stored
    enable_auto_commit=True,
    group_id='my-group', # Consumer group ID
    value_deserializer=lambda x: json.loads(x.decode('utf-8')) # Deserialize JSON data
)

for message in consumer:
    print(f"Received: {message.value}")
```

In this example, the producer script generates website activity events and sends them to Kafka. The consumer script reads these events from Kafka and prints them. The `bootstrap_servers` parameter specifies the address of your Kafka broker. The consumer is part of a `group_id` so Kafka can properly manage offsets for a scalable consuming application.

Key Benefits of Using Kafka:

- **Scalability:** Kafka can handle massive amounts of data and scale horizontally by adding more brokers to the cluster.
- **Fault Tolerance:** Replication ensures data durability even if brokers fail.
- **Low Latency:** Kafka is designed for low-latency data delivery, making it suitable for real-time applications.
- **Decoupling:** Producers and consumers are decoupled, allowing them to evolve independently.
- **Real-time Data Pipelines:** Kafka serves as the backbone for building real-time data pipelines, enabling the flow of data from source to destination with minimal delay.

Kafka is a powerful tool for building data-intensive applications that require real-time data processing and reliable data delivery. Its distributed architecture, fault tolerance, and scalability make it a popular choice for a wide range of use cases.

Apache Flink

- **Apache Flink: A distributed stream processing engine.**
  - Supports stateful computations, fault tolerance, and exactly-once semantics.

Apache Flink is a powerful engine designed for processing data streams in real-time. Think of it as a factory assembly line, but instead of physical objects, it's handling data. This assembly line is spread across many computers (distributed), allowing it to process massive amounts of data quickly and efficiently. Its key strength is its ability to perform complex calculations and transformations on data *as it arrives*, rather than waiting for it to be stored in a database.

- **Supports stateful computations**

"Stateful computations" means Flink can remember things about the data it's processed. Imagine you want to count how many users have visited your website in the last hour. Flink needs to keep track of the current count, so it can increment it whenever a new user visits. This "count" is the state. Without state, Flink would have to recalculate everything from scratch each time, which would be inefficient.

Here's a simplified code snippet (using Flink's Java API) that illustrates a stateful computation:

```
import org.apache.flink.api.common.functions.RichMapFunction;
import org.apache.flink.api.common.state.ValueState;
import org.apache.flink.api.common.state.ValueStateDescriptor;
import org.apache.flink.configuration.Configuration;
import org.apache.flink.streaming.api.datastream.DataStream;
import org.apache.flink.streaming.api.environment.StreamExecutionEnvironment;

public class StatefulExample {

    public static void main(String[] args) throws Exception {
        StreamExecutionEnvironment env = StreamExecutionEnvironment.getExecutionEnvironment();

        DataStream<Integer> input = env.fromElements(1, 2, 3, 4, 5);

        DataStream<Integer> result = input.map(new RichMapFunction<Integer, Integer>() {

            private ValueState<Integer> sumState;

            @Override
            public void open(Configuration config) {
                ValueStateDescriptor<Integer> descriptor =
                    new ValueStateDescriptor<>(
                        "sum", // the state name
                        Integer.class, // the state type
                        0); // default value of the state
                sumState = getRuntimeContext().getState(descriptor);
            }

            @Override
            public Integer map(Integer value) throws Exception {
                Integer currentSum = sumState.value();
                if (currentSum == null) {
                    currentSum = 0;
                }
                Integer newSum = currentSum + value;
```

```
                sumState.update(newSum);
                return newSum;
            }
        });

        result.print();

        env.execute("Stateful Example");
    }
}
```

In this example:

1. We create a `ValueState` called `sumState` to store the running sum.
2. The `map` function retrieves the current sum from the state, adds the current input `value`, updates the state with the new sum, and returns the new sum.

This illustrates the core concept: Flink maintains and updates state as it processes the stream of data.

- **Fault Tolerance**

"Fault tolerance" means that Flink can continue processing data even if one or more of the computers it's running on fails. It achieves this by taking regular snapshots of the state. If a failure occurs, Flink can restart from the latest snapshot, minimizing data loss and downtime.

Imagine our assembly line breaks down. Instead of starting from the beginning, we can go back to the last known good state (the snapshot) and resume from there. This is crucial for applications where data loss is unacceptable, such as financial transactions or fraud detection.

To achieve this Flink uses checkpointing. Checkpointing involves periodically saving the current state of the application to durable storage (e.g., HDFS, Amazon S3). This ensures that in the event of a failure, Flink can recover its state and continue processing from the point of the last successful checkpoint.

Sketch:

```
+----------------------+      +----------------------+      +----------------------+
|  Flink Application    | --> |     State Storage     | --> | Checkpoint (HDFS/S3) |
+----------------------+      +----------------------+      +----------------------+
       |                              |
       | Failure occurs               |
       v                              |
+----------------------+              |
|  Restart Application  | <-- | Load State from        |
+----------------------+      | Checkpoint
```

- **Exactly-Once Semantics**

"Exactly-once semantics" is a guarantee that each piece of data is processed *exactly once*, even in the face of failures. This is a very strong guarantee and is critical for many applications. Without it, you might end up processing the same transaction twice (resulting in double billing) or missing a transaction entirely.

Flink achieves exactly-once semantics through a combination of checkpointing and a technique called "transactional sinks." A sink is the component that writes the processed data to an external system (e.g., a database). Transactional sinks ensure that the data is written atomically. This means that either all the data in a checkpoint is written successfully, or none of it is. If a failure occurs during the write, the transaction is rolled back, and the data is reprocessed from the last checkpoint.

Consider a scenario of updating bank account balance:

1. Flink processes a transaction (e.g., deposit of $100).
2. It updates the account balance in its state.
3. It attempts to write the updated balance to the database.
4. If the write to the database fails (e.g., due to a network issue), Flink rolls back the transaction, reverting to the previous state.
5. When Flink recovers from the failure, it reprocesses the transaction, ensuring that the deposit is applied exactly once.

This combination of features makes Apache Flink a robust and reliable platform for building real-time data processing applications.

Real-Time Data Pipelines

Architecting end-to-end systems for handling data as it arrives, from the moment it's created to when it's stored or acted upon, is the core of real-time data pipelines. These pipelines involve integrating several components to achieve continuous data ingestion, processing, and storage, all within tight latency constraints. It's not just about moving data; it's about deriving value from it *immediately*.

Imagine a scenario: a user clicks a button on an e-commerce website. A real-time data pipeline would capture this click event, process it (perhaps to update product popularity metrics, trigger personalized recommendations, or detect fraud), and store the processed information, all in a matter of milliseconds. Contrast this with a batch processing system that might only analyze these clicks once a day, making real-time actions impossible.

A real-time data pipeline generally consists of the following stages:

1. **Ingestion:** This stage is responsible for collecting data from various sources. These sources can be anything from web servers, mobile apps, IoT devices, databases, and even other applications. The key here is to handle a high volume of data arriving continuously.

   - **Example:** A financial institution ingests stock prices from various exchanges. These prices are constantly changing and need to be captured as soon as they are available.

2. **Buffering:** Often, the incoming data stream is too fast or inconsistent for immediate processing. A buffering layer acts as a shock absorber, smoothing out fluctuations and providing a reliable source of data for downstream processing.

   - **Example:** Apache Kafka is commonly used for this purpose. It acts as a distributed, fault-tolerant message queue, ensuring that no data is lost even if processing components fail.

```
# Simple Kafka producer example (Python)
from kafka import KafkaProducer
producer = KafkaProducer(bootstrap_servers='localhost:9092')
producer.send('user_clicks', b'User ID: 123, Product ID: 456')
producer.flush()
```

Sketch of Buffering Stage

```
[Data Source A] --> [Ingestion] --> [Kafka Buffer] --> [Processing] --> [Storage]
[Data Source B] ----^
```

In this sketch data flows from multiple sources through an ingestion layer into the Kafka buffer, and is pulled out by processing stage, eventually storing it.

3. **Processing:** This is where the actual transformation, enrichment, and analysis of the data occur. This stage typically involves complex computations and requires a powerful stream processing engine.

   - **Example:** Apache Flink is a popular choice for this stage. It allows you to perform stateful computations on the data stream, such as calculating moving averages, detecting anomalies, or joining data from multiple streams. *Stateful computations mean that the processing logic can remember information from previous events and use it to make decisions about current events.*

```java
// Simple Flink example (Java)
import org.apache.flink.streaming.api.datastream.DataStream;
import org.apache.flink.streaming.api.environment.StreamExecutionEnvironment;

public class ClickEventProcessor {
  public static void main(String[] args) throws Exception {
    final StreamExecutionEnvironment env = StreamExecutionEnvironment.getExecutionEnvi

    DataStream<String> clickEvents = env.socketTextStream("localhost", 9999);

    clickEvents.map(event -> "Processed: " + event)
            .print();

    env.execute("Click Event Processing");
  }
}
```

4. **Storage:** The processed data needs to be stored for later analysis, reporting, or other uses. The choice of storage depends on the specific requirements of the application.

   ○ **Example:** For real-time analytics, a NoSQL database like Apache Cassandra or Apache Druid might be used. For longer-term storage and batch processing, a data warehouse like Amazon Redshift or Snowflake might be more appropriate.

5. **Action/Output:** In many real-time pipelines, the processed data is not just stored but also used to trigger actions.

   ○ **Example:** An anomaly detection system identifies a fraudulent transaction and immediately blocks the user's account. The output of the processing stage directly triggers an action in another system.

Building a robust real-time data pipeline requires careful consideration of several factors:

- **Latency:** Minimizing the delay between data arrival and processing is critical.

- **Scalability:** The pipeline must be able to handle increasing data volumes and processing demands.

- **Fault Tolerance:** The system should be designed to handle failures gracefully, ensuring that no data is lost and processing continues uninterrupted.

- **Data Consistency:** Ensuring that data is processed correctly and consistently, especially in the presence of failures, is crucial. Flink's exactly-once semantics are vital here.

Real-time data pipelines are complex systems, but they are essential for organizations that need to react quickly to changing conditions and gain a competitive advantage.

Chapter 12 Data Processing and Analytics-Data Lakes and Warehouses: Modern Storage and Analytics Architectures

Here are 5 bullet points outlining Data Lakes and Warehouses in the context of "Designing Data-Intensive Applications," suitable for a single slide:

- **Data Warehouses:**

    o Structured, schema-on-write. Optimized for analysis with SQL.

- **Data Lakes:**

    o Schema-on-read, store diverse data (structured, semi-structured, unstructured)

- **Modern Data Architectures:**

    o Combine Lakes and Warehouses for flexibility and performance.

- **Trade-offs:**

    o Data quality, governance, and performance need careful consideration.

- **Emerging Trends:**

    o Lakehouses, Data Mesh are trying to address the limitation of the traditional design and make data more accessible.

Data Warehouses

Data warehouses are a cornerstone of traditional business intelligence and analytics. They are designed for analyzing historical data to gain insights and support decision-making.

Structured, schema-on-write.

Data warehouses operate under a "schema-on-write" principle. This means that the structure (schema) of the data must be defined *before* the data is loaded into the warehouse. The data is transformed and cleaned to conform to this predefined schema. This rigorous process ensures data quality and consistency, which is crucial for reliable reporting and analysis.

Think of it like building a house. Before you start placing furniture, you need a blueprint (the schema). You prepare the foundation, walls, and roof according to that blueprint. Only then can you move in furniture that fits the structure. If a piece of furniture is too big or doesn't fit, you either modify the furniture or, in the worst case, modify the house structure. In the context of data warehousing, you modify the data to fit the predefined schema.

For example, consider an e-commerce company storing sales data. A typical data warehouse schema might include tables for:

- `Customers` (customer ID, name, address, etc.)
- `Products` (product ID, name, price, category, etc.)
- `Sales` (sale ID, customer ID, product ID, sale date, quantity, price, etc.)

Before loading sales data, you ensure it conforms to this structure: customer IDs exist in the `Customers` table, product IDs in the `Products` table, and dates are in a consistent format. Missing or inconsistent data is handled according to predefined rules (e.g., rejecting the row, imputing a value, or flagging it for review).

Optimized for analysis with SQL.

Data warehouses are optimized for querying and analyzing data using SQL (Structured Query Language). SQL is a powerful and widely used language for retrieving, manipulating, and analyzing data stored in relational databases. Data warehouses employ specific techniques (e.g., indexing, partitioning, materialized views) to ensure that SQL queries execute efficiently, even on large datasets.

Imagine you have a vast library. A data warehouse is like that library, but the books (data) are perfectly organized and indexed. When you need to find information, you use SQL, which is like the library's card catalog system. It helps you quickly locate the relevant books and chapters you need for your research (analysis).

For instance, to find the total sales for a specific product category in the e-commerce example, you might use the following SQL query:

```
SELECT
    SUM(s.quantity  s.price)
FROM
    Sales s
JOIN
    Products p ON s.product_id = p.product_id
WHERE
    p.category = 'Electronics';
```

This query joins the `Sales` and `Products` tables based on `product_id` and filters the results to include only sales from the 'Electronics' category. The `SUM` function then calculates the total sales amount.

Key characteristics summarized:

- **Purpose:** Optimized for analytical queries, reporting, and business intelligence.
- **Data Type:** Primarily structured data.
- **Schema:** Schema-on-write (structure defined *before* loading data).
- **Query Language:** Primarily SQL.
- **Performance:** High performance for complex analytical queries.
- **Example:** Calculating total revenue by product category, identifying sales trends, creating dashboards for executive decision-making.

In essence, a data warehouse is a curated and structured repository of historical data designed to support informed business decisions. The emphasis on structure and SQL optimization makes it well-suited for scenarios where data quality and analytical performance are paramount.

Structured Data: The Foundation of Data Warehouses

Structured data is the cornerstone of data warehouses, characterized by its well-defined organization and adherence to a rigid schema. This means the data conforms to a pre-defined format, making it easily searchable, analyzable, and manageable. Think of it as neatly organizing books on a bookshelf, where each book has a specific place and label.

Key Characteristics:

- **Predefined Schema:** Before data is loaded into a structured system, its format must be defined. This "schema" specifies the data types (e.g., integers, text strings, dates), relationships, and constraints.
- **Relational Databases:** The most common home for structured data is the relational database. These databases use tables with rows (records) and columns (fields) to organize information.
- **SQL for Access and Manipulation:** Structured Query Language (SQL) is the standard language for interacting with relational databases. It allows users to query, insert, update, and delete data.
- **Schema-on-Write:** This is a critical concept. The schema is applied *before* the data is written into the database. This ensures data consistency and integrity. Any data that does not conform to the schema will be rejected or transformed to fit the schema.

Examples of Structured Data:

- **Customer Information:** A table with columns like Customer ID (integer), Name (text), Address (text), Phone Number (text), and Email (text).
- **Sales Transactions:** A table with columns like Transaction ID (integer), Product ID (integer), Date (date), Quantity (integer), and Price (numeric).
- **Financial Data:** A table with columns like Account Number (integer), Date (date), Transaction Type (text), Amount (numeric).

Code Example (SQL):

Let's imagine a simple table called `Customers` in a relational database.

```
CREATE TABLE Customers (
    CustomerID INT PRIMARY KEY,
    FirstName VARCHAR(255),
    LastName VARCHAR(255),
    City VARCHAR(255),
    Country VARCHAR(255)
);

INSERT INTO Customers (CustomerID, FirstName, LastName, City, Country)
VALUES (1, 'John', 'Doe', 'New York', 'USA');

SELECT  FROM Customers WHERE Country = 'USA';
```

In this example:

- `CREATE TABLE` defines the schema of the `Customers` table. It specifies the column names, data types, and a primary key.
- `INSERT INTO` adds a new row of data that *must* conform to the defined schema.
- `SELECT` retrieves data using SQL, leveraging the structured nature of the data to efficiently find specific information.

Sketch Explanation:

Imagine a spreadsheet. That's a simplified view of structured data. The rows represent records, and the columns represent fields. The heading of each column defines the "schema."

- **Columns (Fields):** Fixed data type (e.g., numbers, text, dates)
- **Rows (Records):** Each row adheres to the column's schema.
- **The overall spreadsheet itself is the table.**

Advantages of Structured Data:

- **Efficient Analysis:** SQL allows for complex queries and aggregations, enabling in-depth analysis.
- **Data Integrity:** Schema enforcement ensures data consistency and accuracy.
- **Mature Tools and Technologies:** A vast ecosystem of tools and technologies exists for managing and analyzing structured data.
- **Compliance:** Structured data simplifies compliance with regulations that require data lineage and auditability.

Limitations of Structured Data:

- **Schema Rigidity:** Changing the schema can be complex and time-consuming, requiring careful planning and execution.
- **Limited Data Variety:** Not suitable for storing unstructured or semi-structured data without significant transformation.

- **Potential for Data Silos:** Can lead to isolated data silos if not properly integrated.

In Summary: Structured data, with its rigid schema and reliance on relational databases and SQL, provides a solid foundation for analytical workloads where data consistency, integrity, and efficient querying are paramount. While its rigidity can be a limitation, the advantages for specific use cases are undeniable, particularly within the data warehouse context.

Data Lakes

Data Lakes offer a different approach to data storage and processing compared to traditional data warehouses. The core concept of a data lake is to store data in its raw, native format, without imposing a rigid schema at the time the data is written (schema-on-read). This flexibility makes data lakes suitable for storing a diverse range of data types.

Schema-on-Read: Embracing Data Variety

Unlike data warehouses, which enforce a predefined structure (schema-on-write), data lakes operate on a "schema-on-read" principle. This means the data's structure is defined only when it's being accessed and analyzed. This provides the freedom to ingest data from various sources, regardless of their original format, and explore the data before committing to a specific schema.

Consider these example data sources feeding into a data lake:

- **Structured Data:** Relational database tables (e.g., customer information, product catalogs).
- **Semi-structured Data:** JSON documents from web APIs, CSV files with varying column counts, log files with key-value pairs.
- **Unstructured Data:** Text documents, images, audio files, video files.

A data lake can accommodate all of these data types. When you want to analyze customer data, you can define a schema for the relevant structured and semi-structured data sources and then combine them. Later, you might define a completely different schema to analyze customer support tickets (unstructured text).

Example: Storing Log Data

Let's say you're collecting web server logs. Each log entry might look something like this:

```
2023-10-27 10:00:00 - GET /product/123 - 200 OK - user_id=456
2023-10-27 10:00:05 - POST /cart/add - 200 OK - user_id=789, product_id=123
2023-10-27 10:00:10 - GET / - 302 Redirect - user_id=456
```

In a data lake, you might store these logs as raw text files. When you want to analyze the logs, you can use tools like Spark or Hive to define a schema on-the-fly:

```
from pyspark.sql import SparkSession

spark = SparkSession.builder.appName("LogAnalysis").getOrCreate()

# Define the schema
schema = "timestamp STRING, method STRING, endpoint STRING, status STRING, details STRING"

# Read the log files
logs = spark.read.text("path/to/your/logs/")

# Split the log lines into columns based on the defined schema

from pyspark.sql.functions import split, regexp_extract
logs_df = logs.select(
    regexp_extract("value", r"(\d{4}-\d{2}-\d{2} \d{2}:\d{2}:\d{2})", 1).alias("timestamp"),
    regexp_extract("value", r"(GET|POST|PUT|DELETE)", 1).alias("method"),
```

```
        regexp_extract("value", r"(\/\S+)", 1).alias("endpoint"),
        regexp_extract("value", r"(\d{3})", 1).alias("status"),
        regexp_extract("value", r"-\s+(.)", 1).alias("details")
)
```

```
logs_df.show()
```

This code snippet demonstrates how you can read unstructured log data, define a schema using regular expressions, and extract relevant information into structured columns for analysis. You didn't need to define this structure beforehand; it's applied at the time of analysis.

Diverse Data Storage

Data Lakes are designed to accommodate different types of data, structured, semi-structured, and unstructured, which makes them a flexible and versatile solution for modern data storage needs. This is the major advantage over a Data warehouse since data warehouse can only accomodate the structure data

- **Structured Data:** Data organized into rows and columns, typical of relational databases. Examples: customer data, sales transactions.

- **Semi-structured Data:** Data that doesn't conform to a rigid table structure but has some organizational properties, like tags or markers. Examples: JSON, XML, CSV files with variable fields.

- **Unstructured Data:** Data without a predefined format. Examples: text documents, images, audio, video files.

Sketch:

```
+---------------------+        +---------------------+        +---------------------+
|   Structured Data   |------->|      Data Lake      |<------|  Semi-structured Data|
|  (e.g., SQL Tables) |        |  (Raw Data Storage) |        |  (e.g., JSON, CSV)  |
+---------------------+        +---------------------+        +---------------------+
                                          |
                                          |
+---------------------+        |          +---------------------+
|  Unstructured Data  |------|          |   Analysis Tools    |
|  (e.g., Text, Images)|        |          |   (Spark, Hive...)  |
+---------------------+        |          +---------------------+
                               |
```

This sketch illustrates how all types of data feed into a central data lake. Analysis tools then pull data and define the schema as needed.

Schema-on-Read

Schema-on-read, also known as late binding, is a data storage and processing approach where the structure of the data is not defined until the data is actually queried. In contrast to schema-on-write (commonly used in data warehouses), where the data's structure must be defined upfront, schema-on-read offers flexibility in dealing with diverse and evolving data types. This approach is a cornerstone of data lakes.

Imagine you are collecting sensor data from various devices. Some devices might send data in JSON format, others in CSV, and some might even send raw text logs. A schema-on-write approach would require you to transform all this data into a consistent, predefined format before storing it. This can be time-consuming and inflexible, especially when new data sources with different formats are added.

With schema-on-read, you store the data as-is in the data lake, regardless of its initial format. When you need to analyze the data, you then apply a schema on the fly. This allows you to explore the data in its raw form, discover patterns, and decide on the most appropriate schema for your analysis.

Example:

Suppose you have a data lake containing web server logs. The logs might have different formats depending on the server configuration or the time period. Some logs might include the user agent string, while others might not.

Using schema-on-read, you can initially store all the log files without enforcing a rigid schema. When you want to analyze the logs to identify the most common browsers used by your visitors, you can apply a schema that extracts the user agent string from the relevant log files. This allows you to perform the analysis even if some log files do not contain the user agent string.

Code Example (Python with Spark):

```python
from pyspark.sql import SparkSession
from pyspark.sql.functions import
from pyspark.sql.types import

spark = SparkSession.builder.appName("SchemaOnReadExample").getOrCreate()

# Assuming you have JSON data in a directory
data_path = "path/to/your/json/data/"

# Read the data without specifying a schema initially
df = spark.read.json(data_path)

# Print the inferred schema
df.printSchema()

# You can now work with the data and define a schema on the fly when needed.
# For example, let's say you want to extract the 'id' and 'name' fields:

# Define a schema for the fields you are interested in.
custom_schema = StructType([
    StructField("id", IntegerType(), True),
    StructField("name", StringType(), True)
])

# Apply the schema while reading the data, specifying the file
df_with_schema = spark.read.schema(custom_schema).json(data_path)

# Print the updated schema
df_with_schema.printSchema()

#Display data
df_with_schema.show()

spark.stop()
```

In this example, Spark infers the schema of the JSON data upon reading. You can then define a custom schema based on your analytical needs and apply it to the data during querying. The schema is not enforced during data ingestion but rather at the time of data access.

Benefits:

- **Flexibility:** Accommodates diverse and evolving data formats.
- **Agility:** Allows for faster data ingestion and exploration without upfront schema design.

- **Cost-Effectiveness:** Reduces the need for costly ETL (Extract, Transform, Load) processes before storing data.

Considerations:

While schema-on-read offers significant advantages, it also presents challenges:

- **Data Quality:** Requires robust data validation and cleansing processes during querying to ensure data integrity.
- **Performance:** Query performance can be affected by the need to infer schema and transform data on the fly.
- **Governance:** Requires careful data cataloging and metadata management to track the structure and meaning of data.
- **Discoverability:** Users need to understand the nature and format of the data to correctly query it. This requires clear documentation and metadata.

Sketch for Explaining Schema-on-Read

A simple sketch can illustrate the concept:

- A container (representing the data lake) filled with various shapes and sizes of objects (representing different data formats: JSON, CSV, Text).
- An "analyzer" tool (representing a query engine) selecting specific objects and applying a "schema filter" (representing the schema) to extract relevant information.

The sketch should highlight that the analyzer determines the schema and extracts information *after* the data is stored, emphasizing the "on-read" aspect. The different shaped objects represent various unstructured, semi-structured, and structured data. The "schema filter" shapes the object for analysis.

Modern Data Architectures

Modern data architectures recognize that neither a pure data warehouse nor a pure data lake is a perfect solution for all use cases. Instead, they advocate for a hybrid approach, combining the strengths of both to achieve greater flexibility and performance.

The core idea is to strategically leverage both data lakes and data warehouses within a single ecosystem. Think of it this way: the data lake acts as a central repository for all kinds of data, regardless of its structure or source. From there, data can be transformed and loaded into the data warehouse for specific analytical purposes. **Analogy :**

Imagine you have a large storage facility (the data lake). Inside, you can store anything – boxes of different sizes, shapes, and contents. Now, imagine you also have a retail store (the data warehouse). You only stock specific items on the shelves that customers frequently buy. The storage facility feeds the retail store, ensuring it has the products customers need, while still keeping all the less-popular or future products in storage.

How it Works

1. **Ingestion to the Data Lake:** Raw data from various sources (e.g., application logs, sensor data, customer databases, social media feeds) is ingested into the data lake in its native format. This adheres to the "schema-on-read" principle. The data lake can handle structured data (like CSV files), semi-structured data (like JSON or XML), and unstructured data (like images or text documents).

2. **Transformation and Enrichment:** Data is then processed and transformed within the data lake. This might involve cleaning the data, standardizing formats, and enriching it with additional information. Tools like Apache Spark or Apache Flink are commonly used for these transformations.

3. **Loading to the Data Warehouse:** After transformation, a subset of the data deemed relevant for specific analytical workloads is loaded into the data warehouse. This data is typically structured and conforms to a predefined schema.

4. **Analysis and Reporting:** The data warehouse is optimized for fast and efficient SQL-based queries. Business analysts and data scientists can use SQL to perform complex analyses, generate reports, and build dashboards.

Diagram

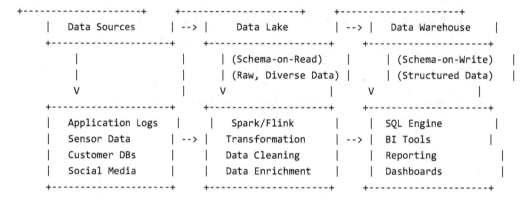

Data Sources: Represents the various origins of data (e.g., logs, sensors, databases, social media). Data Lake: This is the central repository for all kinds of data. Schema is applied on read. Data Warehouse: Contains structured data optimized for analysis.

Example Scenario

Imagine an e-commerce company wants to analyze customer behavior.

- **Data Lake:** The data lake stores all customer data, including website clickstream data (unstructured), order history (structured), and customer reviews (semi-structured JSON).

- **Transformation:** Using Spark, they transform the clickstream data to extract user navigation patterns and combine it with order history to calculate customer lifetime value.

- **Data Warehouse:** The transformed data (customer ID, navigation patterns, lifetime value) is loaded into the data warehouse.

- **Analysis:** Analysts can then use SQL to query the data warehouse and identify high-value customer segments, personalize marketing campaigns, and optimize website design.

Trade-offs

While combining data lakes and warehouses offers numerous advantages, it also introduces trade-offs that require careful consideration. Data quality, governance, and performance are key areas that demand attention.

- **Data Quality:** Maintaining data quality across both the data lake and the data warehouse is crucial. The "garbage in, garbage out" principle applies. Implementing data validation and cleansing processes is essential.

- **Data Governance:** Establishing clear data governance policies is vital to ensure data security, compliance, and consistency. This includes defining data ownership, access controls, and data retention policies.

- **Performance:** Optimizing performance for both the data lake and the data warehouse is critical. This involves choosing the right technologies, tuning queries, and managing data partitioning.

Emerging Trends

Modern data architectures are constantly evolving to address the limitations of traditional designs and make data more accessible. Lakehouses and Data Mesh are two prominent emerging trends.

- **Lakehouses:** Lakehouses aim to combine the best aspects of data lakes and data warehouses into a single system. They provide data warehousing features, such as ACID transactions and schema enforcement, directly on the data lake. This eliminates the need to move data between separate systems, simplifying the architecture and improving performance.

- **Data Mesh:** Data Mesh promotes a decentralized approach to data ownership and management. Instead of a central data team managing all data, domain-specific teams are responsible for their own data products. This fosters greater agility, reduces bottlenecks, and enables better alignment with business needs.

Modern data architectures are no longer about choosing between data lakes and warehouses. They are about strategically combining the strengths of both to build flexible, scalable, and performant data ecosystems that can meet the evolving needs of businesses.

Trade-offs: Data Quality, Governance, and Performance

When choosing between a data warehouse, a data lake, or a hybrid approach, several key trade-offs must be carefully considered. These center around data quality, governance, and performance. Failing to address these adequately can lead to significant problems down the line, including inaccurate insights, compliance issues, and inefficient data processing.

Data Quality

Data quality refers to the accuracy, completeness, consistency, and timeliness of the data. A major trade-off is the level of upfront effort invested in ensuring data quality versus the flexibility offered by a more lenient approach.

- **Data Warehouses:** Because data warehouses enforce a schema-on-write approach, data quality is typically higher. Data is validated and transformed during the ETL (Extract, Transform, Load) process before being loaded into the warehouse. This process involves cleaning the data, standardizing formats, and ensuring that the data conforms to the defined schema.

  - **Example:** Imagine you are loading customer address data. The ETL process might standardize the format of phone numbers (e.g., ensuring all numbers are in the format +1-XXX-XXX-XXXX) and validate postal codes against a known list of valid codes. Any data that fails validation is rejected or flagged for correction.

- **Data Lakes:** Data lakes embrace a schema-on-read approach, which means data is stored in its raw format without upfront validation or transformation. While this provides flexibility to store diverse data types and adapt to evolving business needs, it also shifts the burden of ensuring data quality to the data consumers. Without proper governance and quality checks, data lakes can quickly become "data swamps" – repositories of unusable and untrustworthy data.

  - **Example:** Suppose you are storing social media data. The data lake can store this data in its raw JSON format. You would have to write code to parse and clean this data when you need it. This can be complex and time-consuming.

  - **Sketch:** *Draw a simple diagram. A warehouse as a tidy, labelled cabinet. A data lake as a sprawling pile of unlabeled boxes.*

Data Governance

Data governance encompasses the policies, processes, and standards that ensure data is managed properly throughout its lifecycle. Key aspects include data ownership, access control, data lineage, and data security.

- **Data Warehouses:** Data warehouses typically have well-defined governance policies due to their structured nature and the criticality of the data they contain. Access control is tightly managed, data lineage is carefully tracked, and security measures are robust.

- **Example:** Access to sensitive customer data in a data warehouse might be restricted to specific roles within the organization, such as marketing analysts or customer service representatives. Audit logs track who accessed what data and when, providing accountability and supporting compliance requirements.

- **Data Lakes:** Governing data in data lakes is more challenging due to the variety of data types and the lack of a predefined schema. Implementing effective access control, data lineage tracking, and security measures requires careful planning and investment in specialized tools and processes.

  - **Example:** To manage access to data in a data lake, you might use role-based access control (RBAC) to grant different levels of access to different users or groups. For example, data scientists might have access to raw data, while business analysts only have access to curated and processed data. You can also leverage data catalogs to document metadata and provenance information for data assets, making it easier to discover and understand the data.

  - **Sketch:** *Simple flowchart. Arrows showing data moving from various sources into a messy "Data Lake". Then arrows showing data being cleaned and organized into a more structured "Data Warehouse". Highlight the governance steps that happen along the way.*

Performance

Performance refers to the speed and efficiency with which data can be processed and queried. This is influenced by factors such as data storage format, query optimization techniques, and infrastructure resources.

- **Data Warehouses:** Data warehouses are optimized for analytical queries using SQL. They typically employ techniques such as indexing, partitioning, and columnar storage to improve query performance.

  - **Example:** A query to calculate the average sales per region might involve scanning a large sales table. Indexing the `region` column can significantly speed up the query by allowing the database to quickly locate the relevant rows. Partitioning the table by date can further improve performance by limiting the amount of data that needs to be scanned.

  - **Code Example (SQL):**

    ```sql
    -- Indexing the region column
    CREATE INDEX idx_sales_region ON sales (region);

    -- Partitioning the table by date
    CREATE TABLE sales (
        sale_id INT,
        sale_date DATE,
        region VARCHAR(50),
        amount DECIMAL(10, 2)
    )
    PARTITION BY RANGE (sale_date) (
        PARTITION p202301 VALUES LESS THAN ('2023-02-01'),
        PARTITION p202302 VALUES LESS THAN ('2023-03-01'),
        ...
    );
    ```

- **Data Lakes:** Data lakes can be slower for analytical queries due to the lack of a predefined schema and the need to process raw data. However, modern data lake technologies offer various optimization techniques, such as data partitioning, columnar storage (e.g., using formats like Parquet or ORC), and distributed query engines (e.g., Spark or Presto) to improve performance.

  - **Example:** Storing data in Parquet format allows for efficient columnar storage and compression, which can significantly reduce the amount of data that needs to be read during a query. Using a distributed query engine like Spark allows you to process data in parallel across multiple nodes, which can speed up query execution.

- ○ **Code Example (Spark):**

```
from pyspark.sql import SparkSession

# Create a SparkSession
spark = SparkSession.builder.appName("DataLakeQuery").getOrCreate()

# Read data from Parquet format
df = spark.read.parquet("s3://my-data-lake/sales-data.parquet")

# Calculate average sales per region
avg_sales = df.groupBy("region").agg({"amount": "avg"})

# Show the results
avg_sales.show()

# Stop the SparkSession
spark.stop()
```

The trade-offs between data quality, governance, and performance are interconnected. Improving one aspect may come at the expense of another. The optimal approach depends on the specific requirements of the organization, the nature of the data, and the use cases it needs to support. Understanding these trade-offs is crucial for designing a data architecture that meets both current and future needs.

Chapter 13 Data Processing and Analytics-Data Integration: Change Data Capture (CDC) and ETL Pipelines

- **Data Integration Overview**: Combining data from disparate sources into a unified view.
- **ETL (Extract, Transform, Load)**: Batch processing; extracts data, transforms it to a usable format, and loads it into a data warehouse.
- **Change Data Capture (CDC)**: Real-time or near real-time capture of data changes in source databases.
- **CDC Benefits**: Enables incremental data loading, minimizing latency and resource consumption compared to full ETL runs.
- **CDC & ETL Integration**: CDC feeds data changes into ETL pipelines for continuous data warehousing and analytics, creating a hybrid approach.

Data Integration Overview

Combining data from disparate sources into a unified view.

Data integration is fundamentally about bringing together data from different places and presenting it in a single, consistent way. Think of it like building a house: you have bricks from one supplier, wood from another, and windows from a third. Data integration is the process of assembling all these disparate parts into a functional, coherent home (your unified view).

Why is this important? Because in many organizations, data resides in various systems, databases, and applications that don't naturally talk to each other. Sales data might be in one system, marketing data in another, and customer support data in a third. To get a complete picture of your business – for example, understanding how marketing campaigns impact sales and customer satisfaction – you need to integrate this data.

Let's illustrate with a simple, non-programming example. Suppose you have:

- **Spreadsheet A:** Contains customer names and email addresses.
- **Spreadsheet B:** Contains customer email addresses and purchase history.

Without data integration, you can't easily answer questions like, "Which customers who received a specific marketing email made a purchase?" You'd have to manually compare the lists, which is time-consuming and prone to errors. Data integration would involve merging these spreadsheets (after cleaning and standardizing the data) to create a single table where each customer record contains their name, email, and purchase history.

Consider another example in an e-commerce setting:

- **Inventory System:** Stores product IDs, names, quantities, and prices.
- **Sales System:** Stores customer IDs, order dates, and product IDs of purchased items.
- **Customer Relationship Management (CRM) System:** Stores customer IDs, names, addresses, and contact information.

To analyze sales trends by customer demographics, you need to integrate data from all three systems. Data integration allows you to combine information from these sources to answer questions such as:

- "What are the most popular products among customers in California?"
- "Which marketing campaign led to the highest sales among new customers?"
- "What is the average order value for repeat customers?"

Without a unified view, such analysis would be significantly more difficult, if not impossible. The following shows a possible conceptual diagram of this integration:

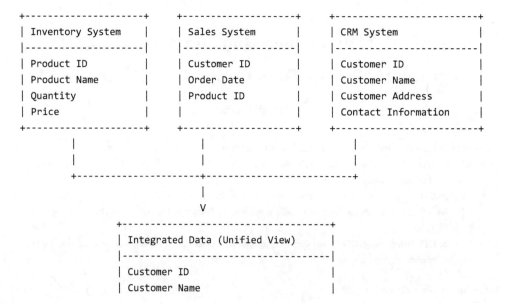

```
| Customer Address                     |
| Product ID                           |
| Product Name                         |
| Order Date                           |
| Price                                |
| Quantity                             |
+--------------------------------------+
```

This simple ASCII diagram outlines how different systems (Inventory, Sales, and CRM) contribute their respective data points into a unified view. The unified view comprises all the essential customer, product, and sales information, providing a holistic dataset for analysis and decision-making.

ETL (Extract, Transform, Load)

ETL, short for Extract, Transform, Load, is a foundational process in data warehousing and business intelligence. It's a batch-oriented approach, meaning it processes data in chunks or scheduled intervals rather than continuously. ETL's primary function is to move data from various source systems into a data warehouse or other target system in a usable and consistent format. Let's break down each stage:

1. Extract:

This is the initial phase where data is read or retrieved from multiple, often heterogeneous, source systems. These sources could be databases (like MySQL, PostgreSQL, Oracle), flat files (CSV, TXT), or even cloud-based applications. The extraction process aims to collect the raw data in its original format.

- **Example:** Imagine a retail company. Its sales data might reside in a MySQL database, customer information in a PostgreSQL database, and website traffic logs in CSV files. The 'Extract' stage involves pulling the data from all these different places.

- **Technical Details:** Extraction methods vary depending on the source. For databases, it could involve running SQL queries. For files, it could involve reading the file line by line.

2. Transform:

The 'Transform' stage is where the raw extracted data is cleaned, standardized, and transformed to meet the requirements of the target data warehouse. This is often the most complex and time-consuming part of the ETL process. Transformations can include:

- **Cleaning:** Handling missing values, correcting errors, and removing duplicates.
  - *Example:* If a customer's phone number is missing, it might be replaced with a default value or the entire record might be flagged for review.

- **Standardization:** Converting data into a consistent format.
  - *Example:* Dates might be in different formats (MM/DD/YYYY, YYYY-MM-DD). Standardization ensures all dates are in a single, uniform format.

- **Filtering:** Selecting only relevant data based on specific criteria.
  - *Example:* Only sales data from the last year might be loaded into the data warehouse.

- **Aggregation:** Summarizing data for reporting purposes.
  - *Example:* Calculating total sales per product category.

- **Joining:** Combining data from multiple sources based on a common key.
  - *Example:* Joining customer data with sales data to analyze purchasing patterns.

- **Data Type Conversion:** Converting the data type of a column to match the target data warehouse schema.

    - *Example:* Converting string representation of numbers to integer or decimal types.

- **Example:** Continuing with the retail company, suppose the sales database uses product codes like 'P123', while the customer database uses 'PRD123'. The 'Transform' stage would standardize these product codes to a single format (e.g., 'PRODUCT_123') before loading them into the data warehouse. Another transformation might involve calculating the 'total revenue' by multiplying 'quantity sold' with 'price per unit'.

- **Technical Details:** The transformation logic is often implemented using scripting languages (like Python), SQL, or dedicated ETL tools.

    - *Code Example (Python):*

    ```python
    import pandas as pd

    # Sample data (replace with your actual data loading)
    sales_data = {'product_code': ['P123', 'P456'], 'quantity': [10, 5], 'price': [20.0, 5(
    sales_df = pd.DataFrame(sales_data)

    # Transformation: Calculate total revenue and standardize product code
    sales_df['total_revenue'] = sales_df['quantity']  sales_df['price']
    sales_df['product_code'] = 'PRODUCT_' + sales_df['product_code'].str.replace('P', '') #

    print(sales_df)
    ```

    Output:

    ```
    product_code  quantity  price  total_revenue
    0  PRODUCT_123        10   20.0          200.0
    1  PRODUCT_456         5   50.0          250.0
    ```

3. Load:

The final stage involves writing the transformed data into the target data warehouse or data store. This is typically done in batches. The loading process needs to be efficient to minimize downtime and ensure data integrity.

- **Example:** The transformed sales data, customer data, and website traffic data are now loaded into a central data warehouse. This data warehouse can then be used for reporting, analytics, and decision-making.

- **Technical Details:** Loading can involve inserting new records, updating existing records, or deleting records, depending on the nature of the data and the requirements of the data warehouse. The 'Load' stage often uses bulk loading techniques to improve performance.

    - **Example:** If using a relational database as the data warehouse, the transformed data can be inserted using SQL `INSERT` statements or bulk loading utilities provided by the database.

ETL Summary:

ETL is a fundamental process, but it's important to remember that it's typically batch-oriented. This means that the data in the data warehouse is only as current as the last ETL run. For real-time or near real-time data needs, Change Data Capture (CDC) techniques (as described elsewhere in the chapter) are often preferred or integrated into the ETL process.

Change Data Capture (CDC)

Change Data Capture (CDC) is a data integration technique focused on capturing changes made to data in a source database in real-time or near real-time. Instead of periodically copying the entire dataset, CDC identifies and extracts only the modifications, such as insertions, updates, and deletions.

Let's consider a scenario: a customer database. Whenever a customer's address is updated, or a new customer is added, CDC detects these changes. These changes are then made available for other systems to consume.

CDC Benefits

The primary benefits of CDC stem from its ability to perform incremental data loading. Traditional ETL (Extract, Transform, Load) processes often involve full data refreshes. A full refresh requires reading the entire source table, which can be very resource-intensive and time-consuming, especially for large databases. CDC avoids this overhead. Because it only processes changed data, CDC significantly minimizes latency and resource consumption.

For example, imagine you have a table with 1 billion rows. An ETL process without CDC would have to scan all 1 billion rows every time it runs, even if only 100 rows have changed. CDC, however, would only need to process those 100 changed rows.

CDC & ETL Integration

CDC is often integrated with ETL pipelines to create a hybrid approach for data warehousing and analytics. CDC provides a continuous stream of data changes, which are then fed into ETL processes for transformation and loading into a data warehouse.

Sketch for CDC & ETL Integration:

```
[Source Database] --> [CDC Process] --> [Data Changes (Inserts, Updates, Deletes)] --> [ETL Pip
```

Here's how it works:

1. **CDC Capture:** The CDC process monitors the source database for changes.
2. **Data Extraction:** When a change occurs, the CDC process captures the relevant data, including details about the type of change (insert, update, or delete).
3. **Data Transformation (ETL):** The captured data changes are passed to the ETL pipeline. The ETL pipeline transforms the data as needed, e.g., applying data cleansing rules, aggregating data, or joining data from different sources.
4. **Data Loading (ETL):** Finally, the transformed data is loaded into the data warehouse, updating the relevant tables with the latest changes.

This integration enables near real-time data warehousing and analytics, as data changes are propagated to the data warehouse with minimal delay. This allows businesses to make decisions based on the most up-to-date information.

Example (Conceptual Code Snippet):

While actual CDC implementation varies depending on the database system and tools used, this is a conceptual representation.

```python
# Assuming we have a stream of CDC events (e.g., from Kafka)
def process_cdc_event(event):
    table_name = event['table']
    operation = event['operation'] # 'insert', 'update', 'delete'
    data = event['data']

    if operation == 'insert':
        insert_into_data_warehouse(table_name, data)
    elif operation == 'update':
        update_data_warehouse(table_name, data)
    elif operation == 'delete':
        delete_from_data_warehouse(table_name, data)

def insert_into_data_warehouse(table, data):
```

```
    # Code to insert data into the data warehouse
    print(f"Inserting into {table}: {data}")

def update_data_warehouse(table, data):
    # Code to update data in the data warehouse
    print(f"Updating {table}: {data}")

def delete_from_data_warehouse(table, data):
    # Code to delete data from the data warehouse
    print(f"Deleting from {table}: {data}")

# Example event
example_event = {
    'table': 'customers',
    'operation': 'update',
    'data': {'customer_id': 123, 'address': 'New Address'}
}


process_cdc_event(example_event)
```

This Python snippet illustrates how CDC events (represented as a dictionary) can trigger different actions in the ETL pipeline, such as inserting, updating, or deleting data in the data warehouse. The actual implementation would involve database-specific code and error handling.

CDC Benefits

Change Data Capture (CDC) offers several key advantages, primarily around efficiency and timeliness when it comes to moving data. These advantages stem from its core principle of tracking and replicating *only* the changes made to data, rather than the entire dataset. Let's explore these in detail.

Enables incremental data loading:

Instead of reloading entire tables every time (which is what traditional ETL often does), CDC identifies and transmits only the rows that have been inserted, updated, or deleted. This is called incremental data loading.

To visualize this, think of a large orders table in an e-commerce database. Imagine thousands of orders are placed each day. Using traditional ETL, you might have to extract *all* orders every night, even if only a few hundred were new or modified. With CDC, you would only extract those few hundred changed records.

```
-- Example: Hypothetical SQL-based CDC tracking table (simplified)
CREATE TABLE Orders_CDC (
    ChangeID INT PRIMARY KEY,
    OrderID INT,
    OperationType CHAR(1), -- 'I' for Insert, 'U' for Update, 'D' for Delete
    ChangeTimestamp DATETIME,
    OrderData VARCHAR(MAX)
);


-- Explanation:
-- When a new order is placed, a row is inserted into the Orders_CDC table with OperationType =
-- When an order is updated, a row is inserted with OperationType = 'U'.
-- When an order is deleted, a row is inserted with OperationType = 'D'.
```

In practice, CDC might use database triggers or transaction logs to populate a similar "CDC table". The ETL process then only reads from this table.

Minimizing latency and resource consumption compared to full ETL runs:

Because CDC works incrementally, it drastically reduces the amount of data that needs to be processed and transferred. This leads to two critical improvements:

- **Lower Latency:** Data changes are reflected in the target data warehouse (or other destination) much faster. With full ETL, there might be a 24-hour delay. With CDC, changes could be reflected in near real-time, perhaps within minutes. This is extremely valuable for applications that need up-to-date information, such as fraud detection or real-time dashboards.

- **Reduced Resource Consumption:** Extracting and transforming *only* the changed data requires significantly less CPU, memory, and network bandwidth than processing the entire dataset. This is especially important for large databases and systems with limited resources. Consider that e-commerce database again; extracting the delta of say 200 MB compared to full table extraction of 2TB drastically impacts resource utilisation. This reduction in resources saves the organization money, which can be diverted to innovate other areas of the business.

To illustrate this concept:

```
Full ETL                          CDC

+----------------------+          +----------------------+
| Extract all data     |------>| Extract changed data   |
| (e.g., entire table) |        | (e.g., new/updated rows)|
+----------------------+          +----------------------+
| Transform entire data |------>| Transform changed data |
+----------------------+          +----------------------+
| Load entire data     |------>| Load changed data      |
+----------------------+          +----------------------+
     More Resources                   Less Resources
     Higher Latency                   Lower Latency
```

This diagram shows that the CDC approach does things faster and easier than full ETL.

CDC & ETL Integration

CDC & ETL Integration represents a powerful hybrid approach to data warehousing and analytics. It combines the strengths of both Change Data Capture (CDC) and traditional Extract, Transform, Load (ETL) processes to achieve continuous and efficient data updates.

CDC feeds data changes into ETL pipelines

Imagine you have an online store. Every time a customer places an order, updates their address, or changes their payment information, that data changes. Traditional ETL would require regularly extracting *all* the data from your store's database and reloading it into your data warehouse. This is time-consuming and resource-intensive, especially when only a small fraction of the data has actually changed.

CDC solves this by capturing only the *changes* to the data in real-time or near real-time. These captured changes are then fed into ETL pipelines. Think of it like this: instead of sending the entire customer database to the warehouse every night, you only send the list of orders placed that day and any address updates that occurred.

For continuous data warehousing and analytics, creating a hybrid approach.

The hybrid approach comes from using CDC *alongside* ETL. CDC provides the stream of real-time data changes. The ETL pipeline receives these changes and integrates them into the data warehouse. This ensures the data warehouse is constantly updated with the latest information without the performance hit of full ETL runs. Consider below diagram to visually see the flow of the data.

```
+------------------+      +------------------+      +------------------+
| Source Database  |----->|  CDC Mechanism   |----->|  ETL Pipeline    |----->| Data Warehouse  |
+------------------+      +------------------+      +------------------+
   (e.g., Orders,        (Captures data         (Transforms and        (Unified,
    Customers)            changes)               loads data)             historical data)
```

For example, consider customer address changes. When a customer updates their address in the source database, the CDC mechanism captures this change. The ETL pipeline then receives this update, transforms it to the correct format for the data warehouse, and loads it, updating the customer's address. This happens without needing to reload the entire customer database. This ensures your analytics dashboards always reflect the most up-to-date customer locations.

This continuous integration provides several benefits:

- **Near Real-Time Data:** Analysts can access the most current data for faster insights and decision-making.
- **Reduced Latency:** Data is available sooner than with traditional batch ETL processing.
- **Lower Resource Consumption:** Incremental loading of only changed data consumes less CPU, memory, and network bandwidth.
- **Improved Scalability:** Handles increasing data volumes more efficiently as only changes are processed.
- **Enhanced Data Quality:** Capturing changes in real-time can help identify and resolve data quality issues sooner.

Let's outline a simplified code example (conceptual) demonstrating how CDC data might feed into an ETL process using Python:

```python
# Simulate CDC data stream (e.g., from Kafka)
cdc_data = [
    {"table": "Orders", "operation": "insert", "data": {"order_id": 123, "customer_id": 456, "ar
    {"table": "Customers", "operation": "update", "data": {"customer_id": 456, "address": "123 M
    {"table": "Orders", "operation": "insert", "data": {"order_id": 124, "customer_id": 789, "ar
]


# Simplified ETL function (in a real-world scenario, this would be far more complex)
def process_cdc_data(data):
    for change in data:
        table = change["table"]
        operation = change["operation"]
        data = change["data"]

        if table == "Orders":
            if operation == "insert":
                print(f"Inserting new order: {data}")
                # Code to insert into data warehouse's Orders table
            elif operation == "update":
                print(f"Updating order: {data}")
                # Code to update order in data warehouse
        elif table == "Customers":
            if operation == "update":
                print(f"Updating customer: {data}")
                # Code to update customer in data warehouse


# Execute the ETL function with CDC data
process_cdc_data(cdc_data)
```

In this example:

- `cdc_data` simulates the stream of changes captured by a CDC mechanism. Each item indicates the table that changed, the type of operation (insert, update, delete), and the specific data involved.
- `process_cdc_data` is a simplified ETL function. It iterates through the changes and performs the corresponding actions on the data warehouse (printing actions for demonstration purposes). In a real ETL pipeline, this would involve more complex transformations and loading into the data warehouse.

This code clarifies how a CDC stream feeds directly into the ETL pipeline, enabling continuous data integration. The benefits of CDC & ETL integration are best realized when your data needs to be updated frequently. It also significantly improves ETL efficiency, especially for large datasets. It is an excellent choice for businesses needing up-to-date insights and agile data analytics.

Chapter 14 Performance, Efficiency, and Optimization-Query Execution and Optimization in Modern Databases

- **Query Optimization Goals:** Minimize resource usage (CPU, I/O, network) and latency.

- **Query Execution Pipelines:** Data flows through operators (filter, join, sort) that transform it.

- **Index Selection:** Choosing the right indexes drastically speeds up common queries.

- **Join Algorithms:** Different join methods (hash join, sort-merge join) have varying performance characteristics depending on data size and distribution.

- **Cost-Based Optimization:** The query planner estimates the cost of different execution plans and chooses the cheapest one.

Query Optimization Goals

The primary goal of query optimization is to make database queries run faster and use fewer resources. This means reducing the time it takes for a query to return results (latency) and minimizing the amount of computing power (CPU), input/output operations (I/O), and network bandwidth required to execute the query.

Minimizing Resource Usage (CPU, I/O, Network):

Databases operate by performing computations (CPU usage), reading and writing data to disks (I/O), and transferring data across networks, especially in distributed systems. Each of these operations consumes resources.

- **CPU Usage:** Complex queries with many calculations, string manipulations, or function calls can consume a lot of CPU. Optimization aims to simplify calculations, avoid unnecessary function calls, and choose algorithms that are computationally efficient. For instance, consider a query that needs to perform a complex calculation on every row of a large table. A better approach might involve pre-calculating and storing the result, or finding a way to perform the calculation only on a subset of the data.

- **I/O:** Reading and writing data to disk is often the slowest part of query execution. Optimization minimizes I/O by using indexes to quickly locate relevant data, reading data in larger chunks, and avoiding full table scans when possible. Imagine a scenario where you're searching for a specific book in a library. If the library has a well-organized index, you can quickly find the book's location without having to search every shelf. Similarly, database indexes help locate data without reading the entire table.

```
-- Example: Query without index (slow)
SELECT  FROM orders WHERE customer_id = 12345;


-- Example: Query with index on customer_id (fast)
CREATE INDEX idx_customer_id ON orders (customer_id);
SELECT  FROM orders WHERE customer_id = 12345;
```

- **Network:** In distributed databases, data is spread across multiple machines. Sending data between machines consumes network bandwidth. Optimization reduces network traffic by pushing computations closer to the data, filtering data early, and sending only the necessary data across the network. For example, if you need to calculate the sum of sales for a specific region, it's more efficient to calculate the sum on each machine in that region and then send only the partial sums to a central location for final aggregation, rather than sending all the raw sales data.

Minimizing Latency:

Latency refers to the time it takes for a query to complete, from the moment it's submitted to the moment the results are returned. Reducing latency is crucial for providing a responsive user experience.

- **Parallelization:** Breaking a query into smaller parts that can be executed concurrently on multiple processors or machines can significantly reduce latency. Consider a query that aggregates data from multiple tables. Instead of processing each table sequentially, the query can be divided into tasks that process each table in parallel.

- **Query Plan Optimization:** Databases use query optimizers to generate different execution plans for a given query and choose the plan with the lowest estimated cost. The cost is typically a combination of CPU usage, I/O, and network traffic. For example, the optimizer might choose to use an index join instead of a full table scan join if it determines that the index join will be faster.

- **Caching:** Storing frequently accessed data in memory can reduce the need to read it from disk, thereby reducing latency. Database systems often use caches to store frequently accessed data and query results. Consider a web application that frequently retrieves user profiles from the database. By caching the user profiles in memory, the application can avoid repeatedly querying the database, resulting in faster response times.

Conceptual Sketch illustrating the Query Optimization Process:

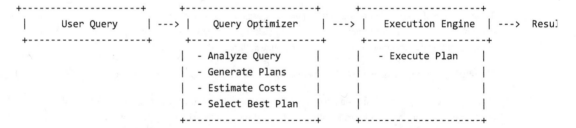

The sketch illustrates the query optimization process. A user submits a query, which is then analyzed by the query optimizer. The optimizer generates different execution plans, estimates the cost of each plan, and selects the best plan based on cost. The execution engine then executes the chosen plan to produce the results.

Query Execution Pipelines

Data in a database doesn't magically transform itself into the answer to your question (your query). Instead, it flows through a series of operations, much like parts moving along an assembly line in a factory. This assembly line for data is called a **query execution pipeline**. Each step in this pipeline is handled by an **operator**.

Data flows through operators (filter, join, sort) that transform it.

Think of an operator as a specialized tool. Some common operators include:

- **Filter:** This operator sifts through the data and keeps only the rows that meet a certain condition (like selecting customers from a specific city).
- **Join:** This operator combines data from two or more tables based on a related column (like linking customer information with their order history).
- **Sort:** This operator arranges the data in a specific order (like sorting products by price).

The pipeline is an ordered sequence of operators. The output of one operator becomes the input of the next. As the data flows through the pipeline, it's transformed step-by-step until the final result is produced.

Example:

Imagine you have a database with two tables: `Customers` and `Orders`. The `Customers` table has columns like `CustomerID`, `Name`, and `City`. The `Orders` table has columns like `OrderID`, `CustomerID`, and `OrderDate`.

You want to find all orders placed after January 1, 2023, by customers living in London.

The query execution pipeline might look like this:

1. **Filter (Customers):** Select customers where `City = 'London'`.
2. **Join:** Join the filtered `Customers` data with the `Orders` table based on `CustomerID`.
3. **Filter (Orders):** Select orders where `OrderDate > '2023-01-01'`.

The data first passes through the Customer filter, reducing it to London residents. This reduced data is then joined with the Orders table using the CustomerID. Finally, the joined data is filtered to only contain orders after the specified date, yielding the final result set.

A Simple Analogy:

Imagine you're making a smoothie. The pipeline is the smoothie-making process. The operators are:

1. **Wash:** Wash the fruits.
2. **Cut:** Cut the fruits into smaller pieces.
3. **Blend:** Blend the fruits together.
4. **Pour:** Pour the smoothie into a glass.

The raw fruits (the data) flow through these operators, getting transformed at each step until you have a delicious smoothie (the query result).

Sketch:

```
+--------+      +--------+      +--------+      +--------+
| Data   | -->  | Filter | -->  |  Join  | -->  | Output |
| Source |      |        |      |        |      |        |
+--------+      +--------+      +--------+      +--------+
```

This diagram shows a simplified pipeline. Data originates from a source, passes through a filter operator, then a join operator, and finally is outputted as the result.

```
+-------------+      +----------------+      +----------------+
| Customers   | ->   | Filter(City)   | ->   | Join (Orders)  |
+-------------+      +----------------+      +----------------+
      |
```

```
           V
+----------------+
| Orders         |
+----------------+
```

Importance

Understanding query execution pipelines is crucial for optimizing database performance. By knowing how data flows and which operators are involved, you can identify bottlenecks and tune your queries and database design to run more efficiently. This often involves choosing the correct indexes, but also understanding the characteristics of the data itself so that the database can choose the most efficient operators and their order of execution.

Index Selection

Choosing the right indexes is crucial for database performance. Indexes dramatically speed up common queries by allowing the database to quickly locate specific data without scanning the entire table. Poorly chosen indexes, however, can slow down write operations (inserts, updates, and deletes) and consume unnecessary storage space. Index selection is about finding the sweet spot: creating indexes that provide significant read performance gains without unduly impacting write performance or storage costs.

To illustrate, consider a table named `Customers` with columns like `CustomerID`, `FirstName`, `LastName`, `City`, and `OrderDate`.

```
CREATE TABLE Customers (
    CustomerID INT PRIMARY KEY,
    FirstName VARCHAR(255),
    LastName VARCHAR(255),
    City VARCHAR(255),
    OrderDate DATE
);
```

Now, suppose a common query searches for customers by `LastName`:

```
SELECT  FROM Customers WHERE LastName = 'Smith';
```

Without an index on `LastName`, the database must perform a full table scan, examining every row in the `Customers` table to find those where `LastName` is 'Smith'. This becomes increasingly inefficient as the table grows.

Creating an index on `LastName` solves this problem:

```
CREATE INDEX idx_LastName ON Customers (LastName);
```

With this index, the database can use a binary search-like approach to quickly locate the 'Smith' entries in the index, and then retrieve the corresponding rows from the `Customers` table. This significantly reduces the time it takes to execute the query.

However, indexes aren't free. Each index adds overhead to write operations. For instance, when a new customer is added, the database must not only insert a new row into the `Customers` table, but also update every relevant index on the `Customers` table. Furthermore, if the table gets updated and the key which is indexed gets updated than indexes must be recreated. Therefore, it's essential to only create indexes that are actually needed.

Consider another common query:

```
SELECT  FROM Customers WHERE City = 'London' AND OrderDate BETWEEN '2023-01-01' AND '2023-01-31'
```

In this case, creating separate indexes on `City` and `OrderDate` might help. However, a composite index on both columns could be even more effective:

```
CREATE INDEX idx_City_OrderDate ON Customers (City, OrderDate);
```

A composite index allows the database to efficiently filter by both `City` and `OrderDate` simultaneously. The database can first use the index to find all customers in 'London', and then quickly filter those customers by `OrderDate`. The below representation shows how a composite index will be used.

```
Index (City, OrderDate):
----------------------------------------------------
| City     | OrderDate    | Row Pointer |
----------------------------------------------------
| London   | 2023-01-05   |    0x1234   |
| London   | 2023-01-10   |    0x5678   |
| London   | 2023-02-15   |    0x9abc   |
| New York | 2023-01-20   |    0xdef0   |
----------------------------------------------------
```

In this example:

- The index is sorted first by `City` and then by `OrderDate` within each city.
- `Row Pointer` represents the physical address of the corresponding row in the `Customers` table.
- When the database executes the query, it first locates the 'London' entries in the index.
- Then, within the 'London' entries, it efficiently filters for `OrderDate` values between '2023-01-01' and '2023-01-31'.
- Finally, it uses the `Row Pointer` to quickly retrieve the corresponding rows from the `Customers` table.

Key Considerations for Index Selection:

- **Query Patterns:** Identify the most frequently executed and performance-critical queries. Focus on creating indexes that benefit these queries.
- **Data Cardinality:** Consider the number of distinct values in a column. Indexes are most effective on columns with high cardinality (many distinct values). Indexing a column with only a few distinct values (like a boolean flag) may not be beneficial.
- **Index Size:** Monitor the size of indexes. Large indexes consume more storage space and can slow down write operations.
- **Write Overhead:** Balance the performance gains from indexes with the overhead they add to write operations. Avoid creating unnecessary indexes.
- **Index Maintenance:** Regularly review and maintain indexes. Remove unused indexes and consider rebuilding fragmented indexes to improve performance.

Effectively choosing indexes requires a deep understanding of query patterns, data characteristics, and the trade-offs involved. Database management systems often provide tools and recommendations to assist with index selection. Continuously monitor query performance and adjust indexes as needed to maintain optimal database performance.

Join Algorithms

Different join methods (hash join, sort-merge join) have varying performance characteristics depending on data size and distribution. Choosing the right join algorithm is crucial for query performance. The database system considers factors like the size of the tables being joined, the available memory, and whether the join columns are already sorted or indexed when selecting the most efficient algorithm.

- **Hash Join:**

  The hash join algorithm is particularly efficient when one of the tables being joined is relatively small and fits into memory. It works by creating a hash table from the smaller table using the join column as the key. Then, it iterates through the larger table, probing the hash table to find matching rows.

  - **How it Works:**

1. **Build Phase:** The algorithm reads the smaller table (the "build" table) and creates a hash table in memory. The join column values are used as hash keys, and the corresponding rows are stored in the hash table.
2. **Probe Phase:** The algorithm reads the larger table (the "probe" table). For each row in the probe table, it calculates the hash value of the join column. It then uses this hash value to look up matching rows in the hash table.
3. **Match Phase:** When a matching row is found in the hash table, the join condition is satisfied, and the corresponding rows from both tables are combined to produce a result row.

○ **Example:** Consider joining two tables: Orders (large table) and Customers (smaller table) on CustomerID.

```
SELECT
FROM Orders o
JOIN Customers c ON o.CustomerID = c.CustomerID;
```

The database might choose hash join. It first builds a hash table using the Customers table (build phase), using CustomerID as the key. Then, it iterates through the Orders table (probe phase). For each OrderID, it looks up the corresponding CustomerID in the hash table to find the matching customer information.

Sketch:

```
Build Phase (Customers):
-----------------------------------------------
|CustomerID| Name      | Other Customer Data|
-----------------------------------------------
|1         | John Doe  | ...                 | -> Hash Table (Key: 1)
|2         | Jane Smith| ...                 | -> Hash Table (Key: 2)
|...       | ...       | ...                 |
-----------------------------------------------


Probe Phase (Orders):
-----------------------------------------------
|OrderID| CustomerID| Other Order Data|
-----------------------------------------------
|101    | 1         | ...              | -> Hash Table Lookup (CustomerID = 1)
|102    | 2         | ...              | -> Hash Table Lookup (CustomerID = 2)
|...    | ...       | ...              |
-----------------------------------------------
```

○ **Pseudo Code:**

```
# Build Phase
hash_table = {}
for row in Customers:
    key = row["CustomerID"]
    hash_table[key] = row

# Probe Phase
results = []
for row in Orders:
    key = row["CustomerID"]
    if key in hash_table:
        customer_row = hash_table[key]
        # Combine order row and customer row
```

```
            results.append(merge_rows(row, customer_row))

    return results
```

- **Sort-Merge Join:**

The sort-merge join algorithm is effective when the tables are already sorted on the join columns or when sorting is a feasible operation. It involves sorting both tables on the join column and then merging them together.

   ○ **How it Works:**

      1. **Sort Phase:** If the tables are not already sorted on the join column, the algorithm sorts both tables. This can be an expensive operation if the tables are large.
      2. **Merge Phase:** The algorithm reads both sorted tables in parallel, comparing the join column values. If the values match, the corresponding rows are joined. If the values do not match, the algorithm advances to the next row in the table with the smaller value.
      3. **Output Phase:** When a match is found, the combined row is produced as output.

   ○ **Example:** Again, consider joining `Orders` and `Customers` on `CustomerID`. Let's assume both tables are already sorted by `CustomerID`.

```
SELECT
FROM Orders o
JOIN Customers c ON o.CustomerID = c.CustomerID;
ORDER BY o.CustomerID, c.CustomerID;
```

The database can use sort-merge join because of the sorted data. It reads both tables simultaneously. It compares the `CustomerID` values in the current row of each table. When the `CustomerID` values match, the rows are joined and output.

Sketch:

```
Sorted Orders:                  Sorted Customers:
-----------------------------   ----------------------------
|OrderID| CustomerID| ...     | |CustomerID| Name      | ...    |
-----------------------------   ----------------------------
|101    | 1         | ...     | |1         | John Doe  | ...    | <- Match!
|102    | 2         | ...     | |2         | Jane Smith| ...    | <- Match!
|103    | 2         | ...     | |3         | David Lee | ...    |
|104    | 3         | ...     | |...       | ...       | ...    |
|...    | ...       | ...     | ----------------------------
-----------------------------
```

   ○ **Pseudo Code:**

```
# Assuming Orders and Customers are already sorted by CustomerID
orders_iter = iter(Orders)
customers_iter = iter(Customers)

order_row = next(orders_iter, None) # None if table is empty
customer_row = next(customers_iter, None)

results = []

while order_row and customer_row:
    if order_row["CustomerID"] == customer_row["CustomerID"]:
```

```
            # Match found! Combine rows
            results.append(merge_rows(order_row, customer_row))
            order_row = next(orders_iter, None)  # move to next order, check for multiple (
        elif order_row["CustomerID"] < customer_row["CustomerID"]:
            order_row = next(orders_iter, None)
        else:
            customer_row = next(customers_iter, None)

    return results
```

- **Nested Loop Join:**

  The nested loop join is the simplest join algorithm, but also the least efficient for large tables. It iterates through each row of the outer table and, for each row, iterates through all rows of the inner table to find matching rows.

  - **How it Works:**

    1. **Outer Loop:** The algorithm iterates through each row of the outer table.
    2. **Inner Loop:** For each row in the outer table, the algorithm iterates through all rows in the inner table.
    3. **Comparison:** For each pair of rows (one from the outer table and one from the inner table), the algorithm checks if the join condition is met.
    4. **Output:** If the join condition is met, the corresponding rows are combined and output.

  - **Example:** Consider joining `Orders` and `Customers` on `CustomerID` using nested loop join.

    ```
    SELECT
    FROM Orders o
    JOIN Customers c ON o.CustomerID = c.CustomerID;
    ```

    The database iterates through each row in the `Orders` table (outer loop). For each `OrderID` in `Orders`, it iterates through every row in the `Customers` table (inner loop) until `CustomerID` matches than returns the results.

    Sketch:

    ```
    Orders (Outer Loop):        Customers (Inner Loop):
    ---------------------------  ---------------------------
    |OrderID| CustomerID| ...    |  |CustomerID| Name    | ...     |
    ---------------------------  ---------------------------
    |101    | 1         | ...    |  |1        | John Doe | ...     | <- Match!
    |102    | 2         | ...    |  |2        | Jane Smith| ...    | <- Match!
    |103    | 2         | ...    |  |3        | David Lee | ...    |
    |104    | 3         | ...    |  |...      | ...      | ...     |
    |...    | ...       | ...    |  ---------------------------
    ---------------------------
    ```

  - **Pseudo Code:**

    ```
    results = []
    for order_row in Orders:
        for customer_row in Customers:
            if order_row["CustomerID"] == customer_row["CustomerID"]:
                # Match found!  Combine rows
                results.append(merge_rows(order_row, customer_row))
    return results
    ```

Cost-Based Optimization selects the most efficient join algorithm based on statistics and cost estimates. The performance differences between these algorithms can be significant, especially for large datasets. The choice depends heavily on table sizes, data distribution, and available resources. Indexes play a critical role in improving join performance, particularly with nested loop joins, where an index on the inner table's join column can drastically reduce the number of rows that need to be examined.

Cost-Based Optimization

Cost-based optimization is a core component of modern database management systems. Its primary function is to determine the most efficient strategy for executing a given query. This optimization process revolves around estimating the 'cost' associated with different possible execution plans and then selecting the plan with the lowest estimated cost. Let's break down what this entails.

The Role of the Query Planner

At the heart of cost-based optimization lies the query planner (sometimes referred to as the optimizer). When a SQL query is submitted to the database, the query planner doesn't immediately execute it. Instead, it explores various ways the query *could* be executed. These different approaches are called execution plans.

Execution Plans and Operators

Consider a simple SQL query like:

```
SELECT
FROM orders
WHERE customer_id = 123
AND order_date > '2023-01-01';
```

There are multiple ways to execute this query. One way might be to first filter the entire `orders` table for `customer_id = 123` and then filter the result for `order_date > '2023-01-01'`. Another way might involve using an index on the `order_date` column to quickly find relevant orders and *then* filter for the specific `customer_id`.

These execution plans are typically represented as trees, where each node in the tree represents an operator. Common operators include:

- **Filter:** Selects rows that meet a specified condition (the `WHERE` clause).
- **Join:** Combines rows from two or more tables based on a related column.
- **Sort:** Arranges rows in a specific order.
- **Index Scan:** Retrieves rows using an index.
- **Table Scan:** Reads every row in a table.

Cost Estimation: A Deep Dive

The crux of cost-based optimization is *estimating* the cost of each potential execution plan. This cost is an abstract measure of the resources required to execute that plan, typically a combination of CPU usage, I/O operations (reading and writing data to disk), and network communication (for distributed databases). The planner uses statistics about the data in the tables to estimate these costs. This statistics stored in system catalogues.

These statistics include:

- **Table size:** The number of rows in a table.
- **Number of pages:** The number of disk pages required to store a table.
- **Index statistics:** Information about the size and distribution of values in an index.
- **Data distribution:** Histograms that show the distribution of values in a column.

For example, consider the filter operation `WHERE customer_id = 123`. If the query planner knows (from statistics) that `customer_id` values are evenly distributed and that there are 1 million rows in the `orders` table, it might estimate that this filter will return approximately 1/N of 1 million rows, N being the numbers of unique `customer_id`. If, on the other hand, there is an index on `customer_id`, the planner will use statistics to estimate the cost of using the index to locate rows matching this criteria, which could be much lower than reading the entire table.

Different operations have different associated costs. A table scan is generally more expensive than an index scan (because a table scan reads every row), but this isn't always the case if the query needs to retrieve almost all rows from the table.

The cost model used by the query planner is a crucial component. It defines how the different factors are combined to arrive at a single cost estimate. A simplified cost model might look something like this:

```
Total Cost = (CPU Cost CPU Weight) + (I/O Cost I/O Weight) + (Network Cost Network
Weight)
```

The weights allow the database administrator to tune the optimizer to prioritize certain types of resources over others.

Choosing the Optimal Plan

Once the query planner has generated several candidate execution plans and estimated their costs, it selects the plan with the lowest estimated cost. This plan is then used to execute the query.

Example

Assume you have the following two tables in your database:

- `Customers (customer_id INT, customer_name VARCHAR, city VARCHAR)`
- `Orders (order_id INT, customer_id INT, order_date DATE, total_amount DECIMAL)`

And you execute the following query:

```
SELECT c.customer_name, SUM(o.total_amount) AS total_spent
FROM Customers c
JOIN Orders o ON c.customer_id = o.customer_id
WHERE c.city = 'New York'
AND o.order_date BETWEEN '2023-01-01' AND '2023-12-31'
GROUP BY c.customer_name
ORDER BY total_spent DESC;
```

The query planner might consider these plans:

Plan A (Hash Join, Filter on Customers first):

1. Filter the `Customers` table to find customers in 'New York'.
2. Perform a hash join between the filtered `Customers` and the `Orders` table on `customer_id`.
3. Filter the joined result for orders within the specified date range.
4. Group the results by customer name and calculate the total spent.
5. Sort the results by total spent in descending order.

Plan B (Index Seek on Orders, Sort-Merge Join):

1. Use an index on `Orders.order_date` to quickly retrieve orders within the specified date range.
2. Perform a sort-merge join between the filtered `Orders` and the `Customers` table on `customer_id`.
3. Filter the joined result to only include customers in 'New York'.
4. Group the results by customer name and calculate the total spent.
5. Sort the results by total spent in descending order.

The query planner would analyze the statistics for the tables and indexes: How many customers are in New York? How many orders are within the date range? Is there an index on `Orders.customer_id`? How large are the tables?

Based on these statistics, the planner will estimate the cost of each step in each plan and choose the plan with the lowest total estimated cost. For example, if there are very few customers in New York, Plan A might be more efficient because it reduces the size of the `Customers` table before the join. However, if there is a very efficient index on `Orders.order_date`, Plan B might be faster.

Illustrative Sketch

To visualize the concepts, consider a simplified diagram:

```
[SQL Query] --> [Query Parser] --> [Query Planner]
                                         |
                                         V
                               [Generate Possible Plans]
                                         |
                                         V
                               [Cost Estimator (Uses Statistics)]
                                         |
                                         V
                     [Select Lowest Cost Execution Plan] --> [Query Executor] --> [Result]
```

In essence, Cost-Based Optimization is a smart strategy that helps the query planner to choose the most efficient way to execute a SQL query.

Limitations

Cost-based optimization isn't perfect. The accuracy of the cost estimates depends on the quality and completeness of the statistics. If the statistics are outdated or inaccurate, the optimizer may choose a suboptimal plan. Additionally, the cost model itself is an approximation of reality. The actual cost of executing a query can be influenced by factors that are difficult to model accurately, such as the current load on the database server or the specific hardware configuration.

Chapter 15 Performance, Efficiency, and Optimization-Indexing and Caching Strategies for Faster Access

Here are 5 bullet points outlining Indexing and Caching strategies for improved performance:

- **Indexes for Query Acceleration:**

- Sparse vs. Dense: Trade-offs in storage overhead and lookup speed.
- B-trees & LSM-trees: Balancing read/write performance for different workloads.

- **Caching Layers:**

    - Client-side vs. Server-side: Location impacts latency and data consistency.
    - Cache invalidation strategies: Balancing staleness with performance gains.

- **Read Optimization:**

    - Materialized Views: Pre-computed results to accelerate complex queries.

- **Write Optimization:**

    - Write-Through vs. Write-Back: Data durability vs. write latency trade-offs.

- **Trade-offs and Considerations:**

    - Data consistency: How to manage the data across various layers.

Indexes for Query Acceleration

Indexes are crucial for speeding up data retrieval in databases. Think of them like the index in the back of a book. Instead of reading the whole book to find a specific topic, you can use the index to jump directly to the relevant pages. In databases, indexes help the system quickly locate the rows that match your query without scanning the entire table.

Sparse vs. Dense: Trade-offs in storage overhead and lookup speed.

Imagine a phone book. A *dense index* would list every single person in the book, along with their phone number and address (a pointer to their full record). A *sparse index* on the other hand, might only list every page of the phone book, and the first person on each page. To find a specific person, you'd first find the correct page using the sparse index, then scan that page.

- **Dense Index:** Offers faster lookups since every record is indexed, but consumes more storage space. It's ideal for smaller tables or columns frequently used in queries. If you have a table of employee details and you often search by employee ID, a dense index on the employee ID column would be beneficial.

- **Sparse Index:** Requires less storage space, but lookups are slower as the database might need to read additional data to find the exact record. Sparse indexes work well on large tables where a dense index would become too large and unwieldy. A good example is the clustering index on a database table, in which you would index on the primary key column and the data on disk is physically sorted according to the indexed field.

Sketch:

```
+------------------+       +------------------+       +------------------+
| Record 1         | -->   | Dense Index      | -->   | Data Page 1      |
+------------------+       | (Record 1 -> Loc)|       | (Record 1...)    |
| Record 2         | -->   | Record 2 -> Loc  |       | Record 2...)     |
+------------------+       | ...              |       | ...              |
| ...              |       +------------------+       +------------------+
| Record N         |       | Record N -> Loc  |
+------------------+       +------------------+


+------------------+       +------------------+       +------------------+
| Record 1         |       | Sparse Index     | -->   | Data Page 1      |
+------------------+       | (Page 1 -> Loc)  |       | (Record 1...)    |
| ...              |       | Page 2 -> Loc    |       | Record 2...)     |
```

```
+------------------+        | ...               |    | ...                       |
| Record N         |        +------------------+    +------------------+
+------------------+
```

B-trees & LSM-trees: Balancing read/write performance for different workloads.

Different indexing structures are optimized for different types of database operations. Two popular choices are B-trees and LSM-trees.

- **B-trees (Balanced Trees):** Are excellent for read-heavy workloads. They maintain sorted data, allowing for efficient range queries and point lookups. However, writes can be relatively slower because the tree needs to be rebalanced as data is inserted or updated. The rebalancing requires to maintain sorting.

  Imagine a physical filing cabinet. A B-tree is like a well-organized filing cabinet where files are neatly sorted alphabetically. Finding a file is quick, but adding a new file in the middle of the cabinet requires shifting other files around, which takes time.

```
//Pseudo Code - Illustration only - Not functional
    BTreeIndex index = new BTreeIndex("employee_id");
    index->insert(123, recordLocation); //Insert Employee ID 123
    index->insert(456, anotherLocation); //Insert Employee ID 456
    Record employee = index->find(123); //Efficient Lookup
```

- **LSM-trees (Log-Structured Merge Trees):** Are optimized for write-heavy workloads. Writes are initially written to memory and then periodically merged into larger, sorted files on disk. This approach provides high write throughput but can result in slower reads due to the need to check multiple levels of data. Because the data in the different trees have not been merged yet into a single tree.

  Think of LSM trees as having multiple filing cabinets. Whenever you have a file to save, you add it to the first cabinet, without necessarily sorting it within that cabinet. After it is full, you then merge these files from the first cabinet into second cabinet and it get sorted. When you need to find a file, you may need to search the filing cabinets. Adding files is really fast, but finding a specific file may take longer.

```
//Pseudo Code - Illustration only - Not functional
    LSMTreeIndex index = new LSMTreeIndex("log_id");
    index->insert(logId1, logRecordLocation); //Fast Insert
    index->insert(logId2, anotherLocation);  //Fast Insert
    LogRecord log = index->find(logId1);        //Lookup might involve multiple levels
```

Sketch:

B-Tree:

```
[50]
        /   \
    [25]    [75]
   /  \    /  \
[10][30][60][90]
```

LSM-Tree:

```
MemTable (Fast Writes) -> Disk Level 1 (Sorted) -> Disk Level 2 (Merged, Sorted) -> ...
```

In summary, the choice between sparse and dense indexes, and between B-trees and LSM-trees, depends heavily on the specific read/write patterns of your application and the size of your data. Understanding these trade-offs is key to designing efficient and performant database systems.

Indexes for Query Acceleration: Sparse vs. Dense

Indexes are crucial for speeding up data retrieval in databases. Think of an index as a table of contents for your data. Instead of reading every page (every row in the database) to find what you need, you can consult the index, which points directly to the relevant information. Two common types of indexes are sparse and dense, each with its own trade-offs.

Dense Indexes:

A dense index contains an entry for *every* record in the data file. Imagine a library where the index lists *every* book, in order, with its exact location on the shelf.

- **Characteristics:** Every key in the data file has a corresponding key in the index.
- **Storage Overhead:** Dense indexes require more storage space because they index every record. This can significantly increase the size of the index, especially for large datasets.
- **Lookup Speed:** Lookups using a dense index are typically very fast. Since every record is indexed, finding a specific record involves a direct lookup in the index, followed by retrieval of the data from the data file.
- **Use Cases:** Dense indexes are best suited for scenarios where you need to quickly retrieve any record in the database. They're also useful for clustered indexes, where the data file is physically sorted according to the index key.

Example:

Consider a table of student records:

| StudentID | Name | Major | GPA | | :-------- | :--------- | :--------- | :--- | | 101 | Alice Smith | Computer Sci | 3.8 | | 102 | Bob Johnson | Physics | 3.5 | | 103 | Carol Davis | Math | 3.9 | | 104 | David Brown | Chemistry | 3.2 |

A dense index on `StudentID` would look like this (simplified representation):

```
Index:
101 -> Row 1
102 -> Row 2
103 -> Row 3
104 -> Row 4
```

Each `StudentID` has a corresponding pointer to the row containing that student's information.

Sparse Indexes:

A sparse index, in contrast, contains entries for only *some* of the records in the data file. This is like a library index that only lists the first book on each shelf. To find a specific book, you look in the index to find the *nearest* entry, then search sequentially from that point.

- **Characteristics:** Only a subset of the keys in the data file have corresponding entries in the index. Generally, sparse indexes are used with sorted data files.
- **Storage Overhead:** Sparse indexes require significantly less storage space than dense indexes because they index fewer records. This is a major advantage for very large datasets.
- **Lookup Speed:** Lookups using a sparse index are generally slower than dense indexes. After finding the nearest index entry, a sequential search may be required to locate the desired record.
- **Use Cases:** Sparse indexes are best suited for scenarios where the data is sorted, and you can tolerate slightly slower lookups in exchange for reduced storage overhead. They are commonly used with large, static datasets where writes are infrequent.

Example:

Assuming the same student records table is sorted by `StudentID`:

| StudentID | Name | Major | GPA | | :-------- | :--------- | :--------- | :--- | | 101 | Alice Smith | Computer Sci | 3.8 | | 102 | Bob Johnson | Physics | 3.5 | | 103 | Carol Davis | Math | 3.9 | | 104 | David Brown | Chemistry | 3.2 |

A sparse index (assuming we index every other record) on `StudentID` would look like this:

```
Index:
101 -> Row 1
103 -> Row 3
```

To find `StudentID` 102, you'd look up 101 in the index, go to Row 1, and then sequentially search until you find 102.

Trade-offs Summarized:

Feature	Dense Index	Sparse Index
Index Coverage	Every record	Subset of records
Storage	Higher	Lower
Lookup Speed	Generally Faster	Generally Slower
Data Order	Not required	Typically Sorted
Write Performance	More Overhead (index updates)	Less Overhead (fewer updates)

Code Example (Conceptual - Python):

While not a direct database index implementation, this illustrates the concept:

```python
# Dense Index (simulated)
data = {101: "Alice", 102: "Bob", 103: "Carol"}
dense_index = {key: key for key in data} #Index values are just keys.
# Lookup Alice
student_id = 101
if student_id in dense_index:
    print(f"Student Name: {data[dense_index[student_id]]}") # Student Name: Alice


# Sparse Index (simulated)
data = {101: "Alice", 102: "Bob", 103: "Carol", 104: "David"} #Added 104 to keep sorted
sparse_index = {101: 101, 103: 103}  #Only 101 and 103 are indexed

def sparse_lookup(student_id):
    nearest_key = None
    for key in sorted(sparse_index.keys()): # Important: Iterate in sorted order
        if key <= student_id:
            nearest_key = key
        else:
            break #Nearest key will point to 101 in the event of Bob.
    #print(nearest_key) #101 in the event of 102
    if nearest_key:
        current_id = nearest_key
        #Linear probing concept. This may or may not work if data is not aligned.
        while current_id <= student_id:
           #  print(current_id) #101 and 102 in the event of 102
            if current_id in data and current_id == student_id:
                return data[current_id] #Bob
            #Linear probing from 101 to Bob
            current_id += 1
    return None
#Lookup Bob
student_id = 102
name = sparse_lookup(student_id)
if name:
    print(f"Student Name: {name}")  # Student Name: Bob
```

```
else:
    print("Student not found")
```

This simplified example illustrates how dense indexes provide direct lookups, while sparse indexes require a sequential search after finding the nearest index entry. In real database systems, these are implemented far more efficiently using structures like B-trees, but the core principle remains the same.

In Summary:

The choice between sparse and dense indexes depends on the specific requirements of your application. If storage space is a primary concern and you can tolerate slightly slower lookups, a sparse index may be appropriate. If fast lookups are critical, and storage space is less of a concern, a dense index may be the better choice. Understanding these trade-offs is crucial for optimizing database performance.

B-trees & LSM-trees: Balancing Read/Write Performance

Choosing the right data structure for indexing is crucial for database performance. Two popular choices are B-trees and LSM-trees, each offering distinct advantages and disadvantages in terms of read and write performance. Understanding their trade-offs is essential for optimizing your database for specific workloads.

B-trees:

B-trees are a classic data structure optimized for both read and write operations. They are widely used in traditional relational databases. Think of a B-tree like a well-organized library card catalog. Each level of the catalog (the tree) helps you quickly narrow down your search.

- **Structure:** A B-tree is a self-balancing tree structure. Data is stored in sorted order within the leaf nodes. Internal nodes act as directories, guiding searches to the correct leaf node. The "B" in B-tree is for "balanced," meaning the tree keeps its structure balanced, ensuring relatively consistent access times for all data.

  Sketch:

  ```
  Root
    /  \
   I1   I2    (Internal Nodes - pointers to child nodes based on key ranges)
   / \  / \
  L1 L2 L3 L4 (Leaf Nodes - contain actual data or pointers to data, sorted)
  ```

  I1, I2 are internal nodes guiding the search based on key ranges. L1, L2, L3, L4 are leaf nodes where the actual data resides.

- **Read Performance:** B-trees generally offer good read performance. To find a specific piece of data, you traverse the tree from the root to the leaf node containing the data. The depth of the tree is relatively small, even for large datasets, meaning lookups are fast. This is similar to quickly finding a book in a library using the organized card catalog.

- **Write Performance:** Writes in B-trees can be more expensive. When you insert or delete data, the tree may need to be re-balanced to maintain its structure. This can involve moving data around and updating multiple nodes, leading to higher write latency. Imagine needing to insert a new card into the middle of a tightly packed section in the card catalog. You might have to shift many cards to make room, which takes time.

- **Example:**

  Let's say you have a database storing user profiles, indexed by user ID, and are using a B-tree.

  ```python
  # Simplified Python example (illustrative)
  class BTreeNode:
      def __init__(self, leaf=False):
  ```

```
        self.leaf = leaf
        self.keys = []
        self.children = []

# (Implementation details of insert, search, delete would go here.  This is a very simplifi

# Example usage (highly simplified)
root = BTreeNode(leaf=True)
root.keys = [1, 5, 10] # User IDs stored
# When searching for user ID 5, the B-tree structure allows quick navigation
# to find the data associated with user ID 5.
```

This simplified code shows the basic structure of a B-tree node. In a real implementation, insert, search, and delete operations would maintain the balanced nature of the tree.

LSM-trees (Log-Structured Merge Trees):

LSM-trees are designed for write-intensive workloads. They optimize for fast writes by sacrificing some read performance. Think of an LSM-tree like a scratchpad where you quickly jot down new information. Later, you organize and merge the information into a more structured format.

- **Structure:** An LSM-tree consists of multiple levels of sorted data. New writes are initially buffered in memory (the "memtable"). Once the memtable reaches a certain size, it is flushed to disk as a sorted file (an "SSTable" or Sorted String Table). These SSTables are then periodically merged together in the background to optimize read performance and reduce storage space.

  Sketch:

```
MemTable (in-memory buffer)
    | (flush to disk)
    V
  SSTable (Level 0) - most recent writes
    | (merge)
    V
  SSTable (Level 1) - older writes
    | (merge)
    V
  SSTable (Level 2) - oldest writes
```

  New writes go to MemTable, then flushed as SSTable at Level 0. SSTables are merged to higher levels periodically.

- **Write Performance:** LSM-trees excel at write performance. Writes are appended to the memtable, which is a very fast operation. This avoids the random writes and re-balancing required by B-trees. Adding information to the scratchpad is quick and easy.

- **Read Performance:** Read performance in LSM-trees can be slower than B-trees, especially if the requested data is scattered across multiple SSTables. To read data, the system needs to check the memtable and potentially multiple SSTables on disk. The merging process helps to improve read performance over time, but it can still be slower than a B-tree for certain workloads. Finding specific information requires checking multiple pages of the scratchpad before consolidation happens.

- **Example:**

  Imagine building a system to track website traffic, where you primarily need to record large volumes of incoming data. An LSM-tree would be well-suited for this.

```python
# Simplified Python example (illustrative)
class MemTable:
    def __init__(self):
        self.data = {}

    def insert(self, key, value):
        self.data[key] = value

    def flush_to_sstable(self):
        # (Code to write self.data to a sorted file on disk - SSTable)
        pass

# Example usage
memtable = MemTable()
memtable.insert("timestamp1", "userA visited page X")
memtable.insert("timestamp2", "userB visited page Y")
# ... more inserts ...
memtable.flush_to_sstable() # Write to SSTable when memtable is full.
```

This simplified code demonstrates how writes are quickly added to the in-memory `MemTable`. The `flush_to_sstable` function would then write the sorted data to disk. The background merging process is not shown in this example, but is a crucial part of how LSM-trees maintain performance.

Summary:

| Feature | B-tree | LSM-tree | |----------------|--|---|| Read Performance | Generally good | Can be slower, improves with compaction || Write Performance| Can be slower due to re-balancing | Excellent, append-only writes || Workload | Read-heavy or balanced read/write | Write-heavy || Complexity | Relatively simpler to implement | More complex due to merging and compaction |

In conclusion, the choice between B-trees and LSM-trees depends heavily on the specific application requirements and workload characteristics. B-trees are a solid choice for balanced read/write workloads, while LSM-trees excel in scenarios where write performance is paramount.

Caching Layers

Caching is a technique used to store frequently accessed data in a faster storage medium to reduce access time and improve overall system performance. Think of it like keeping your most used tools on your workbench instead of in a faraway shed. This section explores the different types of caching layers and the strategies to maintain data validity within these layers.

Client-side vs. Server-side: Location impacts latency and data consistency.

Caching can be implemented on either the client-side (e.g., in a web browser or a mobile app) or on the server-side (e.g., in a web server or a database server). Each location has its own set of benefits and trade-offs concerning latency and data consistency.

- **Client-Side Caching:** This involves storing data on the user's device or browser. The primary advantage is reduced latency since the data is readily available without needing to make a network request to the server. Examples of client-side caching include browser caching of static assets like images, CSS, and JavaScript files, or using local storage in a mobile app to store user preferences.

  - **Example:** Imagine a user repeatedly visiting the same webpage. With client-side caching, the browser downloads the images and other static content on the first visit and stores them locally. Subsequent visits load these assets from the local cache, making the page load much faster without needing to fetch the resources from the server again.

○ **Code Example (Browser Caching):**

```html
<!DOCTYPE html>
<html>
<head>
    <title>Cached Image</title>
    <meta http-equiv="Cache-Control" content="max-age=3600"> <!-- Cache for 1 hour -->
</head>
<body>
    <img src="image.jpg" alt="Cached Image">
</body>
</html>
```

In this example, the Cache-Control meta tag instructs the browser to cache the webpage (and its associated resources like image.jpg) for one hour (3600 seconds).

- **Server-Side Caching:** This involves storing data on the server-side, typically in a memory-based cache like Redis or Memcached. The benefit here is that it reduces the load on the primary data source (e.g., a database) and improves response times for multiple users accessing the same data. However, it introduces some latency compared to client-side caching, as a network request is still required.

    ○ **Example:** Consider a popular e-commerce website. The product catalog and frequently accessed product details can be stored in a server-side cache. When a user requests a product page, the server first checks if the product details are available in the cache. If yes, the server retrieves the data from the cache instead of querying the database, thus reducing the database load and speeding up the response time.

    ○ **Code Example (Server-Side Caching with Redis using Python):**

```python
import redis

# Connect to Redis
redis_client = redis.Redis(host='localhost', port=6379, db=0)

def get_product_details(product_id):
    # Try to get the data from cache
    cached_data = redis_client.get(f"product:{product_id}")

    if cached_data:
        print("Data retrieved from cache")
        return cached_data.decode('utf-8') # Decode from bytes to string
    else:
        # If not in cache, fetch from database (simulated here)
        print("Data retrieved from database")
        product_data = f"Details for product ID {product_id} from database"
        # Store in cache for future use
        redis_client.set(f"product:{product_id}", product_data)
        redis_client.expire(f"product:{product_id}", 3600) # Expire after 1 hour
        return product_data

# Example usage
product_id = 123
details = get_product_details(product_id)
print(details)
```

In this Python example, the `get_product_details` function first checks if the product details are available in the Redis cache. If present, it retrieves the data from the cache. Otherwise, it fetches the data from the database (simulated in this example), stores it in the cache with an expiration time of one hour, and then returns the data.

Cache invalidation strategies: Balancing staleness with performance gains.

Cache invalidation is the process of removing or updating cached data when the original data changes. It is a crucial aspect of caching because outdated data in the cache can lead to incorrect or inconsistent results. The primary challenge is to balance the need for fresh data with the performance benefits of caching. Some common cache invalidation strategies include:

- **Time-To-Live (TTL):** This is the simplest invalidation strategy. Each cached item is assigned a TTL, which specifies how long the item remains valid in the cache. After the TTL expires, the item is automatically removed from the cache or marked as invalid.

    - **Example:** Setting a TTL of 60 minutes for product prices. After 60 minutes, the cached price is considered stale, and the cache will fetch the latest price from the database on the next request.

    - **Code Example (TTL with Redis):**

      ```
      import redis

      redis_client = redis.Redis(host='localhost', port=6379, db=0)

      def cache_data_with_ttl(key, data, ttl):
          redis_client.set(key, data, ex=ttl)  # 'ex' sets the expiration time in seconds

      # Example Usage
      cache_data_with_ttl("user:123", "User details", 3600) # Cache for 1 hour
      ```

      In this Redis example, the `cache_data_with_ttl` function stores data in the cache with an expiration time specified by the `ttl` parameter (in seconds).

- **Write-Through Cache:** With this strategy, every write operation to the primary data store is also immediately written to the cache. This ensures that the cache always contains the most up-to-date data.

    - **Tradeoff:** While it guarantees consistency, it adds latency to every write operation since the system needs to wait for both the database and the cache to be updated.

    - **Scenario:** This strategy is beneficial when data consistency is critical, and the write volume is relatively low. For example, in financial transactions where it's crucial to maintain data integrity at all times.

- **Write-Back Cache (Write-Behind Cache):** With this strategy, write operations are performed only on the cache, and the updates are propagated to the primary data store asynchronously. This improves write performance because the system doesn't need to wait for the database to be updated before acknowledging the write.

    - **Tradeoff:** The main drawback is the risk of data loss if the cache fails before the updates are written to the database. Also, it can lead to data inconsistency if other systems read the data directly from the database before the cache updates are propagated.

    - **Scenario:** This strategy is suitable when write performance is more critical than immediate consistency. For example, in logging systems where high write throughput is required, and occasional data loss is tolerable.

- **Invalidation based on data change notifications:** The caching system listens for change notifications from the data source. When the source data is updated, the corresponding cache entries are invalidated. This is a more sophisticated approach that offers a balance between consistency and performance.

    - **Example:** A database trigger notifies the caching layer when a specific table is updated. The caching layer then removes the corresponding entries from the cache.

    - **Sketch:**

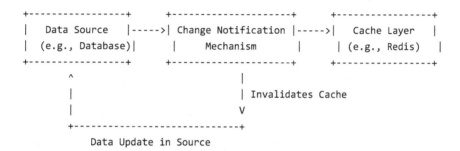

```
+------------------+       +----------------------+       +------------------+
|   Data Source    |----->| Change Notification  |----->|   Cache Layer    |
|  (e.g., Database)|      |     Mechanism        |      |  (e.g., Redis)   |
+------------------+       +----------------------+       +------------------+
         ^                            |
         |                            | Invalidates Cache
         |                            V
    +----------------------------+
           Data Update in Source
```

    In this scenario, when data is updated in the data source, a change notification mechanism (like database triggers or messaging queues) sends a signal to the cache layer, instructing it to invalidate the relevant cache entries.

- **Content Addressing:** The cache key is derived from the content of the data itself. If the content changes, the key changes, and a new cache entry is created, effectively invalidating the old data.

    - **Example:** Hashing the contents of an image file and using the hash as the cache key. If the image changes, the hash changes, so any system requesting the new image will get a cache miss and retrieve the updated version.

Choosing the right cache invalidation strategy depends on the specific requirements of the application, including the desired level of data consistency, the write volume, and the performance goals.

Caching Layers: Client-side vs. Server-side

The location of your cache – whether it resides on the client (e.g., a web browser) or on the server – dramatically impacts performance characteristics and data management strategies. Understanding the trade-offs between client-side and server-side caching is crucial for building responsive and scalable applications.

Client-Side Caching:

Client-side caching involves storing data directly on the user's device or within their application. This offers the potential for extremely low latency, as data can be retrieved without any network request.

- **Location Impacts Latency and Data Consistency:** Since the data is stored locally, retrieval is significantly faster. However, this comes at the cost of potential data staleness. If the server-side data changes, the client-side cache might hold outdated information.

    Imagine a web browser caching an image. When the user revisits the page, the image loads instantly from the local cache. However, if the image has been updated on the server, the user might see the old version until the cache is refreshed.

```
// Example of browser caching (simplified)
// The browser automatically handles caching based on HTTP headers
// set by the server (e.g., Cache-Control, Expires).
// No direct JavaScript manipulation is typically needed for basic caching.
```

In this scenario, the browser examines the `Cache-Control` header sent by the server to understand how long it should cache the image.

- **Cache Invalidation Strategies:** Invalidation is more complex with client-side caches. Several strategies exist, each with its own set of advantages and disadvantages.

  - **Time-Based Expiration:** Set a maximum age for cached data. After this time, the cache entry is considered stale and must be refreshed. This is easy to implement but doesn't guarantee data consistency.
  - **Event-Based Invalidation:** Use push notifications or similar mechanisms to inform clients when the server-side data changes. This provides more immediate invalidation but adds complexity to the application architecture.
  - **Versioning:** Incorporate a version number into the cached data. When the server data changes, the version number is incremented, forcing clients to refresh their caches.

Server-Side Caching:

Server-side caching involves storing data on the server, typically in a dedicated cache layer like Redis or Memcached, which sits in front of the main database. This reduces the load on the database and improves response times.

- **Location Impacts Latency and Data Consistency:** While not as fast as client-side caching, server-side caching still significantly reduces latency compared to querying the database directly. It also provides better data consistency, as the cache is controlled by the server.

  For instance, consider a social media application caching user profiles. When a user requests a profile, the server first checks the cache. If the profile is present and valid (not stale), it's returned directly from the cache, bypassing the database query.

```python
# Python example using Redis for server-side caching
import redis
import time

redis_client = redis.Redis(host='localhost', port=6379, db=0)

def get_user_profile(user_id):
    cached_profile = redis_client.get(f"user:{user_id}")
    if cached_profile:
        print("Profile retrieved from cache")
        return cached_profile.decode('utf-8')  # Decode from bytes

    # Simulate database query
    time.sleep(1) # Simulate a delay to query
    profile_data = f"User profile data for ID: {user_id}"
    print("Profile retrieved from database")
    redis_client.set(f"user:{user_id}", profile_data, ex=60)  # Cache for 60 seconds
    return profile_data

# Example Usage
print(get_user_profile(123))
print(get_user_profile(123))  # Retrieving again will get from cache
```

In this code, the `get_user_profile` function first checks Redis for the user's profile. If found, it returns the cached data. Otherwise, it queries the database (simulated by a delay), stores the result in Redis with an expiration time, and then returns the data.

- **Cache Invalidation Strategies:** Server-side caches offer more control over invalidation. Common strategies include:

  - **Time-To-Live (TTL):** Each cached item has an associated expiration time. After this time, the item is automatically removed from the cache.
  - **Least Recently Used (LRU):** The cache evicts the least recently used items to make room for new data.
  - **Write-Through:** Every write to the database is also written to the cache, ensuring that the cache is always up-to-date. This has higher write latency.
  - **Write-Back:** Writes are made only to the cache. The changes are asynchronously written to the database at a later time. This offers lower write latency but risks data loss if the cache fails before the changes are persisted.

A Simple Visualization

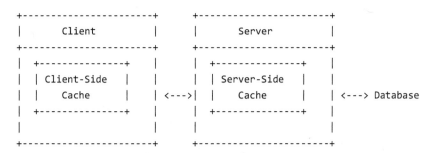

The client-side cache sits directly in the user's application (e.g., browser), allowing for fast retrieval of frequently accessed data. The server-side cache acts as an intermediary between the application server and the database, reducing the load on the database and improving response times.

Choosing between client-side and server-side caching, or using a combination of both, depends on the specific requirements of the application, including the sensitivity of the data, the frequency of updates, and the desired level of performance. A well-designed caching strategy can significantly improve the user experience and reduce the load on the backend infrastructure.

Cache Invalidation Strategies

When you use a cache (a temporary storage area) to speed up data access, you need a way to make sure the data in the cache is up-to-date. This process is called cache invalidation. If the data changes in the main source (like a database), the cache needs to know about it so it doesn't serve old, incorrect information. Choosing the right invalidation strategy is key to balancing performance and data accuracy. Here's a breakdown of common strategies:

- **Balancing staleness with performance gains:** When deciding on a cache invalidation strategy, there's always a tug-of-war. If you invalidate too frequently, you lose the performance benefits of caching because you're constantly fetching fresh data. If you invalidate too rarely, you risk serving stale (outdated) data. The ideal strategy minimizes staleness while maximizing the use of the cache.

  Imagine an e-commerce website that caches product prices. If a price changes in the database and the cache isn't updated, customers might see the wrong price. On the other hand, if the cache invalidates every few seconds, the system might spend more time refreshing the cache than serving data from it.

Now, let's look at specific cache invalidation strategies:

1. **Time-To-Live (TTL)**

   This is one of the simplest strategies. Each piece of data in the cache is assigned a "time to live" (TTL). After that time expires, the cache entry is considered invalid and is removed or refreshed.

- **How it works:** The cache checks the age of an entry. If the age is greater than the TTL, the entry is invalidated.
- **Pros:** Easy to implement.
- **Cons:** Can lead to staleness. Data might change *before* the TTL expires, but the cache will continue to serve the old data until the TTL is reached. You can't guarantee data accuracy.

Sketch:

```
+------------------+       TTL = 60 seconds       +------------------+
| Cached Data      | --------------------------> | Cached Data      |
| (e.g., Price)    |                             | (Invalidated)    |
+------------------+                             +------------------+
Data Stored              60 seconds pass                Data Expired
```

Example Code (Python):

```python
import time

cache = {}
ttl = 60  # seconds

def get_data(key):
    if key in cache and time.time() - cache[key]['timestamp'] < ttl:
        print("Serving from cache")
        return cache[key]['data']
    else:
        print("Fetching from database")
        data = fetch_from_database(key) # Assume this function exists
        cache[key] = {'data': data, 'timestamp': time.time()}
        return data

def fetch_from_database(key):
    #Simulate database call
    return "Data from DB"

# First call: fetches from database
print(get_data('product_price'))

time.sleep(30) # Wait 30 seconds

# Second call: serves from cache
print(get_data('product_price'))

time.sleep(40)  #Wait another 40 seconds, cache must have expired

#Third Call: fetches from database
print(get_data('product_price'))
```

2. **Write-Through Cache**

With this strategy, every time data is written to the main data store (e.g., the database), it is *also* written to the cache.

- **How it works:** Any update to the database is immediately reflected in the cache.
- **Pros:** High data consistency. The cache is always up-to-date with the latest changes.

- **Cons:** Higher write latency. Every write operation takes longer because it has to update both the cache and the database.

Sketch:

```
+-----------+      Write Data     +-----------+     Write Data     +-----------+
|  Client   | ------------------> |   Cache   | ------------------> | Database |
+-----------+                     +-----------+                    +-----------+
```

Example:

Imagine a system tracking user profiles. When a user updates their profile information, the updated data is written to both the database and the cache simultaneously.

This approach is suitable when data consistency is critical, and a slight increase in write latency is acceptable.

3. **Write-Back Cache (also called Write-Behind)**

This is the opposite of Write-Through. Data is first written to the cache, and then written to the main data store at a later time.

- **How it works:** Updates are made to the cache, and those changes are periodically flushed (written) to the database.
- **Pros:** Low write latency. Write operations are very fast because they only update the cache.
- **Cons:** Risk of data loss. If the cache server crashes before the changes are written to the database, the data is lost. Also, can lead to data inconsistencies if not managed carefully.

Sketch:

```
+-----------+      Write Data     +-----------+   (Later) Write Data +-----------+
|  Client   | ------------------> |   Cache   | ----------------------> | Database |
+-----------+                     +-----------+                    +-----------+
```

Example:

Consider a social media platform where users post status updates. To improve the responsiveness of the application, the updates might initially be written to a cache and then asynchronously written to the database. This allows the user interface to respond immediately without waiting for the database write operation. This is usually used when eventual consistency is fine.

4. **Invalidation Based on Data Change (also called Event-Based Invalidation)**

Instead of relying on time or write operations, this strategy invalidates the cache whenever the underlying data changes.

- **How it works:** The system monitors changes in the database. When a change occurs, it sends a signal to the cache to invalidate the corresponding entry.
- **Pros:** High data consistency. The cache is invalidated only when necessary.
- **Cons:** More complex to implement. Requires a mechanism to detect and propagate data changes.

Sketch:

```
+-----------+     Data Change     +-----------+    Invalidate    +-----------+
| Database  | --------------------> | Monitoring| --------------------> |   Cache   |
+-----------+                     +-----------+                    +-----------+
```

Example:

Think of a news website. When a breaking news article is updated in the database, the system sends an event to the cache, which then invalidates the cached version of that article. The next time a user requests the article, it will be fetched fresh from the database and re-cached.

Example Code (Simplified):

```
# Assumes a message queue system is in place (e.g., Redis Pub/Sub, RabbitMQ)

def data_changed_handler(key):
    # This function is called when the data changes in the database
    print(f"Invalidating cache for key: {key}")
    invalidate_cache(key)

def invalidate_cache(key):
    # Remove the data from the cache
    if key in cache:
        del cache[key]
        print(f"Key {key} removed from cache.")
    else:
        print(f"Key {key} not found in cache.")


# Simulated Database update
def update_database(key, new_data):
    # Simulate updating the database
    print(f"Database Updated: {key} with {new_data}")

    # After the update, signal the cache to invalidate
    data_changed_handler(key) # Simulate a trigger that calls data_changed_handler

# Assume cache is a global dictionary
cache = {}

update_database('product_price', '19.99')  # Simulate update the price
```

5. **Least Recently Used (LRU)**

This strategy focuses on the cache itself. When the cache is full and a new item needs to be added, the least recently used item is removed to make space.

- o **How it works:** The cache keeps track of when each entry was last accessed. When the cache is full, the entry that hasn't been used for the longest time is evicted.
- o **Pros:** Simple to implement and often effective.
- o **Cons:** Doesn't consider the importance of the data. An infrequently used item might still be important.

Sketch:

```
[ Item A (last used: 1 min ago) ]
[ Item B (last used: 5 min ago) ]
[ Item C (last used: 30 min ago) ]  <-- LRU Item
Cache is Full.  New Item D needs to be added. Item C is evicted.
```

Example:

Many caching libraries provide built-in support for LRU eviction.

```
from collections import OrderedDict

class LRUCache:
```

```python
    def __init__(self, capacity):
        self.capacity = capacity
        self.cache = OrderedDict()

    def get(self, key):
        if key not in self.cache:
            return None
        else:
            self.cache.move_to_end(key)
            return self.cache[key]

    def put(self, key, value):
        self.cache[key] = value
        self.cache.move_to_end(key)
        if len(self.cache) > self.capacity:
            self.cache.popitem(last = False) #Remove the oldest item

lru_cache = LRUCache(capacity=3)
lru_cache.put('A', 1)
lru_cache.put('B', 2)
lru_cache.put('C', 3)

print(lru_cache.get('A')) #Output: 1

lru_cache.put('D', 4) #This will evict B since B was Least Recently Used before "A" was acc
print(lru_cache.get('B')) #Output: None
```

Each of these strategies has its strengths and weaknesses, and the right choice depends on the specific requirements of your application, including the frequency of data changes, the importance of data consistency, and the acceptable level of latency.

Chapter 16 Performance, Efficiency, and Optimization-Memory Management and Performance Tuning in Large-Scale Systems

- **Understanding Memory Bottlenecks:** Identify memory as a key performance bottleneck in data-intensive applications.
- **Memory Allocation Strategies:** Different memory allocation strategies impact performance.

- **Garbage Collection (GC) Overhead:** GC pauses can introduce latency spikes; minimizing GC overhead is crucial.
- **Off-Heap Memory:** Utilizing off-heap memory for large datasets to reduce GC pressure.
- **Performance Tuning Techniques:**
  - Profiling and monitoring: Essential for identifying memory-related performance issues.

Understanding Memory Bottlenecks

Memory can often become a major obstacle to achieving high performance in applications that handle large amounts of data. These are frequently referred to as data-intensive applications. When an application struggles to access or manage memory efficiently, it creates a "bottleneck," slowing down the entire process.

Think of it like this: Imagine a factory where workers need raw materials to build products. If the supply of raw materials (memory) is limited or the workers (application) have trouble accessing it, production grinds to a halt, even if the workers are highly skilled and the machines are top-of-the-line.

Sketch:

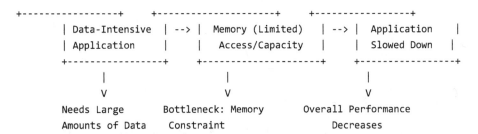

```
+------------------+      +----------------------+      +------------------+
| Data-Intensive   | -->  |  Memory (Limited)    | -->  | Application      |
| Application      |      |   Access/Capacity    |      | Slowed Down      |
+------------------+      +----------------------+      +------------------+
         |                          |                          |
         V                          V                          V
   Needs Large            Bottleneck: Memory         Overall Performance
   Amounts of Data        Constraint                 Decreases
```

In computing terms, a memory bottleneck manifests in various ways:

- **Slow Data Retrieval:** The application spends an excessive amount of time waiting to read data from memory. If the data is not readily available in the fastest memory (like the processor's cache), it needs to be fetched from slower memory (like RAM). This constant back-and-forth slows down processing.

- **Insufficient Memory:** The application simply doesn't have enough memory to store all the data it needs. This forces the application to use slower storage (like the hard drive or SSD) as a temporary "overflow" space, significantly reducing performance. This is often referred to as swapping or paging.

- **Inefficient Memory Access Patterns:** The way the application accesses memory can also contribute to bottlenecks. Accessing memory in a random or scattered manner is much slower than accessing it sequentially.

- **High Memory Latency:** The time it takes to access a specific location in memory is high, which leads to delays in processing data.

To illustrate with a simple example, consider a Java program that processes a very large array of integers:

```java
public class MemoryBottleneckExample {

    public static void main(String[] args) {
        // Create a large array (e.g., 1 billion integers)
        int arraySize = 1_000_000_000;
        int[] largeArray = new int[arraySize];

        // Initialize the array with some values
        for (int i = 0; i < arraySize; i++) {
            largeArray[i] = i;
```

```
    }

    // Perform a simple operation on the array (e.g., sum all elements)
    long sum = 0;
    for (int i = 0; i < arraySize; i++) {
        sum += largeArray[i];
    }

    System.out.println("Sum: " + sum);
    }
}
```

In this example, if the `largeArray` exceeds the available memory, the operating system might start swapping parts of the array to disk. Each access to a swapped-out portion of the array will result in a significant delay, creating a memory bottleneck and slowing down the entire program.

Memory Allocation Strategies

The way memory is assigned and managed by an application has a direct impact on performance. Different strategies suit different use cases, and choosing the wrong one can lead to inefficiencies.

Consider these key factors:

- **Allocation Overhead:** Each time an application requests memory, there is a small overhead associated with finding and allocating a suitable block of memory. If the application frequently allocates small blocks of memory, this overhead can become significant.

- **Fragmentation:** Over time, memory can become fragmented. This means that although there is enough total free memory, it is scattered in small, non-contiguous blocks. When the application needs to allocate a large block of memory, it may fail even if the total free memory is sufficient.

    Sketch:

```
+-------+-------+-------+-------+-------+-------+-------+
| Used  | Free  | Used  | Free  | Used  | Free  | Used  |
+-------+-------+-------+-------+-------+-------+-------+
         ^       ^                       ^
         |       |                       |
    Small Free  Small Free         Small Free
    Blocks      Blocks             Blocks
```

In the above sketch small free blocks represent fragmentation, which makes it difficult to alloc

- **Deallocation Speed:** When an application no longer needs a block of memory, it should be deallocated so that it can be reused. The speed of deallocation can also affect performance.

Common memory allocation strategies include:

- **Stack Allocation:** Used for local variables and function call frames. Allocation and deallocation are very fast because they happen in a predictable order (LIFO - Last In, First Out). However, the stack has a limited size, and memory allocated on the stack is automatically deallocated when the function returns.
- **Heap Allocation:** Used for dynamically allocated memory (e.g., using new in Java or C++). Heap allocation is more flexible than stack allocation, as the size of the allocated memory can be determined at runtime. However, heap allocation is slower than stack allocation and can lead to fragmentation.
- **Memory Pools:** A technique where a fixed-size block of memory is divided into smaller, equal-sized blocks. The application can then allocate and deallocate memory from this pool very quickly, avoiding the overhead

of general-purpose heap allocation. This is particularly useful when the application needs to allocate and deallocate many small objects.

Here's a simple example of memory allocation in C++ using new (heap allocation):

```cpp
#include <iostream>

int main() {
    // Allocate an integer on the heap
    int myInt = new int;

    // Assign a value to the integer
    myInt = 42;

    // Print the value
    std::cout << "Value: " << myInt << std::endl;

    // Deallocate the memory
    delete myInt;
    myInt = nullptr; // Good practice to avoid dangling pointers

    return 0;
}
```

In contrast, a stack allocation would look like this:

```cpp
#include <iostream>

int main() {
    // Allocate an integer on the stack
    int myInt = 42;

    // Print the value
    std::cout << "Value: " << myInt << std::endl;

    // No need to deallocate, memory is automatically deallocated
    // when the function returns

    return 0;
}
```

The key difference is that the heap allocation requires explicit deallocation using delete, while the stack allocation is automatic.

Garbage Collection (GC) Overhead

In languages like Java and C#, memory management is largely automated through garbage collection. The garbage collector periodically identifies and reclaims memory that is no longer being used by the application. While this simplifies development by relieving the programmer of manual memory management, it comes at a cost: garbage collection pauses.

- **GC Pauses:** When the garbage collector runs, it typically needs to pause the application to ensure memory consistency. These pauses can introduce latency spikes, which can be particularly problematic for real-time or interactive applications. The duration and frequency of GC pauses depend on several factors, including the size of the heap, the garbage collection algorithm used, and the allocation rate of the application.

- **Minimizing GC Overhead:** Reducing GC overhead is crucial for achieving optimal performance in garbage-collected environments. Several techniques can be used to minimize GC overhead:

    - **Object Pooling:** Reusing objects instead of creating new ones can reduce the allocation rate and thus reduce GC frequency.
    - **Avoiding Excessive Object Creation:** Being mindful of object creation, particularly in performance-critical sections of code, can significantly reduce GC pressure.
    - **Choosing the Right GC Algorithm:** Different GC algorithms have different performance characteristics. Some algorithms are optimized for low latency, while others are optimized for high throughput. Selecting the right algorithm for the application's needs can improve performance.
    - **Tuning GC Parameters:** Garbage collectors often have configurable parameters that can be tuned to optimize performance. For example, the heap size can be adjusted to balance memory usage and GC frequency.

Here's a Java example that illustrates excessive object creation:

```java
public class GarbageCollectionExample {

    public static void main(String[] args) {
        long startTime = System.currentTimeMillis();

        // Simulate a lot of object creation
        for (int i = 0; i < 1_000_000; i++) {
            String temp = new String("Temporary String"); // Creates a new String object in eacl
        }

        long endTime = System.currentTimeMillis();
        System.out.println("Time taken: " + (endTime - startTime) + " ms");
    }
}
```

In this example, a new `String` object is created in each iteration of the loop. This generates a lot of garbage and can trigger frequent GC cycles. A more efficient approach would be to reuse the same `String` object:

```java
public class GarbageCollectionExampleOptimized {

    public static void main(String[] args) {
        long startTime = System.currentTimeMillis();

        // Reuse a single String object
        String temp = "Temporary String"; // Only one String object is created

        // Simulate operations using the same object
        for (int i = 0; i < 1_000_000; i++) {
            // Perform some operation with the string
            temp.length(); // Example: Accessing the length does not create new objects
        }

        long endTime = System.currentTimeMillis();
        System.out.println("Time taken: " + (endTime - startTime) + " ms");
    }
}
```

This optimized version reduces GC pressure by minimizing object creation.

Off-Heap Memory

Off-heap memory refers to memory that is not managed by the garbage collector. It is allocated directly by the application using mechanisms provided by the operating system or specialized libraries.

- **Utilizing Off-Heap Memory:** Off-heap memory is particularly useful for storing large datasets that would otherwise put significant pressure on the garbage collector. By storing data off-heap, the application can reduce the frequency and duration of GC pauses, leading to improved performance.

- **Manual Memory Management:** However, off-heap memory comes with a responsibility: the application must manage this memory manually. This includes allocating, deallocating, and tracking the memory. Failure to properly manage off-heap memory can lead to memory leaks or other memory-related errors.

- **Serialization/Deserialization:** Data stored off-heap often needs to be serialized (converted into a byte stream) when written to off-heap memory and deserialized (converted back into objects) when read from off-heap memory. This serialization/deserialization process can add overhead, so it's important to choose efficient serialization techniques.

Here's an example using Java's `ByteBuffer` to allocate off-heap memory:

```java
import java.nio.ByteBuffer;

public class OffHeapMemoryExample {

    public static void main(String[] args) {
        int dataSize = 1024  1024  100; // 100 MB
        // Allocate off-heap memory
        ByteBuffer offHeapBuffer = ByteBuffer.allocateDirect(dataSize);

        // Write data to the off-heap buffer
        for (int i = 0; i < dataSize; i++) {
            offHeapBuffer.put((byte) (i % 256)); // Write some data
        }

        // Read data from the off-heap buffer
        offHeapBuffer.position(0); // Reset the position to the beginning
        byte firstByte = offHeapBuffer.get();
        System.out.println("First byte: " + firstByte);

        // No explicit deallocation needed (ByteBuffer will release the memory when garbage col
        // However, it's good practice to release it explicitly if possible
        //   ((sun.nio.ch.DirectBuffer)offHeapBuffer).cleaner().clean(); // Requires internal acc

        System.out.println("Off-heap memory example completed.");
    }
}
```

In this example, `ByteBuffer.allocateDirect()` allocates memory directly from the operating system, bypassing the Java heap and garbage collector. Note that manually releasing the off-heap memory can be tricky and may require using internal APIs (as commented out in the code). Libraries like Chronicle Map and Ehcache provide higher-level abstractions for managing off-heap memory.

Performance Tuning Techniques

Identifying and resolving memory bottlenecks requires a systematic approach. Profiling and monitoring are essential tools in this process.

- **Profiling and Monitoring:**

- o **Memory Profilers:** Tools like VisualVM, JProfiler (for Java), or memory profilers built into IDEs (like those in Visual Studio for .NET) allow you to monitor memory usage, identify memory leaks, and analyze object allocation patterns.
- o **Garbage Collection Monitoring:** Tools that provide insights into GC activity, such as GC logs and monitoring dashboards, can help you understand GC frequency, duration, and the amount of memory reclaimed.
- o **Operating System Monitoring:** Tools like top (Linux/macOS) or Task Manager (Windows) can provide a high-level overview of memory usage at the system level, helping you identify if the application is exhausting available memory.

By carefully profiling and monitoring memory usage, you can pinpoint the specific areas of your application that are contributing to memory bottlenecks. This information allows you to apply targeted optimizations and improve overall performance.

For instance, in Java, you can enable GC logging to analyze GC behavior. Add the following JVM options when starting your application:

```
-verbose:gc -Xloggc:gc.log -XX:+PrintGCDetails -XX:+PrintGCTimeStamps
```

This will generate a gc.log file containing detailed information about garbage collection events, including the amount of memory reclaimed, the duration of GC pauses, and the GC algorithm used. Analyzing this log can help identify GC-related performance issues.

Memory Allocation Strategies

Different memory allocation strategies significantly impact application performance. The way memory is allocated and managed directly influences the speed and efficiency of data access, and thus, the overall responsiveness of the system. Let's explore the key strategies and their implications.

Understanding the Basics

Before diving into specific strategies, it's essential to understand the fundamental process of memory allocation. When a program needs to store data, it requests memory from the operating system (OS). The OS, in turn, provides a block of memory that the program can use. This process, while seemingly simple, involves several layers of complexity and different approaches.

There are two primary ways memory can be allocated: statically and dynamically.

1. Static Allocation

Static allocation happens at compile time. The amount of memory needed is determined *before* the program runs. Variables declared with fixed sizes, global variables, and arrays with predefined dimensions are examples of statically allocated memory.

- **Advantages:**
  - o Fast allocation: Because the size is known in advance, allocation is very quick.
  - o Simple to manage: Memory is allocated once and remains allocated throughout the program's execution.
- **Disadvantages:**
  - o Inflexible: The size cannot be changed during runtime. If you need more or less memory than initially allocated, you're out of luck.
  - o Wasted memory: If the allocated memory is not fully utilized, the unused portion is wasted.

Code Example (C/C++)

```
#include <stdio.h>

int main() {
```

```
int numbers[10]; // Static array of 10 integers

for (int i = 0; i < 10; i++) {
  numbers[i] = i  2;
  printf("numbers[%d] = %d\n", i, numbers[i]);
}

return 0;
}
```

In this example, the numbers array is statically allocated. The compiler knows at compile time that it needs to reserve space for 10 integers.

2. Dynamic Allocation

Dynamic allocation happens at runtime. The program requests memory as needed during execution. This provides flexibility in terms of memory usage.

- **Advantages:**
  - Flexible: Memory can be allocated and deallocated as needed.
  - Efficient: Memory is only allocated when required, reducing wasted space.
- **Disadvantages:**
  - Slower allocation: Allocating memory during runtime incurs overhead.
  - Requires management: The program is responsible for freeing allocated memory to prevent memory leaks.
  - Fragmentation: Over time, memory can become fragmented, making it difficult to allocate large contiguous blocks.

Code Example (C/C++)

```
#include <stdio.h>
#include <stdlib.h>

int main() {
  int numbers;
  int size;

  printf("Enter the number of integers: ");
  scanf("%d", &size);

  numbers = (int) malloc(size  sizeof(int)); // Dynamic allocation

  if (numbers == NULL) {
    printf("Memory allocation failed!\n");
    return 1;
  }

  for (int i = 0; i < size; i++) {
    numbers[i] = i  2;
    printf("numbers[%d] = %d\n", i, numbers[i]);
  }

  free(numbers); // Deallocate memory
  numbers = NULL;
```

```
  return 0;
}
```

In this example, the `numbers` array is dynamically allocated using `malloc`. The size of the array is determined at runtime based on user input. It is crucial to call `free` to release the allocated memory when it's no longer needed.

Specific Memory Allocation Strategies

Within dynamic allocation, several strategies can be employed:

- **First-Fit:** The allocator scans the list of free memory blocks and allocates the first block that is large enough to satisfy the request. Simple to implement but can lead to fragmentation.

- **Best-Fit:** The allocator searches the entire list of free blocks and allocates the smallest block that is large enough. Reduces fragmentation compared to first-fit, but searching the entire list can be slower.

- **Worst-Fit:** The allocator searches for the largest available block and allocates it. The idea is to leave larger free blocks after allocation, reducing the likelihood of small, unusable fragments. However, it often leads to more medium-sized fragments.

- **Buddy System:** Divides memory into power-of-2 sized blocks. When a request comes in, the smallest block that is large enough is repeatedly divided until a block of the required size is obtained. Efficient for allocation and deallocation but can lead to internal fragmentation (unused space within an allocated block).

- **Slab Allocation:** Used in operating systems and some high-performance applications. Caches frequently used objects to avoid repeated allocation and deallocation. Improves performance by reusing pre-initialized objects.

Visual Representation of Allocation Strategies

Here's a simple conceptual sketch to illustrate the difference between First-Fit, Best-Fit, and Worst-Fit:

```
Available Memory: | 100 | 50  | 200 | 75  |
Request Size:     50

First-Fit: Allocates the first 100 block.
          Result: |  50 | 50  | 200 | 75  |

Best-Fit:  Allocates the 50 block.
          Result: | 100 | ALOC | 200 | 75  |

Worst-Fit: Allocates the 200 block.
          Result: | 100 | 50  | ALOC| 75  |    Remaining: 150 in the third one
```

(ALOC means allocated)

This sketch simplifies the visualization. In a real-world scenario, free memory would be more fragmented, and the allocator would have to manage pointers and metadata to track the location and size of free blocks.

Choosing the Right Strategy

The optimal memory allocation strategy depends on the specific application requirements. Factors to consider include:

- **Allocation speed:** How quickly memory needs to be allocated.
- **Fragmentation:** The amount of wasted memory due to fragmentation.
- **Complexity:** The ease of implementing and maintaining the allocator.
- **Predictability:** The consistency of allocation times.

For real-time systems, deterministic allocation strategies (those with predictable allocation times) are often preferred, even if they might lead to some fragmentation. In other applications, minimizing fragmentation might be the primary goal.

Understanding the trade-offs associated with different memory allocation strategies is crucial for optimizing application performance and ensuring efficient resource utilization. Careful consideration of these factors will lead to better performing and more robust software.

Garbage Collection (GC) Overhead

Garbage Collection (GC) is an automatic memory management process that reclaims memory occupied by objects that are no longer in use by a program. While GC simplifies development by freeing programmers from manual memory management, it introduces its own set of performance considerations, collectively known as GC overhead. These overheads primarily manifest as pauses in application execution.

GC Pauses and Latency Spikes:

The primary impact of garbage collection on application performance is the introduction of pauses. During these pauses, the garbage collector halts the execution of the program to identify and reclaim unused memory. These pauses can range from milliseconds to seconds, depending on the garbage collection algorithm, heap size, and the amount of garbage to be collected.

These pauses directly translate to latency spikes in the application. Latency refers to the time it takes for an application to respond to a request. When a GC pause occurs, any requests being processed at that moment are delayed, resulting in a noticeable increase in response time, or a "spike" in latency.

Imagine a scenario where an e-commerce website is processing a customer's order. If a GC pause occurs during this critical transaction, the order processing will be delayed. The customer might experience a slow response, potentially leading to frustration and even abandonment of the purchase. The frequency and duration of these pauses are key metrics to monitor in data-intensive applications.

Minimizing GC Overhead:

Minimizing GC overhead is crucial for achieving consistent and predictable performance, especially in latency-sensitive applications. There are several strategies to reduce GC overhead:

1. **Choosing the Right Garbage Collector:** Different garbage collectors employ different algorithms and are optimized for different workloads. For example, the Garbage First (G1) collector is designed to minimize pause times by collecting garbage in smaller regions of the heap concurrently. The choice of garbage collector depends on the specific application's requirements for throughput, pause time, and memory footprint.

   - **Serial GC:** Simplest GC, uses a single thread to collect garbage. Suitable for small applications with limited memory and running on single-processor machines. Causes long pauses.

   - **Parallel GC:** (also called Throughput Collector) Uses multiple threads to perform garbage collection, reducing overall GC time. However, it can still cause significant pauses.

   - **Concurrent Mark Sweep (CMS) GC:** Tries to minimize pauses by doing most of its work concurrently with the application. Can lead to fragmentation and longer full GC pauses.

   - **G1 GC:** Divides the heap into regions and collects garbage in the regions with the most garbage first. Aims to balance throughput and pause times. Often the preferred choice for large heaps.

2. **Heap Sizing:** Configuring the heap size appropriately is crucial. A heap that is too small will trigger frequent garbage collections, leading to increased overhead. A heap that is too large can increase the duration of garbage collection pauses. Optimal heap size is best determined through performance testing and monitoring.

   Heap Size Configuration Example:

```
java -Xms4g -Xmx8g MyApp
```

-**Xms4g**: Sets the initial heap size to 4 gigabytes. -**Xmx8g**: Sets the maximum heap size to 8 gigabytes.

3. **Object Pooling:** Creating and destroying objects frequently can put a strain on the garbage collector. Object pooling involves reusing existing objects instead of creating new ones, reducing the frequency of garbage collection.

Object Pooling Example (simplified):

```java
import java.util.ArrayList;
import java.util.List;

class ReusableObject {
    // Object properties and methods
}

class ObjectPool {
    private List<ReusableObject> available = new ArrayList<>();
    private List<ReusableObject> inUse = new ArrayList<>();

    public ReusableObject acquire() {
        if (available.isEmpty()) {
            return new ReusableObject(); // Create new if pool is empty
        } else {
            ReusableObject object = available.remove(0);
            inUse.add(object);
            return object;
        }
    }

    public void release(ReusableObject object) {
        inUse.remove(object);
        available.add(object);
    }
}
```

In this example, the `ObjectPool` manages a collection of `ReusableObject` instances. Instead of creating new `ReusableObject` instances every time one is needed, the `acquire()` method checks if there are any available objects in the pool. If so, it returns an existing object. When the object is no longer needed, the `release()` method returns it to the pool for reuse. This approach avoids the overhead of creating and destroying objects repeatedly, reducing GC pressure.

4. **Reducing Object Allocation:** Minimizing unnecessary object creation can significantly reduce the workload on the garbage collector. This can be achieved through techniques such as using primitive data types instead of objects, reusing existing objects, and avoiding the creation of temporary objects.

5. **Short-Lived Objects:** Design the application such that most objects have a short lifespan. Short-lived objects are collected more efficiently by generational garbage collectors.

Sketch of Generational GC:

```
+--------------------+
| Young Generation   |-----> Minor GC (Frequent)
|   +--------------+ |
|   | Eden Space   | |
|   +--------------+ |
```

```
|  | Survivor Space 1|  |
|  +---------------+  |
|  | Survivor Space 2|  |
|  +---------------+  |
+---------------------+
         |Promotion|
         V
+---------------------+
| Old Generation      |-----> Major GC (Less Frequent)
+---------------------+
```

Explanation of the Sketch:

The sketch illustrates the basic principle of Generational Garbage Collection. The heap is divided into two primary generations: the Young Generation and the Old Generation.

- **Young Generation:** This is where new objects are initially created. It's further divided into Eden Space and two Survivor Spaces. Minor GC is performed frequently in this generation, collecting short-lived objects efficiently. Objects that survive multiple minor GC cycles are "promoted" to the Old Generation.
- **Old Generation:** Contains objects that have survived several minor GC cycles, implying they are longer-lived. Major GC is performed less frequently in this generation as it involves a larger scope and more overhead.

By focusing garbage collection efforts on the Young Generation, where most objects die quickly, generational GC reduces the overall GC overhead and improves application performance.

Monitoring and Tuning:

Effective garbage collection tuning requires continuous monitoring of GC performance metrics. Tools like JConsole, VisualVM, and dedicated monitoring solutions provide insights into heap usage, GC pause times, and GC frequency. Analyzing these metrics helps identify areas for optimization and fine-tune GC parameters for optimal performance. Profiling and monitoring tools pinpoint memory leaks and excessive object creation, guiding optimization efforts. Remember that GC tuning is an iterative process. Changes in application code or data patterns may require adjustments to GC configuration.

Off-Heap Memory

Utilizing off-heap memory is a technique used to manage large datasets and reduce the burden on the garbage collector (GC). To understand this, it's important to know how memory is typically managed in environments like the Java Virtual Machine (JVM).

The Problem with On-Heap Memory

Most programming languages, like Java, automatically manage memory using a garbage collector. When you create objects, they are stored in a region of memory called the heap. The garbage collector periodically scans the heap, identifies objects that are no longer in use, and reclaims the memory they occupy.

While garbage collection automates memory management, it comes at a cost. The garbage collector needs to pause the application to perform its work. These pauses, called GC pauses, can introduce latency spikes, which can be detrimental to performance, especially in real-time or high-throughput applications. The more data you store on the heap, the more work the garbage collector has to do, and the longer the GC pauses become.

Imagine the JVM's memory heap is a shared whiteboard. Everyone can write and erase on it. The Garbage Collector is the person responsible for erasing the old and irrelevant writings to free up space. When the whiteboard is almost full, the Garbage Collector needs to pause everyone to do a thorough cleaning.

The Solution: Off-Heap Memory

Off-heap memory provides a way to store data outside of the JVM heap. This means that the garbage collector doesn't need to manage this memory. This approach is beneficial for the following reasons:

1. **Reduced GC Pressure:** By storing large datasets off-heap, you reduce the amount of data the garbage collector has to scan, which in turn reduces the frequency and duration of GC pauses.

2. **Larger Datasets:** The amount of memory available on the heap is often limited by the JVM configuration. Off-heap memory allows you to work with datasets that are larger than the available heap space. The amount of memory available for the heap is often limited by the JVM settings.

3. **Improved Performance:** Storing data off-heap can improve performance by reducing GC overhead and allowing for more efficient memory management.

Consider off-heap memory as having your own private whiteboard. Only you can write and erase it. The Garbage Collector doesn't need to care about your whiteboard at all.

How Off-Heap Memory Works

Off-heap memory is typically allocated using native operating system calls. The programming language provides mechanisms to access and manipulate this memory. For example, in Java, you can use `ByteBuffer` with `allocateDirect` to allocate off-heap memory.

Example (Java):

```java
import java.nio.ByteBuffer;

public class OffHeapExample {

    public static void main(String[] args) {
        // Allocate 10MB of off-heap memory
        int size = 10  1024  1024;
        ByteBuffer buffer = ByteBuffer.allocateDirect(size);

        // Write data to the buffer
        for (int i = 0; i < size; i++) {
            buffer.put(i, (byte) (i % 256)); // Example data
        }

        // Read data from the buffer
        for (int i = 0; i < 10; i++) {
            byte value = buffer.get(i);
            System.out.println("Value at index " + i + ": " + value);
        }

        //Important you should release the memory if you are done!
        //Because this memory is not managed by the Garbage Collector (GC)
        // clean(buffer); //this code should release the memory but it may be unsafe operation,
    }

    /
    private static void clean(ByteBuffer buffer) {
        if (buffer.isDirect()) {
            ((DirectBuffer) buffer).cleaner().clean();
        }
    }
}
```

```
    /
}
```

In this example, `ByteBuffer.allocateDirect(size)` allocates off-heap memory. You can then use the `put` and `get` methods to write and read data from the buffer.

Key Takeaways:

- `ByteBuffer.allocateDirect()` creates a memory region outside the control of the JVM's garbage collector.
- This can reduce GC pressure, but it also means you are responsible for managing the lifecycle of this memory. Failing to release off-heap memory can lead to memory leaks.
- Reading and writing data involves native calls and memory copying, which is faster than garbage collection.
- Accessing off-heap memory typically involves more overhead than accessing on-heap memory, so it's best suited for large datasets where the benefits of reduced GC overhead outweigh the access costs.

Important Considerations

1. **Manual Memory Management:** With off-heap memory, you are responsible for managing the memory yourself. You need to allocate the memory, and you need to free it when you are done with it. Failure to do so can lead to memory leaks. Unlike heap memory, the garbage collector does not automatically reclaim off-heap memory.

2. **Complexity:** Using off-heap memory adds complexity to your code. You need to be careful to avoid memory leaks and other memory-related errors.

3. **Access Overhead:** Accessing off-heap memory can be slower than accessing on-heap memory because it involves native calls. Therefore, off-heap memory is most effective when dealing with large datasets where the benefits of reduced GC overhead outweigh the cost of accessing the memory.

When to Use Off-Heap Memory

Off-heap memory is a valuable tool for specific scenarios:

- **Large Caches:** Applications that maintain large caches of data can benefit from storing the cache off-heap.

- **Data Processing Pipelines:** Data-intensive applications that process large volumes of data can use off-heap memory to reduce GC overhead and improve performance.

- **High-Performance Computing:** Applications that require low latency and high throughput can use off-heap memory to minimize GC pauses.

In summary: Off-heap memory is a powerful technique for managing large datasets and reducing GC overhead. However, it's important to understand the trade-offs involved and use it appropriately. Properly managing off-heap memory involves careful allocation, usage, and deallocation to prevent memory leaks and ensure efficient application performance.

Performance Tuning Techniques

Profiling and monitoring are essential for identifying memory-related performance issues.

Profiling is like being a detective for your program's memory usage. It involves carefully watching how your application uses memory while it runs. This allows you to pinpoint exactly where the problems are. For example, you might find that a specific part of your code is creating a large number of objects that are never used, leading to a memory leak. Or, you might see that certain data structures are growing much larger than expected, consuming excessive memory.

Consider a Java application. You can use profiling tools like VisualVM or the Java Profiler in IntelliJ IDEA to monitor memory allocation and garbage collection. You can use profiling tools that visually show memory allocation over time. If you see a steady increase in memory usage that doesn't decrease (even after garbage collection runs), that's a strong indication of a memory leak. Profilers will let you trace that back to the specific lines of code creating the objects that are not collected.

```java
// Example code (Illustrative)
public class MemoryHog {

    public static void main(String[] args) {
        List<Object> list = new ArrayList<>();
        while (true) {
            list.add(new Object()); // Continously adding Objects to list
        }
    }
}
```

If you run this program and profile it, you will see the memory usage steadily climb until the program runs out of memory. The profiler allows you to identify the `list.add(new Object())` line as the source of the problem.

Monitoring goes hand-in-hand with profiling. While profiling is typically done in a development or testing environment to diagnose specific problems, monitoring is about keeping a continuous eye on your application in production. You're looking for trends and patterns in memory usage, garbage collection times, and other performance metrics. Monitoring helps you detect memory-related problems *before* they cause crashes or slowdowns.

Think of monitoring as setting up alarms in your house. You configure thresholds for memory usage, GC pause times, etc. If these thresholds are exceeded, an alert is triggered, notifying you that something might be wrong. Common monitoring tools include Prometheus, Grafana, and various cloud-provider monitoring services.

Let's consider scenario to implement the monitoring:

1. **Select Metrics:** Choose key metrics to track such as heap usage, non-heap usage, GC time, and the number of GC collections.

2. **Set up Monitoring Tools:** Integrate with tools like Prometheus for data collection and Grafana for visualization.

3. **Define Alerts:** Configure alerts for when memory usage exceeds a threshold (e.g., 80% of heap used) or when GC times are too long.

4. **Example using Micrometer:** Micrometer is a popular library that allows you to easily export metrics to various monitoring systems.

```java
import io.micrometer.core.instrument.MeterRegistry;
import io.micrometer.core.instrument.Metrics;
import io.micrometer.core.instrument.binder.jvm.JvmMemoryMetrics;
import io.micrometer.prometheus.PrometheusConfig;
import io.micrometer.prometheus.PrometheusMeterRegistry;

public class MonitoringExample {

    public static void main(String[] args) {
        // Configure Prometheus registry
        PrometheusMeterRegistry registry = new PrometheusMeterRegistry(PrometheusConfig.DEF

        // Bind JVM memory metrics
        new JvmMemoryMetrics().bindTo(registry);
```

```
    // Make the registry available globally
    Metrics.addRegistry(registry);

    // Simulate memory usage
    List<Object> list = new ArrayList<>();
    while (true) {
        list.add(new byte[1024  1024]); // Allocate 1MB
        try {
            Thread.sleep(100);
        } catch (InterruptedException e) {
            Thread.currentThread().interrupt();
        }
    }

  }
}
```

This sets up Prometheus to collect JVM memory metrics. Then, configure Grafana to visualize these metrics, creating dashboards to monitor memory usage over time. Alert rules can be set to trigger when memory usage exceeds a predefined threshold.

In essence, profiling is detailed, targeted investigation, while monitoring is continuous, broad-based surveillance. Both are essential for maintaining a healthy and performant application.

Profiling and Monitoring: Unveiling Memory Performance

Profiling and monitoring are indispensable tools for identifying and resolving memory-related performance bottlenecks in data-intensive applications. They provide insights into how memory is being used, allowing developers to pinpoint areas where optimization can have the greatest impact. Without these techniques, optimizing memory usage becomes a guessing game.

Why are Profiling and Monitoring Essential?

Think of your application's memory usage as a city's traffic flow. Without traffic cameras and monitoring systems, you wouldn't know where the congestion points are. Similarly, profiling and monitoring act as the "cameras" and "sensors" for your application's memory, showing you exactly where the memory "traffic jams" occur.

- **Pinpointing Bottlenecks:** These techniques reveal which parts of your code are consuming the most memory and which data structures are the largest. For example, a profiler might show that a particular function is allocating a large number of temporary objects that are never explicitly released, leading to memory pressure.
- **Detecting Memory Leaks:** Memory leaks occur when memory is allocated but never freed, gradually depleting available memory. Monitoring tools can detect this slow but steady decline in available memory, alerting you to potential leaks before they cause the application to crash.
- **Understanding Garbage Collection Behavior:** Garbage collection (GC) reclaims memory occupied by objects that are no longer in use. However, GC cycles can pause application execution, leading to latency spikes. Profiling and monitoring can reveal how frequently GC cycles occur, how long they take, and which objects are being collected the most. This information is vital for optimizing GC settings and reducing GC overhead.
- **Validating Optimizations:** After applying memory optimization techniques, profiling and monitoring are crucial for verifying that those techniques actually improved performance. They provide objective data to confirm whether memory usage has been reduced, GC frequency has decreased, or overall application responsiveness has improved.

Practical Examples

Let's illustrate with a Java example, a popular language for data-intensive applications:

```java
import java.util.ArrayList;
import java.util.List;

public class MemoryHog {

    public static void main(String[] args) throws InterruptedException {
        List<String> data = new ArrayList<>();

        for (int i = 0; i < 1000000; i++) {
            data.add("This is a very long string " + i);
        }

        System.out.println("Data loaded into memory.  Press Enter to continue and potentially t
        System.in.read();

        data = null; // Remove reference to the data.

        System.out.println("Reference removed.  Press Enter to exit (and allow GC to clean up).'
        System.in.read();
    }
}
```

In this simplified example, a large amount of string data is loaded into an ArrayList. Profiling this code using tools like VisualVM or JProfiler would immediately highlight the `ArrayList` and the strings it contains as significant memory consumers. Running this code without profiling would not reveal any memory issue until the application crashed.

Profiling Tools and Techniques

Profiling and monitoring require the use of specialized tools. Some common options include:

- **Java:** VisualVM, JProfiler, YourKit, Java Mission Control
- **Python:** cProfile, memory_profiler
- **C++:** Valgrind, gperftools
- **General Purpose:** Perf (Linux), specialized APM (Application Performance Monitoring) solutions.

These tools offer different functionalities, but they generally allow you to:

- **Track memory allocation:** See which parts of the code allocate the most memory.
- **Identify memory leaks:** Detect memory that is allocated but never freed.
- **Monitor garbage collection:** Observe the frequency and duration of GC cycles.
- **Analyze heap dumps:** Examine the contents of the heap to identify large objects and memory fragmentation.

Heap dumps analysis

A heap dump is a snapshot of the memory state of a Java application at a particular point in time. It contains information about all the objects that are currently allocated in the heap, including their types, values, and references to other objects. Heap dumps can be very large, often gigabytes in size for large applications. These snapshots are typically taken in the `.hprof` format.

Here's how a heap dump can be analyzed:

1. **Capturing a Heap Dump:**

    o Using `jmap` (a command-line tool included in the JDK):

    `jmap -dump:live,format=b,file=heapdump.hprof <pid>`

Replace `<pid>` with the process ID of the Java application. The `live` option ensures that only reachable objects are included in the dump, and the `format=b` option specifies the binary format for the file.

- Using VisualVM or other profiling tools: These tools usually have a GUI option to trigger a heap dump.

2. **Analyzing the Heap Dump:**

- Open the `.hprof` file in a heap analyzer such as VisualVM, Eclipse Memory Analyzer Tool (MAT), or JProfiler.
- The analyzer will parse the heap dump and present the information in a structured way.

3. **Common Analysis Tasks:**

- **Identifying Memory Leaks:**
    - Look for objects that are constantly growing in number over time, especially if you suspect that they should have been garbage collected. MAT, for example, has a leak suspect report.
    - Check for retained sizes: the retained size of an object is the amount of heap memory that would be freed if that object was garbage collected. Objects with a large retained size are prime candidates for investigation.
- **Finding Large Objects:**
    - Sort objects by their size to quickly identify the largest memory consumers.
    - Examine the objects to determine why they are so large. Are they holding onto unnecessary data?
- **Analyzing Object References:**
    - Trace the references between objects to understand how they are connected and why they are being retained in memory.
    - This can help identify situations where an object is being kept alive by an unexpected reference from another part of the application.

4. **Example Scenario:**

- **Problem:** Your Java application is experiencing `OutOfMemoryError` exceptions after running for a few hours.
- **Steps:**
    1. Take a heap dump when the application's memory usage is high, but before it crashes.
    2. Open the heap dump in MAT.
    3. Run the leak suspect report. The report might indicate that a certain type of object (e.g., a database connection or a cache entry) is growing without bound.
    4. Examine the references to these objects to determine why they are not being garbage collected. You might find that they are being stored in a static collection that is never cleared, or that they are being held onto by a thread that is still running.
    5. Fix the code to properly release these objects when they are no longer needed.

Code example on Heap Dump

```java
import java.util.ArrayList;
import java.util.List;

public class MemoryLeakExample {

    private static List<Object> leakedObjects = new ArrayList<>();

    public static void main(String[] args) throws InterruptedException {
        while (true) {
            // Create a new object and "leak" it by adding it to the static list.
            Object obj = new Object();
            leakedObjects.add(obj);
```

```
            // Print the current number of leaked objects
            System.out.println("Leaked object count: " + leakedObjects.size());

            // Introduce a small delay to control the rate of object creation
            Thread.sleep(10); // Sleep for 10 milliseconds
        }
    }
}
```

To demonstrate using `jmap` to capture the heap dump, you first need the PID.

`jps`

This command lists all running Java processes along with their IDs.

Once you have the PID (let's assume it's 1234), run `jmap`:

`jmap -dump:live,format=b,file=heapdump.hprof 1234`

This will create a heap dump file named `heapdump.hprof` in the current directory.

Important Considerations:

- **Performance Impact:** Profiling and monitoring can introduce overhead, so it's important to use them judiciously, especially in production environments. Many tools offer sampling modes that reduce overhead while still providing useful insights.
- **Data Interpretation:** Interpreting profiling data requires expertise. Understanding how memory is managed in your chosen language and framework is essential for making accurate diagnoses and applying effective optimizations.
- **Granularity:** Start with high-level monitoring to get an overview of memory usage. Then, drill down into specific areas of the code to identify the root cause of performance issues.
- **Integration with Development Workflow:** Integrate profiling and monitoring into your development workflow from the beginning. Regularly profile your code during development and testing to catch memory-related issues early.
- **Automated Monitoring and Alerting:** Set up automated monitoring and alerting to detect memory leaks and performance degradation in production environments. This allows you to proactively address issues before they impact users.

Conclusion

Profiling and monitoring are indispensable tools for understanding and optimizing memory performance in data-intensive applications. By providing insights into memory usage, garbage collection behavior, and potential memory leaks, they empower developers to build more efficient, reliable, and responsive applications. Embrace these techniques as an integral part of your development process to unlock the full potential of your software.

Chapter 17 Security, Privacy, and Compliance-Data Governance and Regulations: GDPR, CCPA, and Beyond

- **Data Governance Importance:** Establishes policies and procedures for data handling throughout its lifecycle within the application.

- **Security Considerations:** Protect data from unauthorized access, use, disclosure, disruption, modification, or destruction.

- **Privacy Enhancing Technologies (PETs):** Employ techniques like differential privacy, homomorphic encryption, and secure multi-party computation to protect sensitive information.

- **Regulatory Compliance (GDPR/CCPA):** Adhere to regulations like GDPR/CCPA requiring data minimization, consent management, right to be forgotten, and data breach notification.

- **Auditability and Provenance:** Implement mechanisms to track data lineage, modifications, and access events for compliance and debugging.

Data Governance Importance

Data governance is about setting up the rules and processes for how data is handled within an application from beginning to end. It's like establishing a set of policies that dictate what can and cannot be done with data at each stage of its lifecycle.

- **Establishes policies and procedures for data handling throughout its lifecycle within the application.**

Think of it like managing a library. The library needs rules about who can borrow books, how long they can keep them, and what happens if they damage them. Data governance is similar; it defines the rules for using and managing data.

For example, consider an e-commerce application. Data governance policies would specify:

1. How customer data (like names, addresses, and payment information) is collected.
2. Who has access to this data and for what purposes.
3. How long the data is stored.
4. How the data is protected from unauthorized access.
5. What happens to the data when a customer closes their account.

Without these policies, data handling can become chaotic, leading to inconsistencies, errors, and security vulnerabilities.

Imagine an online store where different departments handle customer data in different ways. The marketing team might use outdated addresses, leading to wasted advertising costs. The customer service team might not have access to complete order histories, leading to poor customer service. The development team might accidentally expose sensitive customer data during testing.

Effective data governance addresses these issues by providing a clear framework for managing data.

Here's a simple analogy using a code example (though data governance itself is much broader than just code):

```python
# Without data governance:
def save_customer_data(name, address, payment_info):
    # No validation or security measures
    with open("customer_data.txt", "a") as f:
```

```
        f.write(f"{name},{address},{payment_info}\n")

# With data governance (simplified example):
def save_customer_data(name, address, payment_info):
    # Data validation
    if not isinstance(name, str) or not name:
        raise ValueError("Invalid name")
    if not isinstance(address, str) or not address:
        raise ValueError("Invalid address")

    # Encryption for sensitive data (payment_info) - Simplified
    encrypted_payment_info = encrypt(payment_info)

    # Auditing
    log_data_access("save_customer_data", name)

    # Save to database (more secure than a simple text file)
    save_to_database(name, address, encrypted_payment_info)
```

In the "without data governance" example, data is simply appended to a text file without any validation, encryption, or auditing. The "with data governance" example includes basic validation, suggests encryption for sensitive data, adds auditing (logging who accessed the data), and recommends storing data in a database instead of a plain text file. This illustrates how governance introduces controls to improve data quality and security.

Sketch to represent a "data lifecycle"

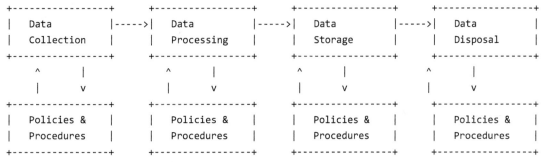

```
+-----------------+       +-----------------+       +-----------------+       +-----------------+
|   Data          |----->|   Data          |----->|   Data          |----->|   Data          |
|   Collection    |       |   Processing    |       |   Storage       |       |   Disposal      |
+-----------------+       +-----------------+       +-----------------+       +-----------------+
      ^       |                 ^       |                 ^       |                 ^       |
      |       v                 |       v                 |       v                 |       v
+-----------------+       +-----------------+       +-----------------+       +-----------------+
|   Policies &    |       |   Policies &    |       |   Policies &    |       |   Policies &    |
|   Procedures    |       |   Procedures    |       |   Procedures    |       |   Procedures    |
+-----------------+       +-----------------+       +-----------------+       +-----------------+
        Data Governance Framework
```

The sketch demonstrates the flow of data through its lifecycle stages: collection, processing, storage, and disposal. Underneath, a "Data Governance Framework" provides the guiding policies and procedures at *each* stage. This framework is what dictates *how* data is handled properly at any point in its existence within the application.

In summary, data governance is crucial for ensuring data is accurate, reliable, secure, and used in compliance with relevant regulations and internal policies. It's the foundation for making informed decisions, improving operational efficiency, and building trust with customers.

Security Considerations

Protecting data within an application is paramount. Security considerations focus on preventing unauthorized access, use, disclosure, disruption, modification, or destruction of data. This section outlines these critical aspects.

Unauthorized Access:

Unauthorized access refers to situations where individuals or systems gain entry to data without proper authorization. This could range from external hackers attempting to breach the system to internal users exceeding their permitted access levels.

Example: Imagine a database containing customer information. Unauthorized access would occur if a marketing employee, who only needs access to customer names and email addresses for campaigns, gains access to customer credit card numbers.

```python
# Example (Conceptual): Python code demonstrating access control (simplified)

def access_data(user_role, data_type):
    if user_role == "marketing" and data_type in ["name", "email"]:
        # Allow access
        print("Access Granted")
    elif user_role == "admin":
        #Allow access to any data
        print("Access Granted")

    else:
        # Deny access
        print("Access Denied")

access_data("marketing", "credit_card")  # Output: Access Denied
access_data("marketing", "email") #output: Access Granted
access_data("admin", "credit_card") #output: Access Granted
```

Unauthorized Use:

Even with authorized access, data can be used inappropriately. This means using the data for purposes other than those explicitly permitted or intended.

Example: A data analyst with access to sales data uses that information to predict stock prices for personal gain, violating company policy and potentially insider trading regulations.

Unauthorized Disclosure:

Unauthorized disclosure involves revealing sensitive data to individuals or entities who are not authorized to see it.

Example: A healthcare provider accidentally sends a patient's medical records to the wrong email address. This is a data breach due to unauthorized disclosure.

Disruption:

Disruption refers to events that prevent authorized users from accessing or using data when they need it.

Example: A denial-of-service (DoS) attack floods a web server with traffic, making it unavailable to legitimate users who are trying to access their accounts and make purchases.

Modification:

Data modification involves altering the contents of data. Unauthorized modification can lead to data corruption, inaccurate reporting, and flawed decision-making.

Example: A hacker gains access to a university's database and changes student grades, resulting in an unfair advantage for some students and a misrepresentation of academic performance.

Destruction:

Data destruction involves permanently deleting or rendering data unusable. This can be caused by malicious attacks, accidental errors, or system failures.

Example: A disgruntled employee deliberately deletes critical files from a company server, causing significant business disruption and data loss.

Sketch Representation:

Here's a sketch concept to represent Security Considerations:

```
 _____
|                                              |    |
|   [ Fortress Wall - Security Considerations ]    |
|                                              |    |
|   Data Inside: (Represented by a box labeled "Data") |
|                                              |    |
|   Attacks coming toward wall:                |
|   - Hacker figure trying to climb the wall (Unauthorized Access)   |
|   - Person inside the fortress misusing data(unauthorized use)          |
|   - Email icon leaking data outside (Unauthorized Disclosure)     |
|   - Hammer hitting data box (Destruction)                    |
|   - Person Modifying the data                             |
|_____|
```

This simple sketch visualizes a fortress protecting data from various threats, representing the security considerations involved. The walls are in place for prevention of any treats, and inside a man is standing there to fix any modification request. Email icon that is leaking data. There is a hammer hitting to distory the box.

Privacy Enhancing Technologies (PETs)

Privacy Enhancing Technologies (PETs) are techniques designed to protect sensitive information while still allowing data to be used for valuable purposes, such as analysis and research. They minimize privacy risks associated with data processing. Let's explore some key PETs: differential privacy, homomorphic encryption, and secure multi-party computation.

Differential Privacy:

Differential privacy adds a carefully calibrated amount of random noise to the data to mask individual information. This ensures that the presence or absence of any single individual's data in the dataset has a limited impact on the outcome of any analysis. In essence, it protects individual privacy while allowing for meaningful statistical analysis.

Concept Sketch:

Original Data --> [Noise Added] --> Publicly Released Data (with differential privacy)

Imagine you have a database of patient records, and you want to release statistics about the average age of patients with a certain condition. Using differential privacy, you would add random noise to the calculation, such that the actual average age is slightly perturbed. This protects any single patient's information from being revealed, even if someone knows all the other patients in the database.

Example (Conceptual Python):

```
def differentially_private_average(data, epsilon):
  """
  Calculates the differentially private average of a dataset.

  Args:
    data: A list of numerical values.
    epsilon: The privacy parameter (smaller epsilon means more privacy).

  Returns:
    The differentially private average.
```

```
"""
    sensitivity = 1.0 # The maximum impact a single data point can have
    noise = np.random.laplace(loc=0, scale=sensitivity/epsilon, size=1)[0]
    average = np.mean(data) + noise
    return average
```

In this simplified example, `epsilon` controls the level of privacy. A smaller `epsilon` means more noise is added, providing stronger privacy but potentially reducing accuracy. The Laplace noise is added to the mean of the data.

Homomorphic Encryption:

Homomorphic encryption allows computations to be performed on encrypted data without decrypting it first. This means data can be processed in a secure environment without ever being exposed in its original form. The results of the computation are also encrypted and can only be decrypted by the data owner.

Concept Sketch:

```
Data (Plaintext) --> [Encryption] --> Encrypted Data --> [Computation on Encrypted Data] --> Enc
```

Think of it like this: you have a locked box (the encryption). You give the locked box to someone who can perform calculations inside it without ever opening it. They return the locked box with the calculated result inside. Only you, with the key, can open the box and see the final result.

Example (Conceptual):

Let's say you want to calculate the sum of several encrypted numbers. With homomorphic encryption, you can perform additions on the encrypted values. The server processing the data never sees the actual numbers, only the encrypted versions. The encrypted sum can be decrypted by the data owner to reveal the true sum. Although practical Homomorphic encryption involves complex mathematical operations, the below sketch gives the key idea:

```
Encrypted(Value1) + Encrypted(Value2) --> Encrypted(Value1 + Value2)
```

Secure Multi-Party Computation (SMPC):

Secure Multi-Party Computation (SMPC) enables multiple parties to jointly compute a function over their private inputs while keeping those inputs secret from each other. Each party only learns the output of the computation, not the individual inputs of the other parties.

Concept Sketch:

```
Party A (Input A)  --|
                     |--> [SMPC Protocol] --> Output
Party B (Input B)  --|
```

Imagine several hospitals want to calculate the average cost of a particular treatment across all their patients, but they don't want to share their individual patient records with each other. Using SMPC, they can jointly compute the average cost without ever revealing their private patient data. Each hospital contributes its data to the SMPC protocol, and the protocol ensures that only the final average is revealed to all parties, while the individual hospital data remains confidential.

These PETs offer different approaches to protecting data privacy, and the choice of which technique to use depends on the specific application and the level of privacy required. When implemented and managed correctly, these tools are very effective in preventing disclosure.

Regulatory Compliance (GDPR/CCPA)

Navigating the landscape of data privacy regulations is critical for any application that handles personal data. Regulations like the General Data Protection Regulation (GDPR) and the California Consumer Privacy Act (CCPA) impose significant obligations on organizations regarding how they collect, process, and store personal information.

Non-compliance can lead to hefty fines and reputational damage. This section outlines key aspects of GDPR/CCPA compliance that must be considered during application development.

Data Minimization:

GDPR and CCPA both emphasize the principle of data minimization. This means that you should only collect and retain the personal data that is absolutely necessary for the specified purpose. Avoid collecting data "just in case" it might be useful later.

Example:

Instead of requesting a user's full address during account creation if only their country is needed for service delivery, collect only the country. Further, ensure the address is not stored once the necessary task of shipping is completed.

Consent Management:

Obtaining valid consent is paramount, especially under GDPR. Consent must be freely given, specific, informed, and unambiguous. Users must have a clear understanding of what data is being collected, how it will be used, and who will have access to it.

Example:

A website collecting browsing data for targeted advertising must present a clear consent banner:

```
"We use cookies to personalize content and ads, to provide social media features and to analyse
[YES] [NO]
Learn More [Link to detailed privacy policy]"
```

The consent should not be bundled with other terms of service. A separate, affirmative action (like clicking "YES") should be required. Pre-ticked boxes are not valid consent.

Right to be Forgotten (Right to Erasure):

GDPR grants individuals the right to request the erasure of their personal data. This means your application must be able to completely remove a user's data from all systems, including backups, when requested.

Implementation Considerations:

1. *Identification:* You must have a reliable way to identify all data associated with a given user.
2. *Deletion Mechanism:* Implement secure and irreversible deletion procedures. Simply marking data as "deleted" is often insufficient. Overwriting the data is often required.
3. *Data Retention Policy:* Implement a data retention policy which is consistent with the regulations and inform users how long their data is going to be held.

Code Example (Conceptual):

```
def delete_user_data(user_id):
    # 1. Find all data records associated with the user_id
    user_records = find_all_records(user_id) # Function to query database

    # 2.  Iterate through each record and securely delete it
    for record in user_records:
        secure_delete(record) #Secure delete overwrite the information

    # 3.  Remove user id from system
    remove_user_id(user_id)
```

Sketch Example:

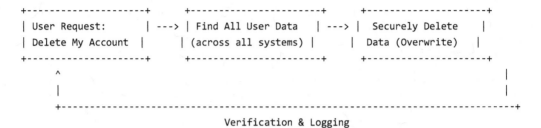

```
+---------------------+       +-----------------------+       +----------------------+
| User Request:       | --->  | Find All User Data    | --->  |   Securely Delete    |
| Delete My Account   |       | (across all systems)  |       |   Data (Overwrite)   |
+---------------------+       +-----------------------+       +----------------------+
       ^                                                                |
       |                                                                |
       +----------------------------------------------------------------+
                        Verification & Logging
```

Data Breach Notification:

GDPR and CCPA require organizations to notify relevant authorities and affected individuals in the event of a data breach that is likely to result in a risk to their rights and freedoms. This notification must be done within a specific timeframe (e.g., 72 hours under GDPR).

Elements of a Data Breach Response Plan:

1. *Detection:* Implement robust monitoring and alerting systems to detect potential breaches.
2. *Assessment:* Quickly assess the scope and severity of the breach, including the type of data affected and the number of individuals impacted.
3. *Notification:* Notify the relevant authorities and affected individuals as required by law.
4. *Remediation:* Take steps to contain the breach and prevent future occurrences, such as patching vulnerabilities and improving security measures.
5. Documentation : Document all data breach responses in detail.

Auditability and Provenance

Auditability and provenance are crucial for responsible data handling, particularly in applications dealing with sensitive or regulated information. They ensure that you can track the history of your data, understand how it has been modified, and identify who has accessed it. This is essential for compliance, debugging, and building trust in your application.

Implement mechanisms to track data lineage, modifications, and access events for compliance and debugging.

This involves setting up systems that automatically record key events in the data lifecycle. Data lineage refers to the origin of the data and the transformations it undergoes. Modifications include any changes made to the data's content or structure. Access events are instances where users or processes interact with the data. Tracking these three elements forms the foundation of auditability and provenance.

For instance, consider an e-commerce application that stores customer orders. Every time an order is placed, updated, or shipped, the system should record:

- Who performed the action (user ID or system process).
- What action was performed (e.g., "order placed," "shipping address updated," "order marked as shipped").
- When the action was performed (timestamp).
- Any relevant data before and after the change (order details, address information, etc.).

To create auditability and provenance in a system we can use logging frameworks, databases to create auditing tables.

```python
import datetime
import logging

logging.basicConfig(filename='data_audit.log', level=logging.INFO,
                    format='%(asctime)s - %(levelname)s - %(message)s')
```

```python
def update_customer_address(customer_id, new_address, user_id):
    """
    Updates the customer's address and logs the change.
    """
    try:
        # Fetch existing customer data (imagine fetching from a database)
        # existing_data = fetch_customer_data(customer_id)
        existing_data = {"customer_id": customer_id, "address": "old address"} # Sample code pur

        # Update the address (imagine updating the database)
        # update_database(customer_id, new_address)

        # Log the event
        log_message = f"User {user_id} updated customer {customer_id}'s address from {existing_
        logging.info(log_message)
        print("Address updated and logged successfully.")

    except Exception as e:
        logging.error(f"Error updating address for customer {customer_id}: {e}")
        print(f"Error updating address: {e}")

# Example Usage:
update_customer_address(123, "123 New Main St", "admin_user")
```

In this example:

- We use Python's `logging` module to record events to a file.
- The `update_customer_address` function simulates updating a customer's address.
- Before updating, we fetch the existing address to record the *before* and *after* states.
- We log the user who made the change, the customer ID, and the details of the change.
- Any errors are also logged for debugging.

You can extend this further and create an audit table to log all the changes that happens to an entity.

Consider a simple database table schema for auditing customer data changes.

```sql
CREATE TABLE customer_audit (
    audit_id SERIAL PRIMARY KEY,
    customer_id INT NOT NULL,
    field_name VARCHAR(255) NOT NULL,
    old_value TEXT,
    new_value TEXT,
    modified_by VARCHAR(255),
    modified_at TIMESTAMP NOT NULL DEFAULT CURRENT_TIMESTAMP
);
```

Here's what each field represents:

- `audit_id`: A unique identifier for each audit entry, automatically incremented.
- `customer_id`: The ID of the customer record that was modified.
- `field_name`: The name of the field that was changed (e.g., 'address', 'email', 'phone').
- `old_value`: The previous value of the field before the change.
- `new_value`: The new value of the field after the change.
- `modified_by`: The user or system process that made the change.
- `modified_at`: The timestamp when the change was made.

This table allows you to track specific changes to individual fields within the customer records over time.

- **Compliance:** Auditability and provenance are crucial for meeting regulatory requirements like GDPR or CCPA. These regulations often mandate the ability to demonstrate how data is handled and processed. Detailed audit logs provide the evidence needed to prove compliance.
- **Debugging:** When errors or inconsistencies arise, audit logs help trace the root cause. By examining the history of data modifications, you can pinpoint the source of the problem and correct it.
- **Building Trust:** Transparency in data handling fosters trust among users and stakeholders. Providing clear information about data lineage and access events demonstrates a commitment to responsible data management.

Implementing auditability and provenance requires careful planning and design. Choose appropriate logging mechanisms, define the scope of what needs to be tracked, and establish procedures for reviewing and analyzing audit logs. By doing so, you can enhance the security, reliability, and trustworthiness of your applications.

Chapter 18 Security, Privacy, and Compliance-Access Control, Encryption, and Secure Data Architectures

- **Access Control:** Limiting data access based on user roles and permissions (e.g., RBAC, ACLs).
- **Encryption:** Protecting data at rest and in transit using cryptographic techniques (e.g., AES, TLS).
- **Secure Data Architectures:** Designing systems with security baked in from the start, considering threat models.
- **Privacy:** Implementing techniques for data anonymization, pseudonymization, and minimizing data collection.
- **Compliance:** Adhering to regulatory requirements (e.g., GDPR, HIPAA) regarding data handling and protection.

Access Control

Access control is about restricting who can see or use specific data. Think of it like keys to different rooms in a house. Not everyone gets a key to every room. Some people might only have a key to the front door and the living room, while others might have keys to all the rooms. In the digital world, access control ensures that only authorized users can access sensitive information. We achieve this by assigning roles and permissions.

Limiting Data Access Based on User Roles and Permissions

This is the core of access control. We define roles (like "administrator," "editor," or "viewer") and assign permissions to each role. Permissions determine what actions a user with that role can perform (e.g., read, write, delete data).

- **Roles:** A role represents a job function or category of users.
- **Permissions:** Permissions specify what a user can do with the data.

For example, in a hospital system:

- A *doctor* role might have permission to view and modify patient records.
- A *nurse* role might have permission to view patient records but not modify them.
- A *billing clerk* role might have permission to view patient insurance information.
- A *patient* role might have permission to view their own health information and messages from their doctors.

RBAC (Role-Based Access Control)

RBAC is a common approach. In RBAC, permissions are associated with roles, and users are assigned to roles. Instead of managing permissions for each user individually, you manage permissions for each role and simply assign users to the appropriate roles. This simplifies administration, especially in large organizations.

```
# Example RBAC implementation (Conceptual)

class Role:
    def __init__(self, name, permissions):
        self.name = name
        self.permissions = permissions

class User:
    def __init__(self, username, role):
        self.username = username
        self.role = role

    def has_permission(self, permission):
        return permission in self.role.permissions

# Define roles
admin_role = Role("admin", ["read", "write", "delete"])
viewer_role = Role("viewer", ["read"])

# Create users
alice = User("alice", admin_role)
bob = User("bob", viewer_role)

# Check permissions
print(f"Alice can delete: {alice.has_permission('delete')}") # Output: True
print(f"Bob can write: {bob.has_permission('write')}")    # Output: False
```

In this simplified Python example, we have `Role` and `User` classes. Roles have permissions, and users are assigned roles. The `has_permission` method checks if a user, based on their role, has a specific permission. Real-world RBAC implementations are significantly more complex and often managed by dedicated software.

ACLs (Access Control Lists)

ACLs are another way to manage access control. Instead of assigning permissions to roles, ACLs associate permissions directly with data objects (like files or database tables). Each object has a list of users or groups and their corresponding permissions for that object.

Consider a file system:

- A file might have an ACL that grants "read" and "write" permissions to the owner and "read" permission to a specific group.
- Another file might have an ACL that grants full access to only the creator.

ACLs can be more granular than RBAC, allowing you to define access rules for individual objects. However, they can be more difficult to manage, especially with a large number of objects and users.

Sketch representation of Access Control List(ACL) and Role-Based Access Control(RBAC)

ACL

```
+-------------------+         +----------------------+
|      Object       |----->|    Access Control    |
|  (e.g., File)     |         | List (ACL)           |
+-------------------+         | User A: Read, Write |
                              | User B: Read         |
                              | Group X: Read        |
                              +----------------------+
```

RBAC

```
+----------+        +---------+        +----------------------+
|   User   |----->|  Role   |----->|     Permissions      |
| (e.g.,Bob)|        | (e.g.,  |        | (e.g., Read, Write)|
|          |        | Editor) |        +----------------------+
+----------+        +---------+
```

The ACL diagram represents an object (like a file) containing a list of who has what access. The RBAC diagram shows that user access is determined by their role and that roles in turn have specific permissions. The arrows indicate direction of relationship (e.g. User points to Role).

Encryption

Encryption is a fundamental security technique for protecting data, both when it's stored (at rest) and when it's being transmitted (in transit). It involves converting data into an unreadable format, called ciphertext, using a specific algorithm and a secret key. Only someone with the correct key can decrypt the ciphertext back into its original, readable form, known as plaintext.

Data at Rest: This refers to data that is stored on a device or system, such as a hard drive, database, or cloud storage. Encryption at rest protects the data if the storage medium is compromised or stolen.

Data in Transit: This refers to data that is being transmitted over a network, such as the internet or a local network. Encryption in transit protects the data from being intercepted and read during transmission. The common encryption algorithms are described below with example.

- **AES (Advanced Encryption Standard):** A widely used symmetric encryption algorithm. Symmetric encryption means the same key is used for both encryption and decryption. AES is known for its speed and security.
- **TLS (Transport Layer Security):** A protocol that provides secure communication over a network. TLS uses encryption to protect data transmitted between a client and a server, such as when you browse a website using HTTPS.

Encryption:

```python
from cryptography.fernet import Fernet

# Generate a key (keep this secret!)
key = Fernet.generate_key()
f = Fernet(key)

# Encrypt a message
message = b"This is a secret message."
```

```
encrypted_message = f.encrypt(message)

print("Original message:", message)
print("Encrypted message:", encrypted_message)

# Decrypt the message
decrypted_message = f.decrypt(encrypted_message)

print("Decrypted message:", decrypted_message)
```

In this example:

1. We use the `cryptography` library, a common Python library for cryptographic operations.
2. `Fernet.generate_key()` creates a new encryption key. It's essential to store this key securely!
3. `Fernet(key)` initializes a Fernet cipher object with the key. Fernet is a recipe built on top of AES (for encryption), along with other cryptographic primitives for message authentication and tamper-proofing.
4. `f.encrypt(message)` encrypts the byte string `message`. The input *must* be bytes, not a regular string.
5. `f.decrypt(encrypted_message)` decrypts the ciphertext back to the original plaintext.

TLS/HTTPS Example (Conceptual Sketch):

Key points illustrated in the sketch:

- **Handshake:** The client and server negotiate a secure connection. This involves the server sending its certificate (containing its public key).
- **Key Exchange:** The client generates a session key and encrypts it with the server's public key. Only the server, with its corresponding private key, can decrypt this session key.
- **Symmetric Encryption:** After the key exchange, all subsequent data is encrypted using a symmetric encryption algorithm (like AES) with the session key. Symmetric encryption is much faster than asymmetric encryption, so it's used for the bulk of the data transfer.
- **HTTPS:** The entire process occurs over HTTP, creating HTTPS (HTTP Secure).

Important Considerations:

- **Key Management:** Securely storing and managing encryption keys is crucial. Compromised keys render the encryption useless. Hardware Security Modules (HSMs) are often used for this purpose.

- **Algorithm Selection:** Choose strong and well-vetted encryption algorithms. Avoid using outdated or weak algorithms. Consult with security experts to determine the appropriate algorithms for your specific needs.
- **Implementation:** Even strong algorithms can be vulnerable if implemented incorrectly. Use established libraries and follow best practices for cryptographic implementation.
- **Performance:** Encryption can impact performance. Choose algorithms and key sizes that provide an acceptable balance between security and performance.

Secure Data Architectures

Designing secure data architectures means building systems where security is a fundamental part from the very beginning, rather than an afterthought. It's like planning the strong foundation of a house before you even start building the walls. This proactive approach involves carefully considering potential threats and vulnerabilities during the design phase and incorporating security measures throughout the entire system. A key aspect of this is threat modeling.

Threat Modeling:

Threat modeling is the process of identifying potential threats and vulnerabilities in a system. It involves systematically analyzing the architecture, identifying assets, and understanding how attackers might try to compromise them. For example, when designing an e-commerce platform, you might identify threats like SQL injection attacks, cross-site scripting (XSS), or distributed denial-of-service (DDoS) attacks.

Think of it like this:

```
System Architecture --> Identify Assets --> Potential Threats --> Security Measures
```

Once you identify the threats, you can design security measures to mitigate them. Here's a basic sketch to illustrate this:

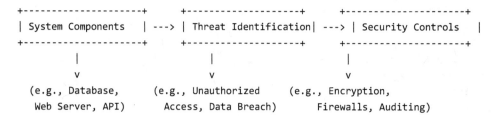

Designing Systems with Security Baked In:

Baking security into the design involves several key principles:

- **Least Privilege:** Granting users and systems only the minimum level of access needed to perform their tasks.
- **Defense in Depth:** Implementing multiple layers of security controls so that if one layer fails, others are still in place.
- **Secure Defaults:** Configuring systems with the most secure settings by default.
- **Regular Security Assessments:** Conducting periodic security audits and penetration testing to identify vulnerabilities.

Examples:

1. **E-commerce Platform:**

   - *Threat*: SQL injection attack on the database.
   - *Security Measure*: Using parameterized queries or an Object-Relational Mapper (ORM) to prevent SQL injection.

   ```
   # Example of parameterized query (Python with psycopg2)
   import psycopg2
   ```

```
conn = psycopg2.connect("dbname=mydb user=me password=secret")
cur = conn.cursor()

user_id = input("Enter user ID: ")

# Instead of:
# cur.execute("SELECT  FROM users WHERE id = " + user_id)  # Vulnerable!

# Use parameterized query:
cur.execute("SELECT  FROM users WHERE id = %s", (user_id,))

results = cur.fetchall()
print(results)

cur.close()
conn.close()
```

In this example, the parameterized query prevents an attacker from injecting malicious SQL code into the query.

2. **Cloud Storage System:**

   - *Threat*: Unauthorized access to stored files.
   - *Security Measure*: Implementing strong authentication mechanisms (e.g., multi-factor authentication), access control lists (ACLs), and encryption of data at rest and in transit.

3. **API Gateway:**

   - *Threat*: DDoS attack overwhelming the API.
   - *Security Measure*: Rate limiting requests, using a Web Application Firewall (WAF), and implementing caching mechanisms.

Considering Threat Models:

A threat model is a structured representation of the threats that are relevant to a system. It helps identify potential attack vectors and prioritize security efforts. The model should take into account:

- **Assets:** What are you trying to protect (e.g., data, systems, infrastructure)?
- **Threat Agents:** Who might want to attack your system (e.g., malicious insiders, external hackers)?
- **Attack Vectors:** How might they try to attack your system (e.g., phishing, malware, vulnerability exploitation)?
- **Impacts:** What would be the consequences of a successful attack (e.g., data breach, service disruption)?

A simple table illustrates a possible threat model:

Asset	Threat Agent	Attack Vector	Impact
Customer Data	External Hacker	SQL Injection	Data Breach
Web Server	DDoS Attacker	Network Flooding	Service Disruption
API Endpoint	Malicious User	API Abuse	Resource Exhaustion

By understanding and modeling these threats, architects can design systems that are resilient to attacks and protect sensitive data. This involves not just technology, but also process and policies. It's a holistic approach to ensuring the safety and integrity of data throughout its lifecycle.

Privacy

Privacy, in the context of data security, focuses on protecting individuals' personal information and ensuring it is handled responsibly. It involves implementing specific techniques and strategies to minimize data collection, anonymize data, and pseudonymize data. The core goal is to empower individuals with control over their information and to prevent its misuse.

Implementing techniques for data anonymization:

Anonymization is the process of removing identifying information from data so that it can no longer be linked to a specific individual. This is not simply removing names and addresses; it involves a more comprehensive approach to eliminate any attributes that could potentially be used to re-identify someone.

- **Example:** Consider a dataset of customer transactions. Anonymization might involve:

    - Removing customer names and addresses.
    - Replacing specific dates of birth with age ranges (e.g., instead of "1990-05-15," use "30-35 years old").
    - Generalizing location data (e.g., replacing a specific address with a city or region).

```
import pandas as pd

# Sample customer data (replace with your actual data)
data = {'CustomerID': [1, 2, 3, 4],
        'Name': ['Alice Smith', 'Bob Johnson', 'Charlie Brown', 'David Lee'],
        'Age': [32, 45, 28, 51],
        'City': ['New York', 'Los Angeles', 'Chicago', 'Houston']}

df = pd.DataFrame(data)

# Anonymization techniques
df['Name'] = 'Customer'  # Replace names with "Customer"
df['Age'] = df['Age'].apply(lambda age: f'{age // 10  10}-{age // 10  10 + 10}' ) # Convert
df['City'] = 'Metropolis'  # Replace all cities with 'Metropolis'
print(df)
```

In this example the pandas library used to transform the name, city and age column of the data frame.

Sketch Visualization:

```
Original Data:
+-----+-------------+-----+----------+
| ID  | Name        | Age | City     |
+-----+-------------+-----+----------+
| 1   | Alice Smith | 32  | New York |
| ... | ...         | ... | ...      |
+-----+-------------+-----+----------+


Anonymized Data:
+-----+-------------+-----+----------+
| ID  | Name        | Age | City     |
+-----+-------------+-----+----------+
| 1   | Customer    | 30-40 | Metropolis|
| ... | ...         | ... | ...      |
+-----+-------------+-----+----------+
```

Implementing techniques for data pseudonymization:

Pseudonymization involves replacing identifying information with pseudonyms or aliases. Unlike anonymization, pseudonymized data can potentially be linked back to the original individual if the pseudonymization key is available. However, without the key, the data appears anonymous.

- **Example:** A hospital might replace patient names with unique patient IDs in their research database. Researchers can then analyze the data without knowing the patients' actual identities. However, the hospital retains a separate key that links the patient IDs back to the corresponding patient records if needed for clinical purposes.

```
import hashlib

# Sample patient data
patient_data = {'PatientID': 12345, 'Name': 'Eve Williams', 'Condition': 'Diabetes'}

# Pseudonymization using SHA-256 hashing
def pseudonymize(data):
    pseudonymized_data = {}
    for key, value in data.items():
        if key == 'Name':
            # Hash the name to create a pseudonym
            pseudonym = hashlib.sha256(value.encode()).hexdigest()
            pseudonymized_data['PatientPseudonym'] = pseudonym
        else:
            pseudonymized_data[key] = value
    return pseudonymized_data

pseudonymized_patient_data = pseudonymize(patient_data)
print(pseudonymized_patient_data)
```

Here, SHA-256 hashing is used to generate a pseudonym for the patient's name. The original name is not stored in the pseudonymized data. A separate, secure system would need to maintain the link between the original name and the pseudonym if re-identification is ever necessary (which should be carefully controlled and justified).

Sketch Visualization:

```
Original Data:
+-------------+-----------------+-----------+
| PatientID   | Name            | Condition |
+-------------+-----------------+-----------+
| 12345       | Eve Williams    | Diabetes  |
+-------------+-----------------+-----------+


Pseudonymized Data:
+-------------+------------------------------------+-----------+
| PatientID   | PatientPseudonym                   | Condition |
+-------------+------------------------------------+-----------+
| 12345       | e5b7... (SHA-256 Hash)             | Diabetes  |
+-------------+------------------------------------+-----------+


Separate Key (Securely Stored):
+------------------------------------+----------------+
| PatientPseudonym                   | Name           |
+------------------------------------+----------------+
| e5b7... (SHA-256 Hash)             | Eve Williams   |
+------------------------------------+----------------+
```

Minimizing Data Collection:

Data minimization means only collecting and retaining the data that is absolutely necessary for a specific purpose. This principle helps to reduce the risk of privacy breaches and misuse of personal information.

- **Example:** An e-commerce website should only collect the data required to process an order (e.g., name, address, payment information). It should not collect unnecessary information such as the customer's browsing history or social media profiles unless there is a legitimate business reason and the customer has provided explicit consent.

```python
class UserProfile:
    def __init__(self, username, password, email, address, phone_number, browsing_history, so
        self.username = username
        self.password = password
        self.email = email
        self.address = address
        self.phone_number = phone_number
        self.browsing_history = browsing_history
        self.social_media = social_media


class OrderInformation:
    def __init__(self, name, address, payment_information):
        self.name = name
        self.address = address
        self.payment_information = payment_information


# Minimizing data collection
class UserProfile:
    def __init__(self, username, password, email):
        self.username = username
        self.password = password
        self.email = email


class OrderInformation:
    def __init__(self, name, address, payment_information):
        self.name = name
        self.address = address
        self.payment_information = payment_information
```

The minimized version contains only the name, address, and payment_information. This adheres to the principle of data minimization by collecting only what's necessary for order processing.

Sketch Visualization:

```
Original Data Collection (Excessive):

[ User Profile: Username, Password, Email, Address, Phone, Browsing History, Social Media ]
                                     +
[ Order Details: Name, Address, Payment Info ]


Minimized Data Collection (Necessary Only):

[ User Profile: Username, Password, Email ]
                         +
[ Order Details: Name, Address, Payment Info ]
```

Privacy is a multifaceted concept. Careful consideration and implementation of anonymization, pseudonymization, and data minimization techniques are essential to protect individuals' privacy and build trust in data-driven systems.

Compliance

Compliance, in the context of data security and privacy, refers to adhering to a set of rules, regulations, laws, and industry standards governing how data is handled and protected. It's not simply about following guidelines; it's about demonstrating a commitment to responsible data management. Failure to comply can lead to significant legal penalties, reputational damage, and loss of customer trust.

Different regions and industries have distinct compliance requirements. For example, if your organization handles personal data of European Union citizens, you must comply with the General Data Protection Regulation (GDPR). Similarly, if you deal with protected health information in the United States, you need to comply with the Health Insurance Portability and Accountability Act (HIPAA). The Payment Card Industry Data Security Standard (PCI DSS) applies to organizations that handle credit card information. Each of these regulations has specific stipulations that organizations must implement.

To illustrate, consider GDPR. GDPR mandates several key principles, including:

- **Lawfulness, Fairness, and Transparency:** Data processing must be lawful, fair, and transparent to the data subject.
- **Purpose Limitation:** Data should be collected only for specified, explicit, and legitimate purposes.
- **Data Minimization:** Only necessary data should be collected.
- **Accuracy:** Data should be accurate and kept up to date.
- **Storage Limitation:** Data should be kept only as long as necessary.
- **Integrity and Confidentiality:** Data should be processed in a manner that ensures appropriate security.
- **Accountability:** The data controller is responsible for demonstrating compliance with GDPR.

Let's examine how compliance might be implemented in practice with a simplified code example, focusing on data minimization. Suppose you are building a user registration system.

```python
class User:
    def __init__(self, user_id, username, password, email, full_name, address, phone_number, dat
        self.user_id = user_id
        self.username = username
        self.password = password
        self.email = email
        self.full_name = full_name
        self.address = address
        self.phone_number = phone_number
        self.date_of_birth = date_of_birth
        self.gender = gender
        self.nationality = nationality


# Non-compliant approach: Collects all available data.
user1 = User(1, "johndoe", "password123", "john@example.com", "John Doe", "123 Main St", "555-1:

# Compliant approach: Collects only necessary data (e.g., for basic account functionality).
class MinimalUser:
    def __init__(self, user_id, username, password, email):
        self.user_id = user_id
        self.username = username
        self.password = password
        self.email = email

user2 = MinimalUser(2, "janedoe", "securepass", "jane@example.com")
```

In this scenario, the initial User class collects a wide range of potentially unnecessary information. A more compliant approach, as demonstrated by the MinimalUser class, is to collect only the data strictly required for the purpose (e.g., account creation and authentication). This directly addresses the GDPR principle of data minimization.

Another important aspect of compliance is establishing clear data handling policies and procedures. For instance, you should have a documented procedure for responding to data subject access requests (DSARs), which allow individuals to request access to their personal data, request rectification, erasure, or restriction of processing.

Here's a simplified sketch illustrating the flow of a DSAR:

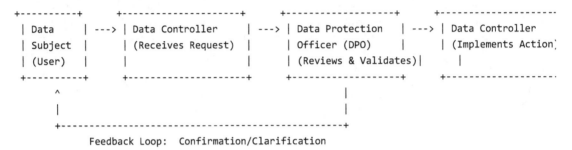

```
+----------+      +---------------------+      +--------------------+      +--------------------
| Data     | ---> | Data Controller     | ---> | Data Protection    | ---> | Data Controller
| Subject  |      | (Receives Request)  |      | Officer (DPO)      |      | (Implements Action)
| (User)   |      |                     |      | (Reviews & Validates)|    |
+----------+      +---------------------+      +--------------------+      +--------------------
      ^                                                  |
      |                                                  |
      +--------------------------------------------------+
          Feedback Loop:  Confirmation/Clarification
```

The user (data subject) initiates the request. The data controller receives it and typically involves a Data Protection Officer (DPO) to validate and process the request. Finally, the controller implements the required action (e.g., providing the data, deleting it) and confirms completion with the user.

Achieving and maintaining compliance requires ongoing effort. Regular audits, risk assessments, and updates to data protection practices are necessary to adapt to evolving regulations and threat landscapes. Staff training is also crucial to ensure that everyone understands their responsibilities in protecting data and adhering to compliance requirements. By prioritizing compliance, organizations can build trust with their customers, avoid legal repercussions, and foster a culture of responsible data stewardship.

Chapter 19 Future Trends and Real-World Architectures-AI and Data-Intensive Systems: The Rise of Intelligent Databases

Here are 5 bullet points outlining "Future Trends and Real-World Architectures - AI and Data-Intensive Systems: The Rise of Intelligent Databases," suitable for a single slide presentation:

- **AI Integration:**
    - Embedded AI/ML: Databases directly incorporating machine learning models for tasks like anomaly detection, prediction, and automated indexing.

- **Autonomous Database Management:**

- Self-Tuning: Databases automating optimization tasks (e.g., index creation, query plan selection) with minimal human intervention.

- **Vector Databases:**

  - Similarity Search: Specialized databases designed for storing and efficiently querying high-dimensional vector embeddings, crucial for AI applications.

- **Real-time Feature Stores:**

  - ML Feature Serving: Systems managing and serving features for machine learning models in production, ensuring consistency and low latency.

- **Explainable AI (XAI) in Databases:**

  - Data Provenance: Integrating explainability techniques within the database to understand the factors influencing AI-driven decisions based on data.

AI Integration

Embedded AI/ML: Databases directly incorporating machine learning models for tasks like anomaly detection, prediction, and automated indexing.

Consider a traditional database. It stores and retrieves data based on explicit instructions you give it, like "find all customers who bought product X." Now, imagine a database that can also *learn* from the data and proactively identify unusual patterns or predict future customer behavior. That's the essence of AI integration in databases, specifically through embedding AI and Machine Learning (ML) models.

Anomaly Detection:

Think of a credit card company tracking transactions. They want to quickly identify fraudulent activity. Without AI, they'd rely on predefined rules like "flag transactions over $10,000" or "flag transactions from country Y." These rules are static and can be easily circumvented.

With AI integration, the database can learn the typical spending patterns of each customer. It builds an ML model for each customer (or groups of similar customers). If a transaction significantly deviates from that learned pattern, it's flagged as an anomaly. This is more sophisticated than simple rules because it adapts to individual behavior and can detect subtle fraudulent activities that rules might miss.

Sketch:

```
[Customer Data (Spending Habits)] ----> [ML Model (Learned Pattern)] ----> [Incoming Transactior
```

Code Example (Conceptual - using Python and a hypothetical database library):

```python
# Assume 'db' is an object connected to the database
# Assume 'customer_data' is a table of transactions for a specific customer

import sklearn.ensemble

# Fetch customer's transaction data
customer_data = db.query("SELECT  FROM customer_transactions WHERE customer_id = '123'")

# Train a machine learning model (e.g., Isolation Forest for anomaly detection)
model = sklearn.ensemble.IsolationForest()
model.fit(customer_data[['transaction_amount', 'transaction_time']])

# Function to predict if a new transaction is an anomaly
def predict_anomaly(transaction):
```

```
score = model.decision_function([[transaction['transaction_amount'], transaction['transaction_
return score # Lower score means more likely an anomaly

# Example usage:
new_transaction = {'transaction_amount': 10000, 'transaction_time': '2024-01-01 12:00:00'}
anomaly_score = predict_anomaly(new_transaction)

if anomaly_score < -0.5: # Adjust threshold as needed
  print("Possible anomaly detected!")
```

Prediction:

Retailers want to predict which products a customer is likely to buy next. Instead of relying on simple "customers who bought X also bought Y" analysis, an AI-integrated database can use more sophisticated techniques. It can learn from a customer's past purchases, browsing history, demographics, and even social media activity (if available).

This data is fed into an ML model embedded within the database. The model might be a recommendation engine that predicts the probability of a customer purchasing different products. The database can then proactively suggest these products to the customer, increasing the likelihood of a sale.

Sketch:

```
[Customer Data (Purchases, Browsing)] + [Product Data (Descriptions, Categories)] ----> [Recomme
```

Automated Indexing:

Databases use indexes to speed up query performance. Creating the right indexes is crucial but can be a complex and time-consuming task for database administrators. An AI-integrated database can *learn* which queries are frequently executed and automatically create indexes to optimize them.

For instance, if a database notices that queries filtering data by "date" and "region" are common, it can automatically create a composite index on those columns. This significantly speeds up those queries without requiring manual intervention. The system continuously monitors query patterns and adjusts the indexes over time, ensuring optimal performance.

Sketch:

```
[Query Log] ----> [Query Pattern Analysis (ML Model)] ----> [Index Recommendations] ----> [Autor
```

In essence, embedding AI/ML allows databases to move beyond simply storing and retrieving data to becoming intelligent systems that proactively analyze, predict, and optimize their own performance. This shift transforms databases from passive repositories to active participants in data-driven decision-making.

AI Integration: Embedded AI/ML

Databases are evolving beyond simple data storage and retrieval systems. They are now actively incorporating Artificial Intelligence (AI) and Machine Learning (ML) models directly within their architecture. This embedding allows databases to perform intelligent tasks, analyze data in real-time, and automate traditionally manual processes.

Let's break down what "Embedded AI/ML�? actually means in the context of modern databases. It signifies a fundamental shift where the database itself becomes an active participant in data analysis, rather than simply a passive repository.

One of the primary drivers for embedding AI/ML is the ability to perform *anomaly detection*. Imagine a large e-commerce platform. Every transaction is recorded in the database. Traditionally, identifying fraudulent transactions would require a separate system that periodically scans the database, applies some rules, and flags suspicious activities. With embedded AI/ML, a machine learning model trained to recognize fraudulent patterns sits directly within the database. As new transactions are added, the model instantly scores each transaction for its likelihood of being fraudulent.

```
-- Example (Conceptual): Trigger an ML model on new transactions

CREATE TRIGGER check_fraud
AFTER INSERT ON transactions
FOR EACH ROW
EXECUTE FUNCTION fraud_detection_model(NEW.transaction_data);

-- Function fraud_detection_model might call an embedded ML model
-- and return a fraud score. Transactions above a certain score are flagged.
```

The advantage is speed and reduced complexity. No more ETL (Extract, Transform, Load) processes to move data to a separate analytics system. The detection happens *in situ*, as data arrives. This is crucial for real-time fraud prevention.

Another key application is *prediction*. Consider a retail company wanting to predict future sales. Historical sales data resides in the database. An embedded ML model can analyze this data to predict future demand for specific products in different regions.

```
-- Example (Conceptual): Predict sales using an embedded ML model

SELECT
    region,
    product_id,
    predict_sales(region, product_id, current_date + interval '1 month') AS predicted_sales
FROM
    products;

-- The function 'predict_sales' would interact with an embedded ML model
-- trained on historical sales data to generate the prediction.
```

These predictions can then be used to optimize inventory management, adjust pricing strategies, and improve overall business efficiency. The database becomes a proactive decision-making tool, not just a store of historical records.

Automated indexing is another significant benefit. Indexing is crucial for query performance, but manually creating and managing indexes can be a complex and time-consuming task. Embedded AI/ML can automatically analyze query patterns and data distributions to identify optimal indexing strategies. The database essentially learns how users are querying the data and creates indexes to speed up the most common and important queries.

Sketch representing traditional vs embedded approach

Traditional:

```
[Data Source] --> [ETL Process] --> [Analytics System] --> [Insights]
  ^_____|
```

Embedded:

```
[Data Source] --> [Database with Embedded AI/ML] --> [Real-time Insights & Actions]
```

The sketch visually illustrates the difference. The traditional approach requires a separate analytics system and ETL processes, creating latency and complexity. The embedded approach streamlines the process, enabling real-time insights and actions directly from the database.

In summary, embedded AI/ML is transforming databases into intelligent data management systems. They can now proactively analyze data, make predictions, and automate optimization tasks, all within the database itself. This leads to improved performance, reduced complexity, and faster insights, empowering organizations to make data-driven decisions more effectively.

Autonomous Database Management

Autonomous database management represents a significant leap forward in database technology, shifting the burden of routine administration from human database administrators (DBAs) to the database system itself. This is achieved through sophisticated automation of various tasks, leading to reduced operational costs, improved performance, and increased reliability.

Self-Tuning:

Self-tuning is a core aspect of autonomous database management. It involves the database system automatically optimizing its configuration and operation based on observed workloads and performance metrics. This includes tasks such as:

- **Index Creation and Management:** Indexes are crucial for query performance, but creating and maintaining them manually can be time-consuming and error-prone. An autonomous database can analyze query patterns and automatically create, modify, or drop indexes to optimize query execution times.

    - **Example:** Consider a table `Orders` with columns `CustomerID`, `OrderDate`, and `TotalAmount`. Suppose frequent queries involve filtering by `OrderDate`. An autonomous database might detect this and automatically create an index on the `OrderDate` column.

- **Query Plan Selection:** When a query is submitted, the database needs to determine the most efficient way to execute it. This involves choosing an optimal query plan from a potentially vast number of alternatives. Autonomous databases use machine learning techniques to learn from past query executions and dynamically select the best plan for each query.

    - **Explanation:**

    Query: `SELECT  FROM Orders WHERE CustomerID = 123 AND OrderDate > '2023-01-01';`

    The database has multiple ways to execute this:

    1. Scan the entire `Orders` table and filter based on the conditions.
    2. Use an index on `CustomerID` to find matching rows and then filter by `OrderDate`.
    3. Use an index on `OrderDate` to find matching rows and then filter by `CustomerID`.
    4. Use a composite index on both columns (`CustomerID, OrderDate`).

    The autonomous system analyzes the data distribution, index availability, and past performance of similar queries to select the most efficient execution plan.

- **Resource Allocation:** Autonomous databases can dynamically allocate resources (e.g., CPU, memory, storage) based on workload demands. This ensures that critical tasks receive sufficient resources while avoiding resource waste.

    - **Example:** During peak business hours, an e-commerce database might automatically increase CPU allocation to handle a surge in online orders. During off-peak hours, the CPU allocation can be reduced to conserve resources.

- **Parameter Tuning:** Databases have numerous configuration parameters that affect performance. Manually tuning these parameters is a complex and time-consuming task. Autonomous databases can automatically adjust these parameters based on workload characteristics.

    - **Example:** The `buffer_pool_size` parameter in PostgreSQL controls the amount of memory allocated to caching data. An autonomous system can monitor the buffer pool hit ratio and adjust the `buffer_pool_size` to optimize caching performance.

- **Data Partitioning:** Partitioning involves splitting a large table into smaller, more manageable pieces. An autonomous database can automatically partition tables based on access patterns and data characteristics.

  - **Example:** A time-series database might automatically partition data based on time intervals (e.g., daily or monthly partitions) to improve query performance and simplify data management.

- **Statistics Gathering:** Accurate statistics about data distribution are essential for query optimization. Autonomous databases automatically collect and update statistics to ensure that the query optimizer has the information it needs to make informed decisions.

  - **Explanation:** The query optimizer relies on statistics like the number of rows in a table, the number of distinct values in a column, and the distribution of values to estimate the cost of different query plans. By automatically gathering and updating these statistics, the autonomous database ensures that the optimizer has accurate information to work with.

- **Minimal Human Intervention:** A key characteristic of autonomous databases is their ability to perform these tasks with minimal human intervention. The goal is to free up DBAs from routine maintenance tasks so that they can focus on more strategic initiatives.

  - **Benefit:**

```
Human DBA
-> Focuses on Strategic work, such as:
      1. Security compliance, auditing
      2. Disaster recovery planning
      3. Data architecture optimization
      4. Application performance Analysis
      5. Capacity planning
```

- **Sketch:**

```
+----------------------+    Workload Analysis   +----------------------+
|     Application      |   -------------------> | Autonomous Database  |
+----------------------+                        | Management System    |
                                                +----------------------+
 |                                                        |
 | Automatic Tuning (Indexes, Query Plans, Resources)     |
 V                                                        |
+----------------------+    Feedback Loop       +----------------------+
|  Optimized Database  | <-------------------- | Performance Metrics   |
+----------------------+                        +----------------------+
```

The sketch above shows how an autonomous database management system analyzes the workload and uses that information to automatically tune the database. The system then monitors performance metrics and uses them to further optimize the database. This creates a feedback loop that ensures the database is always performing at its best.

Autonomous Database Management: Self-Tuning

Self-tuning databases represent a significant leap in database technology, moving away from manual administration towards autonomous operation. This capability focuses on automating optimization tasks that traditionally require expert human intervention. The core idea is to minimize the need for database administrators (DBAs) to constantly monitor and adjust database settings for optimal performance. This is achieved by embedding intelligence within the database system itself.

What is Self-Tuning?

Self-tuning refers to the database's ability to automatically adjust its internal parameters and configurations to achieve optimal performance without requiring manual intervention. The database effectively learns from its workload and adapts its behavior to match the changing demands of applications and users.

Examples of Self-Tuning in Action

- **Index Creation:** A common bottleneck in database performance is inefficient query execution due to missing or poorly designed indexes. A self-tuning database analyzes query patterns and automatically creates or drops indexes based on observed access patterns.

  - **Scenario:** Imagine an e-commerce application where users frequently search for products based on "category" and "price." Without an appropriate index, these queries would require a full table scan, which is slow. A self-tuning database would recognize this pattern and automatically create a composite index on "category" and "price" to speed up these searches.

  - **Without Self-Tuning:**

```
-- Without index:  Query likely to be slow
SELECT product_name FROM products WHERE category = 'electronics' AND price < 100;
```

  - **With Self-Tuning (Automatic Index Creation):**

```
-- Self-tuning database automatically creates an index similar to:
CREATE INDEX idx_category_price ON products (category, price);

-- Subsequent queries will be much faster
SELECT product_name FROM products WHERE category = 'electronics' AND price < 100;
```

- **Query Plan Selection:** SQL queries can be executed in various ways, each resulting in a different query plan. The database's query optimizer is responsible for choosing the most efficient plan. However, with complex queries and large datasets, the optimizer may not always make the optimal choice. A self-tuning database continuously monitors query execution and learns which plans perform best under different conditions, adjusting its optimization strategy accordingly.

  - **Scenario:** A database might initially choose a nested loop join for joining two large tables. However, a self-tuning database might observe that a hash join consistently performs better for these tables given the data distribution and memory availability. It then automatically switches to using a hash join for similar queries in the future.

  - **Sketch:**

```
[Initial Query] --> [Query Optimizer (Chooses Plan A - Nested Loop Join)] --> [Execution (S
```

- **Resource Allocation:** Self-tuning databases can also dynamically adjust resource allocation (CPU, memory, disk I/O) to different parts of the database system based on workload demands. If a particular set of queries is consuming a large amount of resources, the database can automatically allocate more resources to those queries to improve their performance.

  - **Scenario:** During peak hours, online transaction processing (OLTP) queries might require more CPU resources, while during off-peak hours, batch reporting jobs might be more resource-intensive. A self-tuning database automatically adjusts CPU allocation to prioritize OLTP during peak hours and reporting during off-peak hours.

- **Configuration Parameter Tuning:** Databases have numerous configuration parameters that affect performance. Manually tuning these parameters is a complex and time-consuming task. Self-tuning databases automatically adjust these parameters based on observed workload patterns and performance metrics.

Benefits of Self-Tuning Databases

- **Reduced Administrative Overhead:** Automating optimization tasks frees up DBAs to focus on more strategic initiatives, such as database design and security.
- **Improved Performance:** Self-tuning databases can achieve better performance than manually tuned databases by continuously adapting to changing workloads.
- **Lower Total Cost of Ownership (TCO):** By reducing the need for manual administration and improving performance, self-tuning databases can lower the overall cost of owning and operating a database system.
- **Increased Scalability:** Self-tuning databases can automatically adapt to changing workloads, making it easier to scale database systems to meet growing demands.
- **Faster Problem Identification:** Self-tuning mechanisms are also capable of identifying and mitigating resource bottlenecks to ensure higher uptime for databases and minimal performance degradation.

Underlying Technologies

Self-tuning databases leverage various machine learning and statistical techniques to analyze workload patterns, predict performance, and optimize database settings. These techniques include:

- **Reinforcement Learning:** Used to learn optimal query execution plans and resource allocation strategies.
- **Regression Analysis:** Used to predict performance based on workload characteristics and configuration parameters.
- **Time Series Analysis:** Used to detect anomalies and trends in workload patterns.
- **Genetic Algorithms:** Used to explore a wide range of configuration parameter settings and find the optimal combination.

In Summary

Self-tuning databases represent a significant advancement in database technology, enabling autonomous optimization and reducing the need for manual administration. By leveraging machine learning and statistical techniques, these databases can continuously adapt to changing workloads and achieve optimal performance. This ultimately leads to reduced costs, improved scalability, and increased efficiency. They are a key component of intelligent database systems, contributing to their ability to handle the demands of AI and data-intensive applications.

Vector Databases

Similarity Search: Specialized databases designed for storing and efficiently querying high-dimensional vector embeddings, crucial for AI applications.

Vector databases are a unique type of database specifically crafted to handle the complex data structures used in many modern AI applications. Instead of storing information in traditional tables with rows and columns, they store data as *vectors*. Think of a vector as a list of numbers representing different characteristics or features of an item. This allows the database to understand and compare items based on their similarity, which is essential for tasks like image recognition, natural language understanding, and recommendation systems.

To understand this better, consider the following:

Imagine you want to build a system that recommends movies to users. You can't just compare movie titles alphabetically. You need to understand what the movie is *about*. Let's say you extract the following features for each movie:

- **Genre:** Comedy, Action, Drama, Romance, Sci-Fi (represented as numerical values)
- **Keywords:** Robots, Love, Space, Detective (again, as numerical values)
- **Actors:** Tom Cruise, Angelina Jolie, etc. (represented by IDs, which are numerical)
- **Box Office Revenue:** (a single numerical value)
- **Average Review Score:** (a single numerical value)

You can then combine all of these numbers into a single vector. For instance:

```
Movie A = [0.2, 0.8, 0.0, 0.1, 0.0, 0.0, 0.0, 0.9, 0.0, 1, 100000000, 4.5]
```

```
Movie B = [0.0, 0.1, 0.7, 0.1, 0.0, 0.0, 0.0, 0.0, 0.1, 0, 150000000, 4.2]
```

Now, `Movie A` has a vector representation, and `Movie B` also has a vector representation. A vector database allows you to store these vectors and quickly find other movies with similar vectors. The closer the vectors are to each other mathematically, the more similar the movies are assumed to be.

This "closeness" or similarity is typically measured using metrics like:

- **Cosine Similarity:** Measures the angle between two vectors. A smaller angle indicates higher similarity.
- **Euclidean Distance:** Calculates the straight-line distance between two vectors. Smaller distance indicates higher similarity.

Illustration

```
Movie A Vector  ------------------->
                     / \
                    /   \  Angle
                   /     \
Movie B Vector  ------------------->
```

- Smaller Angle between vectors represents greater similarity.

A simplified example of a vector search using Python and a library (like `faiss`, but presented conceptually without relying on a specific library):

```python
# Simplified representation (no actual library usage for demonstration)
def cosine_similarity(vec1, vec2):
  """Calculates cosine similarity between two vectors."""
  dot_product = sum(x  y for x, y in zip(vec1, vec2))
  magnitude_vec1 = sum(x2 for x in vec1)0.5
  magnitude_vec2 = sum(x2 for x in vec2)0.5
  if magnitude_vec1 == 0 or magnitude_vec2 == 0:
    return 0  # Handle zero-magnitude vectors
  return dot_product / (magnitude_vec1  magnitude_vec2)


# Example movie vectors (simplified)
movie_vectors = {
  "MovieA": [0.8, 0.2, 0.1],
  "MovieB": [0.2, 0.9, 0.3],
  "MovieC": [0.7, 0.3, 0.2],
  "MovieD": [0.1, 0.1, 0.8]
}


def find_similar_movies(query_vector, movie_vectors, top_n=3):
  """Finds the most similar movies to a query vector."""
  similarities = {}
  for movie, vector in movie_vectors.items():
    similarities[movie] = cosine_similarity(query_vector, vector)

  # Sort movies by similarity in descending order
  sorted_movies = sorted(similarities.items(), key=lambda item: item[1], reverse=True)
  return sorted_movies[:top_n]


# Example query vector
query_vector = [0.75, 0.25, 0.05]  # User likes Action, a bit of Comedy, no Sci-Fi
```

```
# Find the top 2 most similar movies
similar_movies = find_similar_movies(query_vector, movie_vectors, top_n=2)

print("Recommended movies:", similar_movies) #It will print MovieA, MovieC
```

In the above code, a similarity search can be done without vector database, but that is not a real world scenario and it will be computationally costly. In real-world scenarios, these vectors would have hundreds or thousands of dimensions, and the dataset would contain millions of vectors. This is where specialized vector databases excel. They use sophisticated indexing techniques to perform similarity searches *extremely* quickly, even with massive datasets. These indexing techniques might involve hierarchical clustering, graph-based approaches, or specialized tree structures optimized for high-dimensional data.

Why are vector databases important for AI?

Many AI models, particularly in areas like natural language processing and computer vision, represent data as high-dimensional vectors. For example:

- **Word Embeddings:** Words are represented as vectors capturing their semantic meaning. "King" and "Queen" will have vectors that are close to each other because they are semantically related.
- **Image Embeddings:** Images can be processed by a deep learning model to generate a vector representing the image's content. Similar images (e.g., different photos of cats) will have similar vectors.

Vector databases are essential for efficiently searching and retrieving information based on these vector representations. They are a key component in building AI-powered applications that require understanding relationships and similarities in complex data. Example use cases including recommendation engines, fraud detection, and image-based search.

Vector Databases: Similarity Search

Concept: Vector databases are specialized databases designed for storing and efficiently querying high-dimensional vector embeddings, crucial for AI applications. Similarity search is the fundamental operation performed in these databases. It involves finding vectors that are "close" or similar to a given query vector. The notion of "closeness" is defined by a distance metric, such as Euclidean distance or cosine similarity.

Why are Vector Databases Important?

Traditional databases excel at exact match queries (e.g., "find all customers with name 'Alice'"). However, many modern AI applications require finding data based on *similarity* rather than exact matches. For example:

- **Image Retrieval:** Find images similar to a query image. Instead of searching for images with the exact same pixels, you want images with similar content (e.g., other pictures of cats).
- **Recommendation Systems:** Recommend products similar to items a user has already purchased. These "similar" products might not share any explicit attributes but are semantically related.
- **Natural Language Processing:** Find documents similar to a query document. This is useful for tasks like plagiarism detection, document clustering, and semantic search.

Representing data as vectors is a way to quantify semantic similarity, which a vector database can then exploit to find relevant results.

How Similarity Search Works

1. **Embeddings:** The first step is to convert your data (images, text, etc.) into vector embeddings. An embedding is a numerical representation of the data, capturing its semantic meaning. Pre-trained models, such as those in TensorFlow or PyTorch, are frequently used to create these embeddings.

2. **Indexing:** Vector databases employ specialized indexing techniques to organize the vectors for efficient search. These techniques allow the database to avoid comparing the query vector against every vector in the database. Common indexing methods include:

- **Approximate Nearest Neighbor (ANN) algorithms:** These algorithms sacrifice some accuracy for speed, finding "near" neighbors rather than the absolute closest neighbors. Examples include:

  - **Hierarchical Navigable Small World (HNSW):** Builds a multi-layered graph where each layer is a progressively smaller subset of the data. Searching starts at the top layer and navigates down to the bottom layer to find the nearest neighbors.

  - **Product Quantization (PQ):** Divides the vector space into smaller sub-spaces and quantizes each sub-vector. This allows for efficient distance calculations using pre-computed lookup tables.

  - **Tree-based methods:** Similar to KD-trees, but adapted for high-dimensional spaces.

3. **Querying:** When a query is submitted, the database uses the index to quickly identify candidate vectors that are likely to be similar to the query vector.

4. **Distance Calculation:** The database calculates the distance between the query vector and the candidate vectors using a chosen distance metric.

5. **Ranking and Retrieval:** The database ranks the candidate vectors based on their distance to the query vector and returns the top k most similar vectors (where k is a user-defined parameter).

Example: Python Code with `faiss`

`faiss` is a popular library for efficient similarity search. Here's a simplified example:

```python
import faiss
import numpy as np

# 1. Create sample data (replace with your embeddings)
dimension = 128  # Dimensionality of the vectors
num_vectors = 10000
data = np.float32(np.random.rand(num_vectors, dimension))

# 2. Build the index
index = faiss.IndexFlatL2(dimension)  # L2 distance (Euclidean)
# Another alternative
#index = faiss.IndexHNSWFlat(dimension,32)

index.add(data)

# 3. Create a query vector
num_queries = 1
query = np.float32(np.random.rand(num_queries, dimension))

# 4. Search the index
k = 5  # Number of nearest neighbors to retrieve
distances, indices = index.search(query, k)

# 5. Print the results
print("Indices of nearest neighbors:", indices)
print("Distances to nearest neighbors:", distances)
```

Explanation:

- We create random data to simulate vector embeddings. In a real application, you would load embeddings generated by a pre-trained model.

- `IndexFlatL2` creates an index that performs an exhaustive search, calculating the L2 distance (Euclidean distance) between the query vector and all vectors in the database. For larger datasets, you would typically use an approximate nearest neighbor index (e.g., `IndexHNSWFlat`) for faster search. `IndexHNSWFlat` uses the HNSW algorithm. The constructor argument 32 refers to the M parameter, which controls the number of connections each node has in the graph. A larger value of M generally leads to better search accuracy but also increases memory usage.
- `index.add(data)` adds the vectors to the index.
- `index.search(query, k)` searches the index for the k nearest neighbors to the query vector. It returns the distances and indices of the nearest neighbors.
- The output shows the indices of the 5 most similar vectors in the database, along with their corresponding distances from the query vector.

Distance Metrics

Choosing the right distance metric is crucial for accurate similarity search. Common metrics include:

- **Euclidean Distance (L2 distance):** The straight-line distance between two points. Sensitive to the magnitude of the vectors.
- **Cosine Similarity:** Measures the angle between two vectors. Insensitive to the magnitude of the vectors, focusing on the direction. Often used when the magnitude of the vectors is not meaningful.
- **Dot Product:** The dot product of two vectors. Related to cosine similarity but is sensitive to the magnitude of the vectors.

Real-World Considerations

- **Scalability:** Vector databases must be able to handle massive datasets. Distributed architectures and optimized indexing techniques are essential.
- **Performance:** Similarity search can be computationally expensive. Choosing the right indexing method and hardware is crucial for achieving low latency.
- **Accuracy vs. Speed:** Approximate nearest neighbor algorithms offer a trade-off between accuracy and speed. Choosing the right algorithm depends on the specific requirements of the application.
- **Update Frequency:** The frequency with which vectors are updated in the database impacts the choice of indexing algorithm. Some algorithms are better suited for dynamic datasets.

Conclusion

Similarity search using vector databases is a powerful tool for building AI applications that require finding data based on semantic similarity. With the growth of AI and machine learning, vector databases are becoming increasingly important for a wide range of applications.

Chapter 20 Future Trends and Real-World Architectures-Lessons from Large-Scale

Architectures: Case Studies from Leading Tech Companies

- **Case Studies Context:** Illustrate architectural patterns from the book using real-world examples from companies like Google, Amazon, and Netflix.

- **Practical Application:** Show how theoretical concepts (e.g., CAP theorem, consistency models) are applied in production systems.

- **Architectural Evolution:** Demonstrate how these companies' architectures have evolved over time to meet increasing scale and complexity.

- **Trade-off Analysis:** Highlight the trade-offs made in choosing specific technologies and architectures (e.g., eventual consistency vs. strong consistency).

- **Future Implications:** Discuss emerging trends and technologies that are shaping the future of data-intensive applications (e.g., serverless, edge computing).

Case Studies Context

This section uses real-world examples from prominent tech companies – Google, Amazon, and Netflix – to illustrate the architectural patterns discussed in this book. Instead of abstract theories, we delve into concrete implementations, showcasing how these patterns manifest in large-scale, data-intensive systems.

The goal is to provide a practical understanding of how different architectural patterns are used in the industry. We will see how these companies have solved common problems related to scale, performance, reliability, and data management by adapting these patterns.

For instance, consider Google's use of MapReduce. The MapReduce pattern is fundamental to processing vast amounts of data in parallel. Google developed it to index the web. In simple terms, imagine counting the occurrences of each word in a large collection of documents.

- **Map Phase:** The input data (the documents) is divided into smaller chunks, and each chunk is processed by a "mapper." The mapper extracts words and emits key-value pairs, where the key is the word and the value is 1 (representing one occurrence).
- **Reduce Phase:** The key-value pairs are grouped by key (i.e., all the occurrences of the same word are grouped together). A "reducer" then sums the values for each key to get the total count for each word.

While the original MapReduce is less frequently used now in its initial form, the underlying principle of distributing processing across many machines remains crucial and has evolved into systems like Apache Spark.

Amazon, on the other hand, relies heavily on microservices. Their e-commerce platform is built on a modular architecture, where each service handles a specific business function.

- For example, there's a "Product Catalog Service" responsible for storing and managing product information.
- A "Recommendation Service" provides personalized product recommendations based on user behavior.
- An "Order Management Service" handles order processing and fulfillment.

This microservice architecture allows Amazon to scale individual services independently based on demand. If the Recommendation Service experiences a surge in traffic, they can scale it up without affecting other services.

Netflix's architecture is designed to handle massive streaming requests. They use a combination of techniques, including content delivery networks (CDNs) and a distributed database system (Cassandra). CDNs store copies of content closer to users, reducing latency and improving streaming performance. Cassandra, a NoSQL database, provides high availability and scalability for storing user data and video metadata.

These examples highlight how each company has adapted architectural patterns to suit their specific needs and challenges. Instead of simply stating the theory of the architectural patterns, we will examine working examples, allowing you to understand the actual code and configurations that drive massive data-intensive application

Practical Application: From Theory to Production

This section delves into the practical application of theoretical concepts crucial to building robust data-intensive applications. We move beyond abstract definitions to examine how these concepts are implemented and managed in real-world production systems. We'll explore how companies wrestle with these challenges and the solutions they employ.

Let's consider two vital theoretical concepts: the CAP theorem and consistency models.

CAP Theorem in Production Systems

The CAP theorem states that in a distributed system, you can only guarantee two out of three properties: Consistency, Availability, and Partition Tolerance. Partition Tolerance, the ability of the system to continue operating even when some nodes can't communicate with others, is generally non-negotiable in distributed systems. Thus, architects often face the difficult choice between Consistency and Availability.

- **Choosing Availability over Consistency:** Consider an e-commerce website like Amazon. During a network partition, if a customer adds an item to their cart, Amazon might prioritize availability by allowing the order to proceed even if the system can't immediately confirm that the item is in stock. This means there's a *possibility* that the order might be cancelled later if the stock check fails. This is an example of prioritizing Availability over Consistency. They might use a technique like optimistic locking or compensation transactions to handle potential inconsistencies.

  Let's say we are taking a real-world e-commerce scenario. In following scenario a user is trying to add product to their cart. *User Activity Flow*

  1. **User adds a product to their cart:** The user browses the e-commerce site and selects an item they want to purchase. They click the "Add to Cart" button.
  2. **Cart service receives request:** The request to add the product to the cart is sent to the cart service. The request includes the user's ID and the product ID.
  3. **Cart service checks inventory:** The cart service needs to ensure that there is sufficient inventory available for the selected product. It sends a request to the inventory service to check the stock level.
  4. **Inventory service responds:** The inventory service checks its database and sends a response back to the cart service with the current stock level for the product.
  5. **Cart service updates cart:** If the inventory level is sufficient, the cart service updates the user's cart in its database.
  6. **Cart service sends confirmation:** The cart service sends a confirmation message back to the user's browser, indicating that the product has been successfully added to the cart. The updated cart information is displayed to the user.

  Technical Implementation (Illustrative)

  In the backend, the application servers of e-commerce stores might use programming code like the below(python example):

```python
def add_to_cart(user_id, product_id, quantity):
    try:
        # 1. Get current cart state (optimistic locking)
        cart = get_cart(user_id)
        old_version = cart.version

        # 2. Check inventory (compensating transaction logic)
        inventory_available = check_inventory(product_id, quantity)
```

```
        if not inventory_available:
            raise InsufficientInventoryError("Not enough items in stock.")

        # 3. Update cart (potential race condition)
        cart.items[product_id] = cart.items.get(product_id, 0) + quantity
        cart.version += 1

        # 4. Save updated cart (check for optimistic lock failure)
        save_cart(cart, old_version)

        # 5. Asynchronously update inventory service (eventual consistency)
        publish_inventory_update_event(product_id, -quantity) #reduce quantity
        return True
    except OptimisticLockError:
        # Handle race condition (retry or inform user)
        return False
    except InsufficientInventoryError:
        #Inform User
        return False
    except Exception as e:
        # Log error and potentially trigger a compensating action
        print(f"An error occurred: {e}")
        return False
```

Explanation of the code:

- **Optimistic Locking:** The function attempts to read cart version and it tries to write it after incrementing the cart version. Before writing cart the function will check if cart version is changed.
- **Compensating Transaction:** If reduce quantity event fail to publish than the function must rollback the cart.
- **Eventual Consistency:** Cart Service will send a message to the reduce inventory quantity, in case of failure Cart Service will trigger a compensating action to notify the user.

The above implementation shows a simplified, practical example of how an e-commerce system may handle adding products to a cart while dealing with concurrency, potential inventory shortages, and consistency challenges in distributed systems.

- **Choosing Consistency over Availability:** Banking systems often prioritize consistency. Imagine transferring money between accounts. It's critical that the transaction is either fully completed (money debited from one account and credited to another) or entirely rolled back. During a network partition, the system might choose to become temporarily unavailable to ensure data integrity, meaning users might be unable to access their accounts during the outage. Techniques like two-phase commit (2PC) or Paxos/Raft consensus algorithms are often used in such scenarios to achieve strong consistency.

Consistency Models in Practice

Different applications require different levels of data consistency. Choosing the appropriate consistency model is a critical decision.

- **Eventual Consistency:** Many social media platforms like Twitter or Facebook rely on eventual consistency. When you post a status update, it might not be immediately visible to all your friends. It will eventually propagate across the system. This trade-off allows for high availability and scalability. Updates are applied to individual nodes quickly, and inconsistencies are resolved over time.

Consider a *sketch* of an eventual consistency example within a social media context:

```
[User A] --(Post Update)--> [Cache Server 1] --(Async Replication)--> [Cache Server 2]
    |
    | (Immediate Ack)
    V
User A's Timeline
```

In the sketch, User A posts an update. That update is immediately written to a local cache server (Cache Server 1). User A receives immediate confirmation that the update was posted. The update is then asynchronously replicated to other cache servers (like Cache Server 2). Another user viewing User A's timeline might initially see an older version of the timeline if they are served by Cache Server 2 before the replication completes. Eventually, all caches will converge on the same, consistent data.

- **Strong Consistency:** Financial systems and inventory management systems often require strong consistency. Every read should return the most recent write, regardless of which server you query. Achieving strong consistency can impact performance and availability, so it's typically used only when absolutely necessary. **Example:** When processing a financial transaction, it's essential to ensure that funds are either successfully transferred from one account to another or the transaction is completely rolled back, leaving both accounts untouched.

Implementation

```python
import threading

class Account:
    def __init__(self, account_id, balance):
        self.account_id = account_id
        self.balance = balance
        self.lock = threading.Lock()  # Lock to ensure thread safety

    def withdraw(self, amount):
        with self.lock:
            if self.balance >= amount:
                self.balance -= amount
                return True
            else:
                return False

    def deposit(self, amount):
        with self.lock:
            self.balance += amount
            return True

    def get_balance(self):
        with self.lock:
            return self.balance


def transfer(from_account, to_account, amount):
    with from_account.lock, to_account.lock:  # Acquire locks on both accounts

        if from_account.withdraw(amount):
            to_account.deposit(amount)
            return True
        else:
```

```
# If the withdrawal fails, ensure the transaction is rolled back
return False
```

Explanation

- ○ **Locking Mechanism**: A locking mechanism is used to maintain the consistency and integrity of the data when multiple threads are accessing and modifying shared data.
- ○ **Atomic Operation:** The transfer funds is implemented using thread locking to ensure that both withdraw and deposit operations happen atomically. The fund will not be partially completed.

By understanding these practical applications of theoretical concepts, you can make informed decisions about the architecture and technologies you choose for your data-intensive applications, balancing factors like consistency, availability, performance, and scalability.

Architectural Evolution

This section explores how the architectures of data-intensive applications evolve over time, focusing on real-world examples from companies like Google, Amazon, and Netflix. The evolution is driven by the need to handle increasing scale, complexity, and changing business requirements. We will look at what trigger such evolutions and some common patterns observed.

Companies often start with simpler, monolithic architectures. A monolithic architecture is like a single, large application where all components are tightly coupled. For example, a simple e-commerce application might have all its code (handling user logins, product catalogs, order processing, etc.) in one big codebase.

```
Sketch of Monolithic Architecture:


+-------------------------------------------------------+
|                 Monolithic Application                |
+-------------------------------------------------------+
| User Interface | Product Catalog | Order Processing |
| Login          | Search          | Payment          |
+-------------------------------------------------------+
|                     Database                          |
+-------------------------------------------------------+
```

This approach is easier to develop and deploy initially. However, as the application grows, it becomes increasingly difficult to manage, scale, and update. Deploying new changes requires redeploying the entire application, even if only a small part has been modified. Code conflicts become more frequent as more developers work on the same codebase.

To address these challenges, companies often transition to microservices. Microservices involve breaking down the monolithic application into smaller, independent services that communicate with each other, often over a network. Each microservice focuses on a specific business capability, such as user authentication, product recommendation, or order management.

```
Sketch of Microservices Architecture:
```

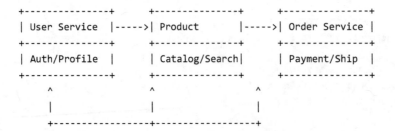

Consider Netflix. Initially, they had a monolithic architecture. As their user base and content library grew, they faced performance and scalability issues. They migrated to a microservices architecture, breaking down their application into services like video streaming, recommendation engine, user management, and billing. Each service could be developed, deployed, and scaled independently.

Similarly, Amazon evolved from a monolithic application to a service-oriented architecture (SOA) and then to a microservices architecture. This allowed them to handle the massive scale of their e-commerce platform and innovate faster.

Google, with its diverse range of products and services, also employs microservices extensively. For example, Google Search is a complex system built on top of numerous microservices. Each service handles a specific task, such as indexing web pages, ranking search results, or displaying ads.

The evolution isn't just about moving from monoliths to microservices. It's also about adopting new technologies and architectural patterns to meet specific needs. For example, companies may adopt NoSQL databases to handle unstructured data or event-driven architectures to improve responsiveness.

Consider the evolution of data storage. Early applications relied on relational databases like MySQL or PostgreSQL. However, as data volumes grew and applications needed to handle more diverse data types, companies started using NoSQL databases like Cassandra, MongoDB, and DynamoDB.

Here's a simple example. If we are tracking user activities in an application, and we start with traditional SQL database like.

```sql
CREATE TABLE user_activities (
    user_id INT,
    activity_type VARCHAR(255),
    timestamp TIMESTAMP,
    details TEXT
);
```

As data volumes increase and we need to store unstructured data (e.g. user clicks, social media posts) a NoSQL like MongoDB becomes more suitable

```
// Example MongoDB document
{
    user_id: 123,
    activity_type: "click",
    timestamp: ISODate("2024-01-01T12:00:00Z"),
    details: {
        page_url: "/product/123",
        element_id: "buy_button"
    }
}
```

The architectural evolution is also influenced by the need to improve resilience and fault tolerance. Cloud platforms like AWS, Azure, and GCP provide a wide range of services that make it easier to build resilient applications. Companies may use techniques like redundancy, replication, and circuit breakers to prevent failures and ensure that their applications remain available even when individual components fail.

The architectural evolution is a continuous process. As technology advances and business requirements change, companies must adapt their architectures to remain competitive. This often involves adopting new technologies, refactoring existing code, and embracing new architectural patterns.

Trade-off Analysis

When designing data-intensive applications, there are rarely universally "correct" solutions. Instead, architects constantly navigate trade-offs, carefully weighing the pros and cons of different technologies and architectural choices to meet specific requirements. A core aspect of this process is understanding the implications of these trade-offs on factors like consistency, availability, latency, cost, and complexity. Let's explore these considerations.

Consistency vs. Availability:

One of the most fundamental trade-offs is between consistency and availability, often illustrated by the CAP theorem. The CAP theorem states that in a distributed system, you can only guarantee two out of the following three:

- **Consistency:** Every read receives the most recent write or an error.
- **Availability:** Every request receives a (non-error) response, without guarantee that it contains the most recent write.
- **Partition Tolerance:** The system continues to operate despite arbitrary partitioning due to network failures.

In practice, partition tolerance is non-negotiable for most large-scale systems, leaving architects to choose between consistency and availability.

- **Strong Consistency:** Systems that prioritize consistency ensure that all clients see the same data at the same time. This is often achieved through techniques like distributed transactions and consensus algorithms (e.g., Paxos, Raft).

  - **Example:** A banking application requires strong consistency to ensure that transactions are processed correctly and account balances are always accurate. If a user transfers money from one account to another, the system must guarantee that the money is deducted from the first account and added to the second account before either transaction is considered complete.
  - **Trade-off:** Achieving strong consistency can reduce availability, especially during network partitions. If one part of the system cannot communicate with another, it may need to halt operations to avoid inconsistent data. This increased latency can also affect the user experience.

- **Eventual Consistency:** Systems that prioritize availability allow for temporary inconsistencies. Data will eventually become consistent across all replicas, but there may be a delay.

  - **Example:** A social media platform can tolerate eventual consistency for some features, such as displaying the number of likes on a post. If a user likes a post, the update may not be immediately visible to all other users. However, the system will eventually converge to the correct number of likes.
  - **Trade-off:** While eventual consistency improves availability and responsiveness, it introduces the risk of stale data. Applications must be designed to handle these inconsistencies, which can add complexity.
  - **Code Example:** A simple example of handling eventual consistency in code might involve versioning data. When updating a record, increment a version number. During reads, compare the version numbers of different replicas and choose the latest version. While this example is not comprehensive, it illustrates the need for application-level logic to manage potential inconsistencies.

```
class DataRecord:
    def __init__(self, value, version):
        self.value = value
        self.version = version


def read_data(replica1, replica2):
    """
    Read data from two replicas and return the most recent version.
    """
    if replica1.version > replica2.version:
        return replica1
```

```
    else:
        return replica2

# Example usage
replica1 = DataRecord("initial value", 1)
replica2 = DataRecord("initial value", 1)

# Update replica1
replica1.value = "updated value"
replica1.version = 2

# Read the data
latest_data = read_data(replica1, replica2)
print(f"Latest value: {latest_data.value}, Version: {latest_data.version}") #output Latest value
```

Latency vs. Throughput:

Another common trade-off involves latency (the time it takes to complete a single operation) and throughput (the number of operations that can be processed per unit of time).

- **Low Latency:** Systems that require low latency prioritize fast response times, even if it means sacrificing some throughput.

  - **Example:** An online gaming platform needs low latency to provide a responsive and immersive experience. Players expect immediate feedback when they perform actions, such as moving their character or firing a weapon.
  - **Trade-off:** Achieving low latency often requires optimizing code, using fast storage devices (e.g., SSDs), and caching frequently accessed data. These optimizations can reduce the overall throughput of the system.

- **High Throughput:** Systems that require high throughput prioritize processing a large volume of data, even if it means increasing latency for individual operations.

  - **Example:** A data warehousing application needs high throughput to process large batches of data efficiently. The system may not need to respond immediately to individual queries, but it must be able to ingest and process data quickly.
  - **Trade-off:** Achieving high throughput often involves techniques like batch processing, parallel processing, and distributed computing. These techniques can increase latency for individual operations, as data needs to be aggregated and processed across multiple nodes.

Cost vs. Performance:

The cost of infrastructure and operations is a significant consideration for any data-intensive application. Architects must balance the need for performance with the cost of resources.

- **High Performance:** Systems that require high performance may need to use expensive hardware, such as high-end servers, SSDs, and fast network connections.

  - **Example:** A financial trading platform requires high performance to process transactions quickly and accurately. The system may need to use specialized hardware to minimize latency and maximize throughput.
  - **Trade-off:** High-performance hardware can be expensive to purchase, maintain, and operate. Architects must carefully consider whether the performance gains justify the cost.

- **Low Cost:** Systems that need to minimize costs may need to sacrifice some performance. This can be achieved through techniques like using commodity hardware, optimizing code, and caching data.

- **Example:** A blog hosting platform may need to minimize costs to offer affordable hosting plans. The system may use commodity hardware and caching to reduce the load on the servers.
- **Trade-off:** Reducing costs can impact performance, especially during peak traffic periods. Architects must carefully monitor the system to ensure that it can handle the load without sacrificing user experience.

Complexity vs. Maintainability:

As systems become more complex, they become more difficult to maintain and operate. Architects must balance the need for advanced features and functionality with the need for simplicity and maintainability.

- **Advanced Features:** Systems that require advanced features may need to use complex technologies and architectures.

  - **Example:** A recommendation engine may need to use machine learning algorithms and complex data pipelines to provide accurate and personalized recommendations.
  - **Trade-off:** Complex systems can be difficult to understand, debug, and maintain. They may also require specialized skills and expertise.

- **Simplicity:** Systems that prioritize simplicity may need to sacrifice some features and functionality.

  - **Example:** A simple key-value store may be sufficient for applications that only need to store and retrieve data.
  - **Trade-off:** Simpler systems may not be able to meet all of the requirements of the application. Architects must carefully consider whether the simplicity outweighs the limitations.

Sketch Example:

Below is a sketch representing the consistency vs. availability trade-off based on the CAP Theorem.

CAP Theorem

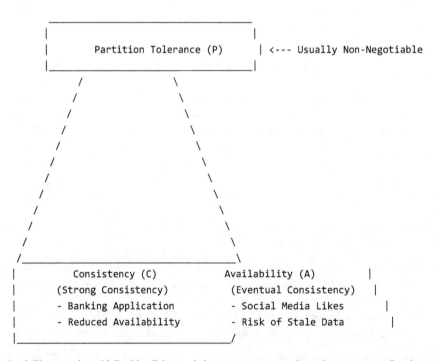

```
     _____
    |                               |
    |      Partition Tolerance (P)  |  <--- Usually Non-Negotiable
    |_____|
          /                \
         /                  \
        /                    \
       /                      \
      /                        \
     /                          \
    /                            \
   /                              \
  /                                \
 /_____\
 |      Consistency (C)      Availability (A)      |
 |     (Strong Consistency)   (Eventual Consistency)  |
 |     - Banking Application   - Social Media Likes   |
 |     - Reduced Availability  - Risk of Stale Data   |
 |_____/
```

This sketch illustrates that with Partition Tolerance being a must, one must choose between strong Consistency or high Availability.

In summary, trade-off analysis is a critical part of designing data-intensive applications. Architects must carefully weigh the pros and cons of different technologies and architectural choices to meet the specific requirements of the application. By understanding these trade-offs, architects can make informed decisions that result in scalable, reliable, and cost-effective systems.

Future Implications

This section explores emerging trends and technologies that will significantly shape the future of data-intensive applications. We will discuss serverless computing and edge computing, examining their potential impact on how we build, deploy, and manage these applications.

Serverless Computing:

Serverless computing represents a paradigm shift in how we think about infrastructure. Instead of provisioning and managing servers, developers focus solely on writing code. The cloud provider handles the underlying infrastructure, automatically scaling resources as needed.

- **Key Benefits:** Serverless computing offers several advantages:

    - *Reduced Operational Overhead:* Developers no longer need to worry about server maintenance, patching, or scaling. This allows them to focus on building features and delivering value.
    - *Cost Efficiency:* You only pay for the resources you consume. If your application is idle, you pay nothing.
    - *Automatic Scaling:* The cloud provider automatically scales resources to handle varying workloads. This ensures that your application can handle sudden spikes in traffic.
    - *Faster Development Cycles:* Reduced operational overhead and automatic scaling enable faster development cycles. Developers can quickly prototype and deploy new features without worrying about infrastructure.

- **Example:** Imagine a photo processing application. With traditional infrastructure, you would need to provision servers to handle incoming photo uploads and processing. With serverless computing, you can use a function-as-a-service (FaaS) platform like AWS Lambda or Azure Functions. Each time a photo is uploaded, a function is triggered to process it. The cloud provider automatically scales the function to handle the load.

    Here's a simplified code example (using Python and AWS Lambda):

```python
import boto3
import os

def lambda_handler(event, context):
    # Get the object from the event and show its content type
    bucket = event['Records'][0]['s3']['bucket']['name']
    key = event['Records'][0]['s3']['object']['key']

    try:
        s3 = boto3.client('s3')
        response = s3.get_object(Bucket=bucket, Key=key)
        content = response['Body'].read()
        print("CONTENT TYPE: " + response['ContentType'])
        # Your image processing logic here
        return 'Image processed successfully!'
    except Exception as e:
        print(e)
        print('Error getting object {} from bucket {}. Make sure they exist and your bucket
        raise e
```

In this example, the `lambda_handler` function is triggered whenever a new object is uploaded to an S3 bucket. The function retrieves the object, processes it, and returns a result. The developer doesn't need to worry about the underlying infrastructure.

- **Challenges:** Serverless computing also presents some challenges:

  - *Cold Starts:* When a serverless function is invoked after a period of inactivity, it may experience a "cold start" delay.
  - *Debugging and Monitoring:* Debugging and monitoring serverless applications can be more challenging than traditional applications.
  - *Vendor Lock-in:* Serverless platforms are often vendor-specific, which can lead to vendor lock-in.
  - *Statelessness:* Serverless functions are typically stateless, which means they cannot store data between invocations. This can make it difficult to build complex stateful applications.

Edge Computing:

Edge computing brings computation and data storage closer to the source of data. Instead of sending data to a central cloud, processing occurs on devices or servers located at the edge of the network.

- **Key Benefits:** Edge computing offers several advantages:

  - *Reduced Latency:* By processing data closer to the source, edge computing can significantly reduce latency. This is critical for applications that require real-time responsiveness, such as autonomous vehicles and industrial automation.
  - *Bandwidth Optimization:* Edge computing can reduce the amount of data that needs to be transmitted over the network. This can save bandwidth costs and improve network performance.
  - *Increased Reliability:* Edge computing can improve the reliability of applications by allowing them to continue operating even when the network connection is unreliable.
  - *Enhanced Security:* Edge computing can enhance security by keeping sensitive data on-premises.

- **Example:** Consider a smart factory with thousands of sensors collecting data on machine performance. Sending all of this data to the cloud for processing would consume a significant amount of bandwidth and introduce latency. With edge computing, data can be processed locally on edge servers. These servers can analyze the data in real-time and identify potential problems before they cause a breakdown.

  Here's a basic sketch to illustrate:

```
[Sensors] --> [Edge Server] --> [Cloud]
   (Data)      (Processing)    (Aggregation & Analysis)
```

The sensors send data to the edge server, which performs initial processing and analysis. Only aggregated or critical data is sent to the cloud for further analysis and long-term storage.

- **Challenges:** Edge computing also presents some challenges:

  - *Complexity:* Edge computing environments can be complex to manage, especially when dealing with a large number of devices.
  - *Security:* Securing edge devices can be challenging, as they are often deployed in physically insecure environments.
  - *Resource Constraints:* Edge devices typically have limited resources, such as processing power and memory.
  - *Connectivity:* Maintaining connectivity between edge devices and the cloud can be challenging, especially in remote areas.

Combined Impact:

Serverless and edge computing are not mutually exclusive. They can be combined to create powerful data-intensive applications. For example, a serverless function could be deployed on an edge device to process data locally.

- **Future Trends:**

  - *AI at the Edge:* Combining edge computing with artificial intelligence (AI) will enable new applications, such as autonomous robots and smart surveillance systems.
  - *5G and Edge Computing:* The rollout of 5G networks will provide the high bandwidth and low latency needed to support many edge computing applications.
  - *Blockchain and Edge Computing:* Blockchain can be used to secure data and transactions at the edge.
  - *Quantum Computing and Edge Computing:* Quantum computing may enhance computation performance on the edge.

These emerging trends and technologies are poised to revolutionize how we build and deploy data-intensive applications. By understanding the benefits and challenges of serverless and edge computing, developers can create innovative solutions that meet the demands of the future.

www.ingramcontent.com/pod-product-compliance
Lightning Source LLC
LaVergne TN
LVHW060121070326
832902LV00019B/3078